UNIMAT 3 LATHE ACCESSORIES

Bob Loader

Special Interest Model Books

Special Interest Model Books Ltd
P.O.Box 327
Poole
Dorset BH15 2RG
England

www.specialinterestmodelbooks.co.uk

First published by
Nexus Special Interests Ltd 2001

This edition published by
Special Interest Model Books Ltd 2009

ISBN 978 185486 213 6

Printed and bound in Malta by Melita Press

Acknowledgements

My thanks to Ted Jolliffe, who used my first few articles, Stan Bray, who used one of mine in the first 'Model Engineers' Workshop', Harold Hall and Geoff Sheppard, for their constant support, encouragement and kindness and Bill Burkinshaw, who had to edit this.

A big thank you to my wife, who is my proof-reader, illustrations editor, photographer when I haven't got a free hand (some of the photographs in this book are her work), also my extra pair of hands when I am using both of mine. She is the very best administration assistant I could wish for and many improvements in the layout and planning of this manuscript are hers.

I have had to leave out many people who have helped me in my long, and still continuing, learning process. So thanks to everyone I have worked with over the years.

Finally, if it is possible to thank a machine; I do so. The Unimat range has a tradition of usefulness and versatility. I can vouch for both. Although my first love is the Unimat 3, which I have used since 1985, I know that the Unimat 4 is a worthy next stage in the series, having had the privilege of testing it. I have no doubt that the Millennium model, now in limited production, will follow the tradition. I will always, however, have a soft spot for my favourite. Thank you, Unimat 3, for being such a wonderful machining centre.

Bob Loader
Milton Keynes, March 2000.

Contents

Introduction

I have been an engineering craftsman, in one way or another, for 50 odd years. In that time I have worked in workshops as different as those of the civil service, to two men, a dog and a boy companies.

I didn't intend to be an engineering craftsman and wanted to be a trainee reporter on the local paper, but in 1947 nothing pleased a working class father more than a son who was an apprentice. In those days going against parental advice, especially about jobs, wasn't done. So I left a small country grammar school, with a marginal school certificate, and was taken on as a craft apprentice at a radar research establishment of what was then, the Ministry of Supply.

A grammar school teaches pupils to be articulate, so I had all the standard answers for the interviewers off-pat: Yes, I did like making things, no, I didn't mind getting my hands dirty, yes, I did realise that the pay would be poor, till I became a skilled man, and so forth.

Perhaps the pay would have been no poorer at the local paper, and perhaps I'd have been happier juggling words than shaping materials, but I would have missed out on some great times, great people and lots of laughs.

The year of 1947 was very much austerity time, one small bar of chocolate a week, and you had to know the tobacconist pretty well if you smoked. Ice cream had a funny texture and taste, record players were called gramophones and had to have a needle changed for each side of a breakable 10 or 12in record.

Many of my friends were apprentices in various trades and the girls we pursued were apprentice hairdressers, tracers, or worked in shops or offices. It was, in spite of everything, a great time to have left school, get a job with prospects and be earning a pittance.

We apprentices were a motley lot, but we soon became absorbed into the scheme of things; the training workshop, typical of its time, with machines which had been seen on scrap heaps, or seen better days. There were plenty of files and hacksaws in better condition. We filed a lot, the usual- boil 'em down jobs, a gap gauge, tap wrench, G clamps and a 3in square. The piéce de resistance was the cube, a 1in. cube to be filed to an accuracy of 0.002in all over. My chosen material, not my own, was a softish aluminium alloy. I learned about files 'pinning'. I also learned what 'black hot' meant, when I picked up a job which I had just silver soldered and was in that condition. I learned all sorts of useful things, all part of the process of making a square peg, as I was, fit the round hole.

One day a week we spent in the drawing-office or a classroom. The first few weeks of the class room element were conducted by one of the senior engineers who was trying out a book he had written. It was called, 'Hand Sketching for Engineers', or something similar. I came across it years later when I was looking for another book. It took me right back to that September, which was a series of hot afternoons. I remembered the fog he made with his pipe and the frying and bubbling noises it made, on the frequent re-lights. I read the book again and very good it was.

The drawing office was the favourite time of the week. The section we worked in was right against the partition separating the tracing office and the girls who worked there. We used full-sized boards, sharpened our pencils to chisel points and learned the difference between first and third angle projection, we called them English and American. We constructed ellipses, cycloids, involutes, parabolas and other constructions, and drew the standard proportions for bolts, nuts, rivets, rolled steel sections and other useful objects.

We had an excellent grounding in the engineering business and I wouldn't have missed it. Some of the experiences are still easy to recall, some have faded with time, all of them helped to make me a competent craftsman. I thank all the many people who have made it so.

Chapter 1

A Milling Table For The Unimat 3

Some years ago I did an evening class at my local college. The main project was a vertical head for my Unimat 3. I finished it but it wasn't all that good, as an extra I made a milling table for the same machine: it has been far more useful than the vertical head.

Calculate your working time

For those who are thinking about a model engineering class, there are some things to think of. For starters, estimate the work you expect to do in the time available and divide by two. A nominal two-hour class is unlikely to be more than one and a half hours' useful time. There are tools to be booked out and returned, looking for things, waiting for the machine someone else is using and clearing up at the end of the session. The machine you have waited for will almost certainly need re-setting and your lecturer will have some students who will need a lot of attention, so be patient when you need help or advice.

Have alternatives

As well as the job you really want to do, have another one which can be done mostly by fitting and with hand tools because most colleges have plenty of bench space. The big queues are for lathes, milling machines and surface grinders. That was why I had the milling table to work on when I couldn't get on the machine I wanted.

I made it simple to save time, which is why it has no T slots, it simplifies the construction so much. The details are shown in **Fig.1.1**; the rows of tapped holes do exactly the same job as the T slots without the hassle of machining the slots. It is just a matter of finding the right bolt and a washer, always an easier task than finding a T nut of the right size.

To stop the holes getting clogged with swarf and other debris, they can be blocked with short cheese-headed screws with shallow heads, made so that they are under flush with the surface. This is optional and the bungs could be made from nylon or a suitable synthetic material, or if you don't mind the cleaning out, forget them.

Machining the table

The table can be machined by holding the blank in a four-jawed chuck. If it is held by the flanks of the jaws, as

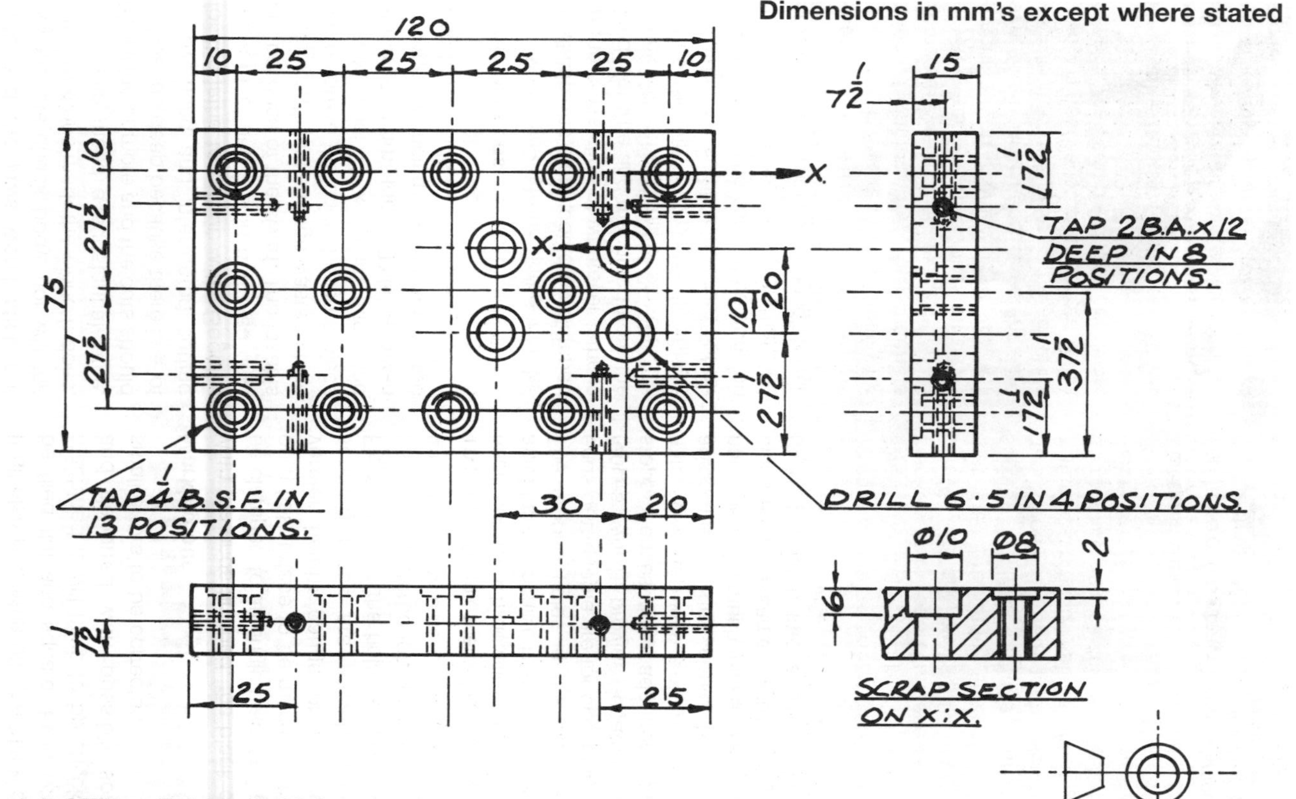

Fig. 1.1. Milling Table - B.M.S

shown in the drawing, it will be quite safe and the jaws won't stick out beyond the chuck body, nor will the jaw serrations mark the work. It does, of course, need a substantial lathe, 6in swing or more and the cuts should not be too deep because there is a lot of overhang and interrupted cutting for the lathe to put up with. Goggles are a must and a shirt buttoned right up, because of the swarf. The ideal is a blank with just enough waste to take off to square the ends. I used a piece of mild steel 75 x 15mm thick and about 122mm long. This allowed enough for facing, without taking too long to machine.

Other methods

Should a nice strong lathe not be available, the blank could be clamped to the cross slide of whatever lathe is used, set true and machined from the chuck with an end mill or slot drill. Do not try this with a fly cutter; fly cutters are alright for some things, but not for this. The trimming can not be done on a machine the size of a Unimat; the cross slide does not have enough travel.

Last resort

If all else is written off, the blank can be filed flat and square. Even when machined it will have to be checked and deburred with possibly some small errors to be corrected.

Marking out

With the ends finished, the blank can be clamped to an angle plate and put on a flat surface to be marked out. A vernier height gauge or rule and scribing block are equally useful. Fig.1.1 shows the hole positions as I used them although they can be different if wanted.

The 6.5mm holes are for 6mm cap-head screws which will fit the T nuts and clamp the table to the cross slide. The tapped holes in the sides and ends of the table are for clamping the fences which provide locators and stops. Fences are made from 3mm mild steel strip with slotted holes for adjustment. They could be case-hardened. If a much thicker piece was clamped in the same position, it could make the table into a sort of angle

Fig. 1.2. Work clamped to the side of the table to mill a Vee slot.

Dimensions in mm's except where stated

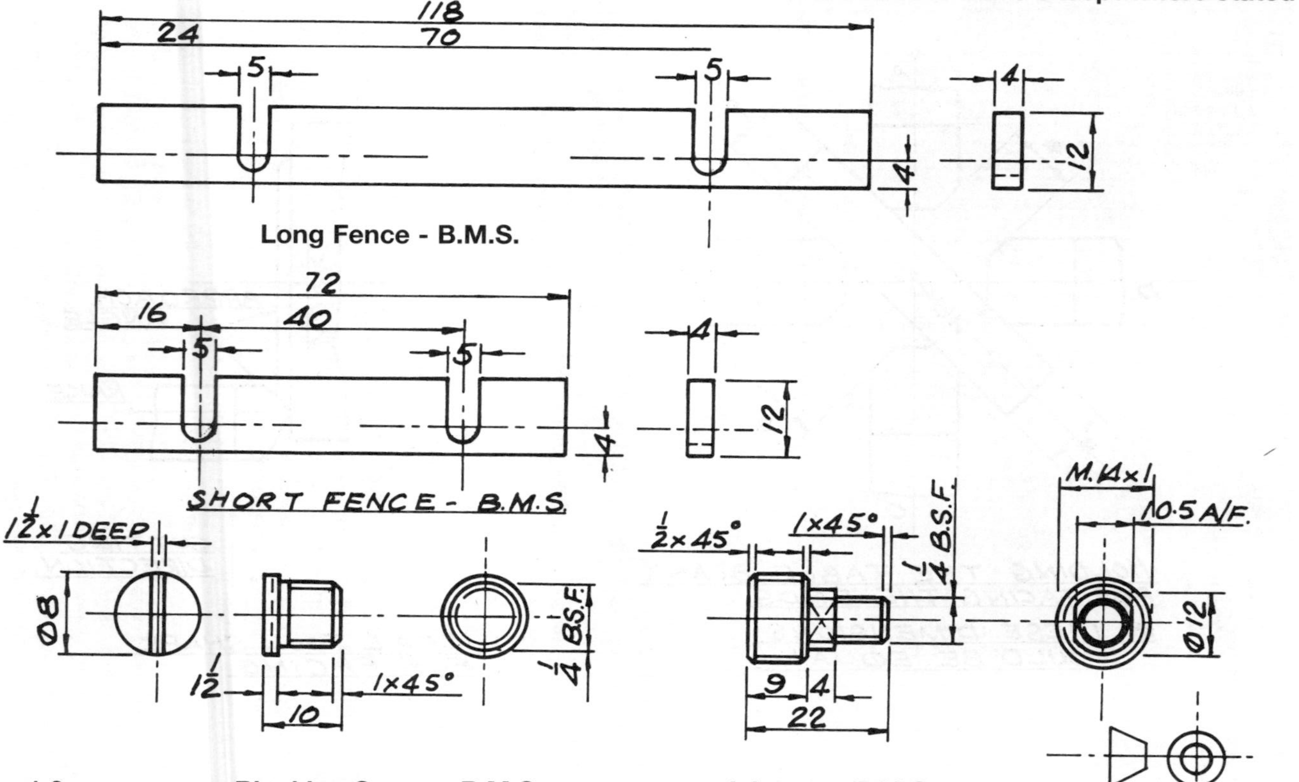

Long Fence - B.M.S.

SHORT FENCE - B.M.S.

Blanking Screw - B.M.S.

Adaptor - B.M.S.

Fig. 1.3

A.B.C.D. - Chuck Jaws

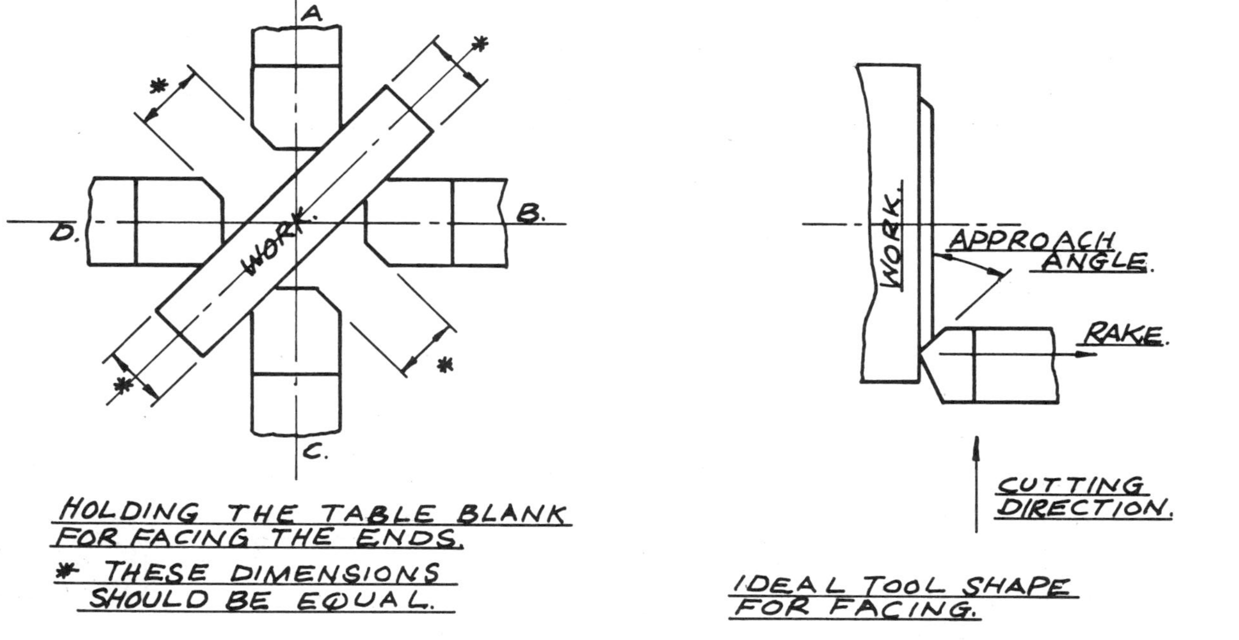

Fig. 1.4

plate and if the sides are flat and square enough, work can be clamped directly to them with a large clamp as in **Fig. 1.2** which shows a V-slot being machined this way.

Clamping holes

The clamping holes are tapped 1/4in BSF because I have plenty of bolts of this size in various lengths. It is a good clamping thread but 6mm would do just as well.

Counterboring was done before tapping and if the holes are drilled clearance size for 2mm depth and lightly countersunk, the threads will be burr free. The tapping size holes were drilled right through.

Finishing off

I was lucky and able to grind my table flat, square and true. It isn't necessary to go to those lengths but the machine was available and it made everything accurate. I scraped the top because I like the look of a scraped surface; it is a hand skill worth preserving. The screws for clamping the fences are 2BA cap heads.

Optional extras

The other components shown in **Fig. 1.3** are the blanking screws to seal those holes not being used, and an adapter for fastening the Unimat chuck to the table for machining circular work. The adapter was made from 15mm diameter mild steel, turned to 14mm and threaded M14 x 1. If the equipment is to hand it can be screw cut, if not, taps and dies are easy to find. The blank for the adapter should be made longer than needed, so that there is enough to hold in the chuck while it is threaded and the 12mm and 1/4in diameters are turned. Once the 1/4in BSF thread has been cut, the adapter can be cut off, faced and chamfered.

The flats are to fit a spanner and if made to the dimensions shown, an 0BA spanner will fit.

Since I made the table, I have used it for milling and drilling and found it most useful, especially as I use the Unimat for all the drilling and milling jobs as well as the normal turning. So if you are limited to a small lathe which has to do everything, make a table; it is well worthwhile. **Fig. 1.4** shows the machining method for the table ends. **Fig. 1.5** is the table in position on the lathe cross slide and **Fig. 1.6**. the table with fences in position and stopper screws left out.

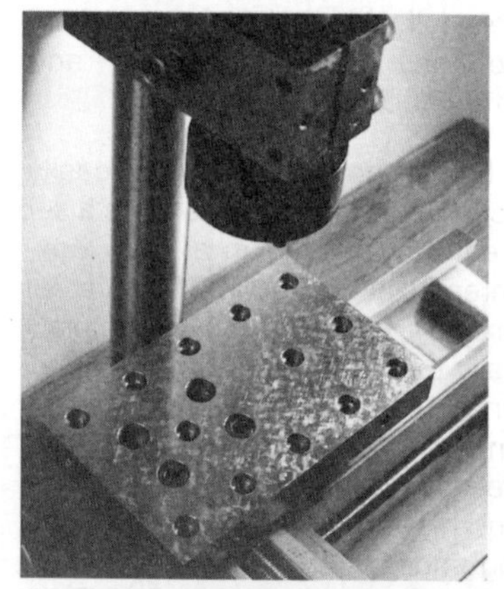

Fig. 1.5. The table in position on the lathe cross slide with the (unfinished) milling/drilling head.

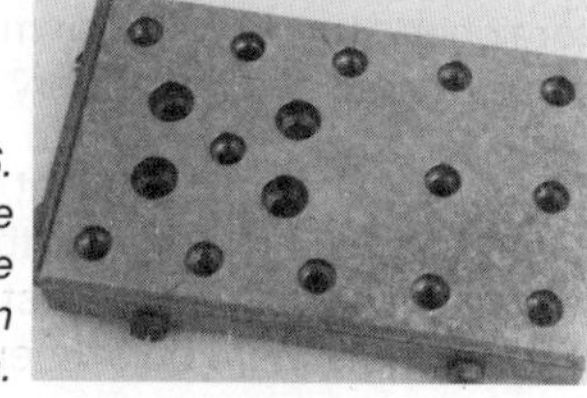

Fig. 1.6. The table with the fences in position.

Chapter 2

Cheap and Cheerful Tap Wrenches

Once, when I was moving from one job to another, my tap wrenches vanished and my set of hexagonal keys went walkabout at the same time. These things happen when small tools have to be recovered from borrowers, hunted for in the depths of drawers full of junk and fetched from where they were last used and forgotten about.

The hexagonal keys were easily replaced, but the wrenches were a set of three: not a set as in a fancy box, but three sizes which would cover all the sizes of taps and hand reamers I normally came across, from the small BA ones to about 10mm. They were nothing special, except to me, made on the same pattern as the one in **Fig. 2.1** and nickel plated by a chap in the plating shop who owed me a favour; that's how the world goes round. They held a tap nice and firmly and at a pinch could be used as lathe carriers. The biggest one was the first 'foreigner' I made when on my stint on the turning section. I was very fond of it.

For a long time I used what they had in the stores. Poor things they were, sometimes worn to the most amazing shapes, the square hole where the tap fitted anything but square and the threaded end, which bears against the tap to hold it in, so burred over that it was impossible to unscrew it more than a couple of threads.

Over the years I made or had given, enough to get by on but recently I made a replacement for the smallest missing one. I did this because it is the smaller taps which need the most care and are easiest to break. Fig.2.2 shows a selection of the ones I use now. The biggest one was made by an apprentice who did not want it; it is a very good one, well made and cyanide hardened. I bought the tee wrench and it is useful but slips occasionally and the size range is small. My favourites are the two obviously home-made ones. They grip positively and will hold a good range of sizes.

A cheap and cheerful wrench

The simplest is often the best and you cannot get simpler than the wrench in **Fig. 2.3.** It can be made very quickly. The only tricky bit is to make sure that the holes for the screws go truly through the middle of the arms, and that the arms are drilled together, so that they line up lengthways as well.

Dimensions in millimetres

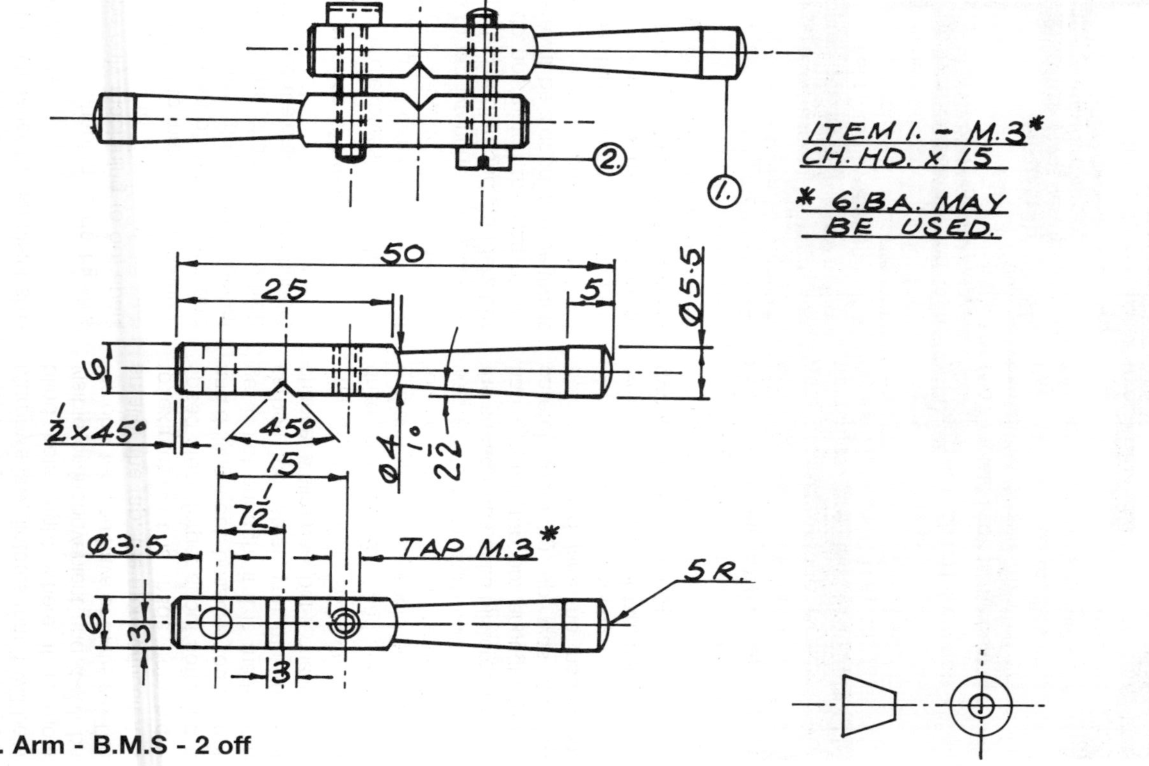

Fig. 2.1. 1. Arm - B.M.S - 2 off

When the holes have been drilled and tapped, the two arms can be clamped together and a pilot hole drilled in the centre. The hole can then be filed square for whatever the smallest size it will fit will be.

As there is no shaping to do for this type, the only machining to do, apart from drilling, is to tidy up the ends. When I've had to make one in a hurry, I have just sawn off two lengths and filed the ends tidy, with special attention to the sharp edges which would cut into the palms of the hands.

The importance of swing

There is an expression in the jazz business that, 'it don't mean a thing if it ain't got that swing'. The same thing applies to tap wrenches; they can be nickel plated or diamond studded, but if they do not match the size of the tap, there will be a good chance that it will be very hard to turn or that it will break the tap. Swing is vital. The wrench in **Fig. 2.3** has a swing of 145mm and I use it for sizes between 5mm and 8mm (2BA to 5/16in). The smaller one in Fig.2.1 has a swing of 75mm ideal for taps down to 12BA. Use too big a wrench on small taps and sooner or later you will break one. Murphy's law dictates that it will be a blind hole, right where it is most visible or inconvenient and it will be the only tap you have of that size. The smaller the tap, the more difficult it is to extract. If it is made from high-speed steel, forget about softening it and drilling it out, because you will not get it hot enough: if it is made from carbon tool steel, you may have a chance; a slim one, but a chance.

The smallest tap I have softened and drilled out was 4BA. I had the use of a gas/air torch which could be adjusted to a very small, very hot flame. The job was made from aluminium alloy and the surface was quite blistered when I had got the tap hot enough. Some careful touching up was needed before it could face the inspection. The moral is, always suit the size of wrench to the size of tap, and have a good range of wrenches.

Fig. 2.2.
The tap wrenches, one for most sizes.

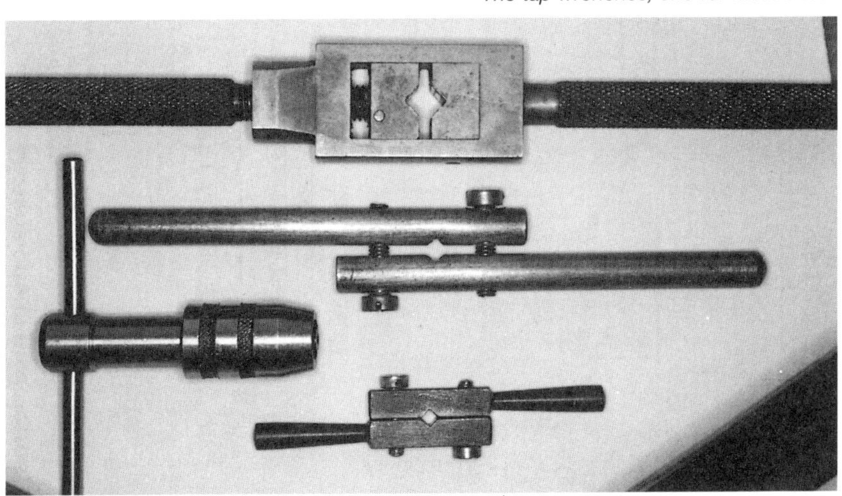

Dimensions in millimetres

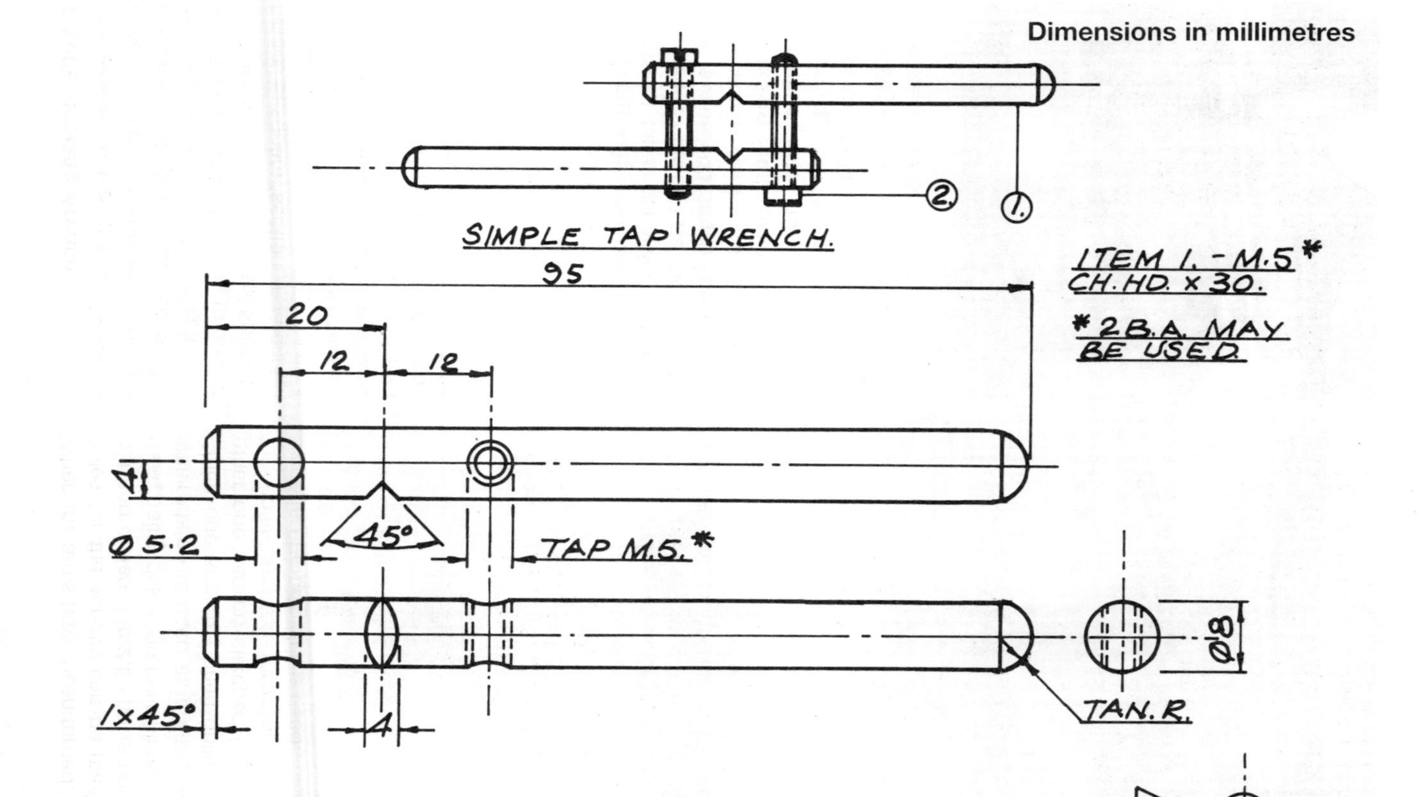

Fig. 2.3.

1. Arm - B.M.S. - 2 off

A better-looking wrench

The wrench in **Fig. 2.1** is almost as easy to make as the previous one and can be scaled up for bigger sizes. The one drawn is the smallest practicable size. There is a bit of turning to do and the best way is to make a split bush to hold the square section in a three-jawed chuck. This saves fiddling about with a four-jawed chuck, even if one can be found which will close enough to hold the size. The split bush is easy to make and the inside diameter should be a bit bigger than the distance across the diagonal of the square. The outside diameter should give a wall thickness of about 1 to 1.5mm. Split it with a hacksaw and de-burr the inside and it will hold a treat. **Fig. 2.4** shows one of the arms having its taper cut using the bush. The centre hole can be left in as long as it is nice and small. The finishing cut needs to be light, at high speed with a slow feed. The split bush will hold the arm for facing and chamfering, as long as it isn't expected to hold large cuts.

Fig. 2.4. Turning the taper on one of the small wrench arms.

When the arms have been turned, the holes for the screws can be marked out and drilled. **Fig.2.5** shows one of them being drilled on the Unimat. The small clamp is used as a hand vice. When one arm has been drilled, the other one can be clamped to it and the holes spotted through. At this stage the tapping drill is used.

Fig. 2.5. Drilling the tapping-size in the small arm.

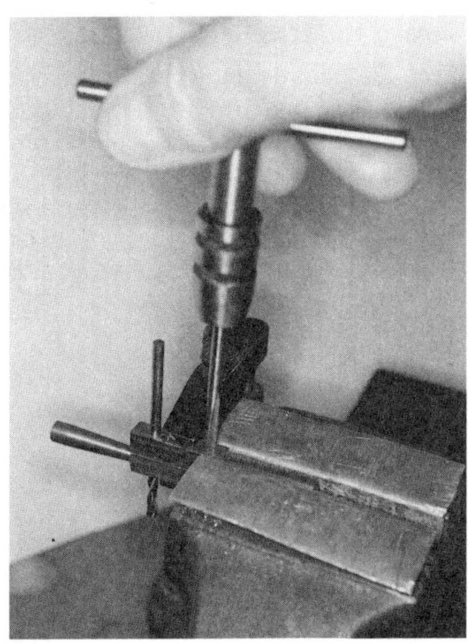

Fig. 2.6. Tapping the small arm, using a tapping-size drill to line up.

Fig.2.6 shows the next operation. The tapping drill is passed through one set of holes to hold the arms in position while they are clamped in the vice and one pair of holes tapped right through. A screw is tightened in the tapped pair and the process repeated for the other pair. With this done, one hole of each arm is opened out to the clearance size. With the screws in, the arms should line up precisely and a pilot hole can be drilled ready for filing the square **Fig.2.7**.

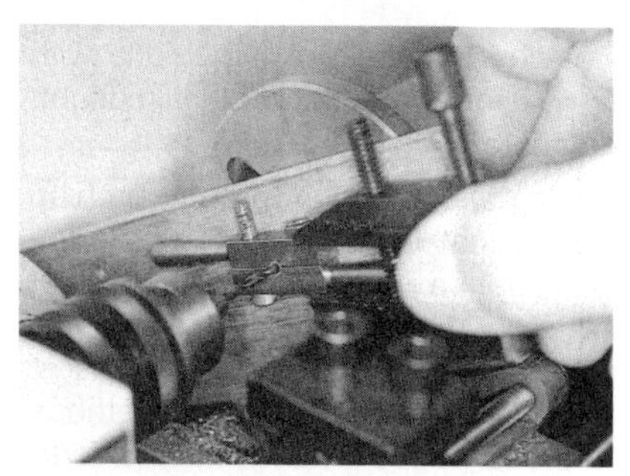

Fig. 2.7. Drilling the pilot hole for the square.

Making the square for the tap

From the pilot hole the square can be roughed out one arm at a time with a small square file. **Fig. 2.8**. To finish off, the two arms are assembled with a thin piece of card or a shim trapped between the arms, the square is then filed to fit the smallest tap which will be used, **Fig. 2.9**.

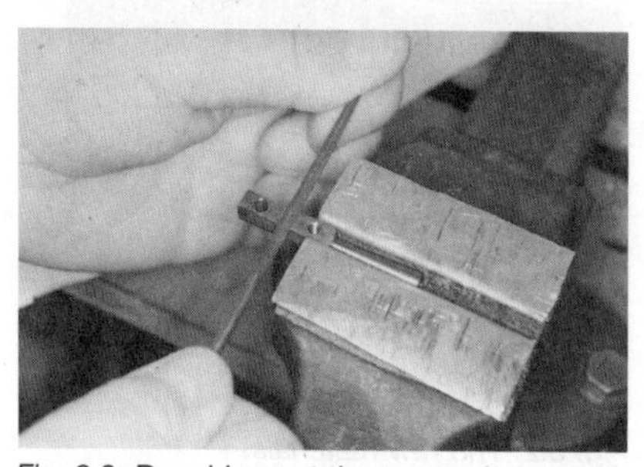

Fig. 2.8. Roughing out the square in one arm.

Fig. 2.9. Finishing the square with a square Swiss file.

The small gap left will allow the wrench to close enough to hold firmly.

Finishing off

The completed wrench or wrenches can be case-hardened, if the facility is available. I oil-blackened the smaller one and it looks quite presentable. **Fig. 2.10** shows it being used to drive a 10BA tap. It grips nicely and I can get a better feel with it than with the tee pattern wrench in **Fig.2.2.**

A set of tap wrenches is very useful, especially if they cover a good range. They can often be made from the odds-and-ends box.

Fig. 2.10. The finished small wrench being used.

Chapter 3

A 90mm Face Plate For The Unimat 3

I have often wished that the Unimat face plate was better designed. It is excellent for a catch plate when turning between centres, but not so good for what I mainly use it - as a support when I use the lathe as a drilling machine.

Changes needed

I have three main complaints. Firstly, it isn't big enough; 90mm is better than the 70mm one provided. Secondly, there is a rim at the periphery and ribs in the casting which get in the way of clamping. Thirdly, it has three clamping slots which rarely coincide with where I want to put the bolts. **Fig.3.1** shows the rim and ribs. Four slots would be far better.

Fig. 3.1. The blank for the quadrants screwed to the Unimat faceplate.

I decided to make a larger one with four T-slots and a flat back. If in doubt, fabricate.

Having one machine to do everything means that fabrication is usually the best option and saves the Unimat from too much milling. It does not like milling and makes graunching noises. So I intended to use similar methods to those I used when I made a four-jawed chuck. I thought I could use some of the left over bits from the chuck job, and wasted some time trying. Common sense prevailed and I began the job proper with the materials shown in **Fig. 3.2**, a cast iron blank just over 90mm diameter and 12mm thick, a 50mm diameter piece of duralumin and a piece of mild steel

Fig. 3.2. The raw materials.

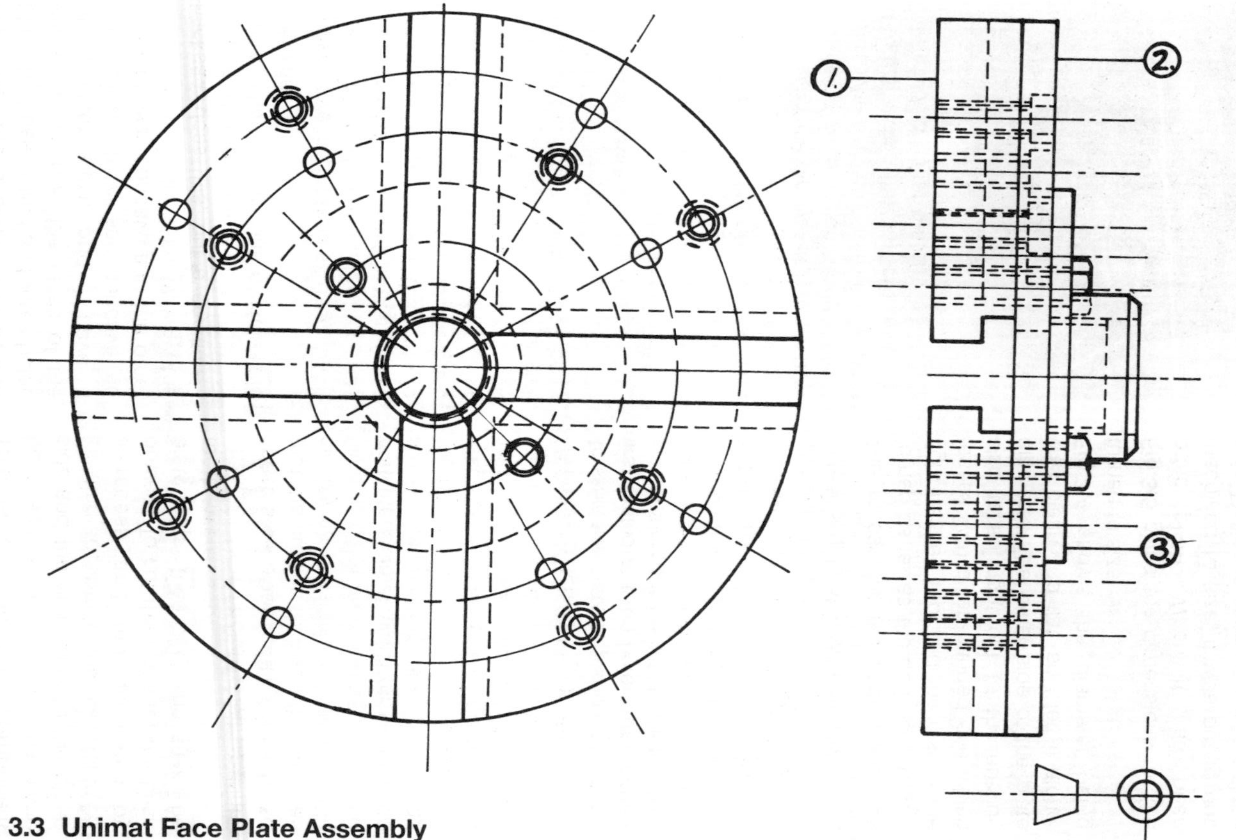

Fig. 3.3 Unimat Face Plate Assembly

plate 130 x 100mm x 5mm. The photo was taken after a face of the cast iron blank had been trued and three holes drilled. In the raw, the faces of the blank were sawn and I have a hacksaw which will saw concave, so one face was concave and the other one convex. I don't know why the hacksaw does this, but every time I have to slice bits off large diameters, that is what it does: one of life's little mysteries.

Those were the materials I used, but it was what I had to hand. If other ones are preferred, it doesn't matter. Apart from screws and dowels, the parts to be made are: the back plate, the base plate and a disc to make four quadrants from. **Fig.3.3** shows the assembly. The cap-head screws and some of the hidden detail have been left out to avoid clutter.

Fig. 3.4. The final cut off the base-plate.

Base plate

This is an important component because the back plate fastens to one side and the quadrants to the other, locating accurately, the back plate by a recess and the quadrants by dowels. To cut the circle for the base plate I first tried a coping saw. The teeth were soon worn flat, so I changed to a hacksaw with a high-speed steel blade, cutting bit by bit so that the cut line followed the curve as closely as possible. It wanted a little filing to get it as round as I could, so that the Unimat wouldn't protest too much: a large diameter exerts a large force against the tool, and small irregularities can make the belt slip. When this happens, sparks flash in the motor switch housing, so I go carefully with large diameters.

To skim the plate to just over 90mm, I first drilled a 1/4in hole in the centre and mounted it on a 1/4in bolt with a large thick washer under the head. The washer was 3/4in diameter and 7/32in thick. It gripped tightly and accurately in the chuck, running quite true and the skimming went well, with only a couple of small belt slips.

The recess for the back plate was turned as far as the bolt head with a right-handed tool and the rest of the recess with a left-handed one which also faced right out to the outside diameter. The other side of the plate was clean and flat, so I left it alone. **Fig.3.4** shows the diameter being turned to size.

Fig.3.5 gives the dimensions for the base plate. When it had been machined to size, it was put to one side. Drilling is done later, when all the parts can be drilled together.

Dimensions in mm's except where stated

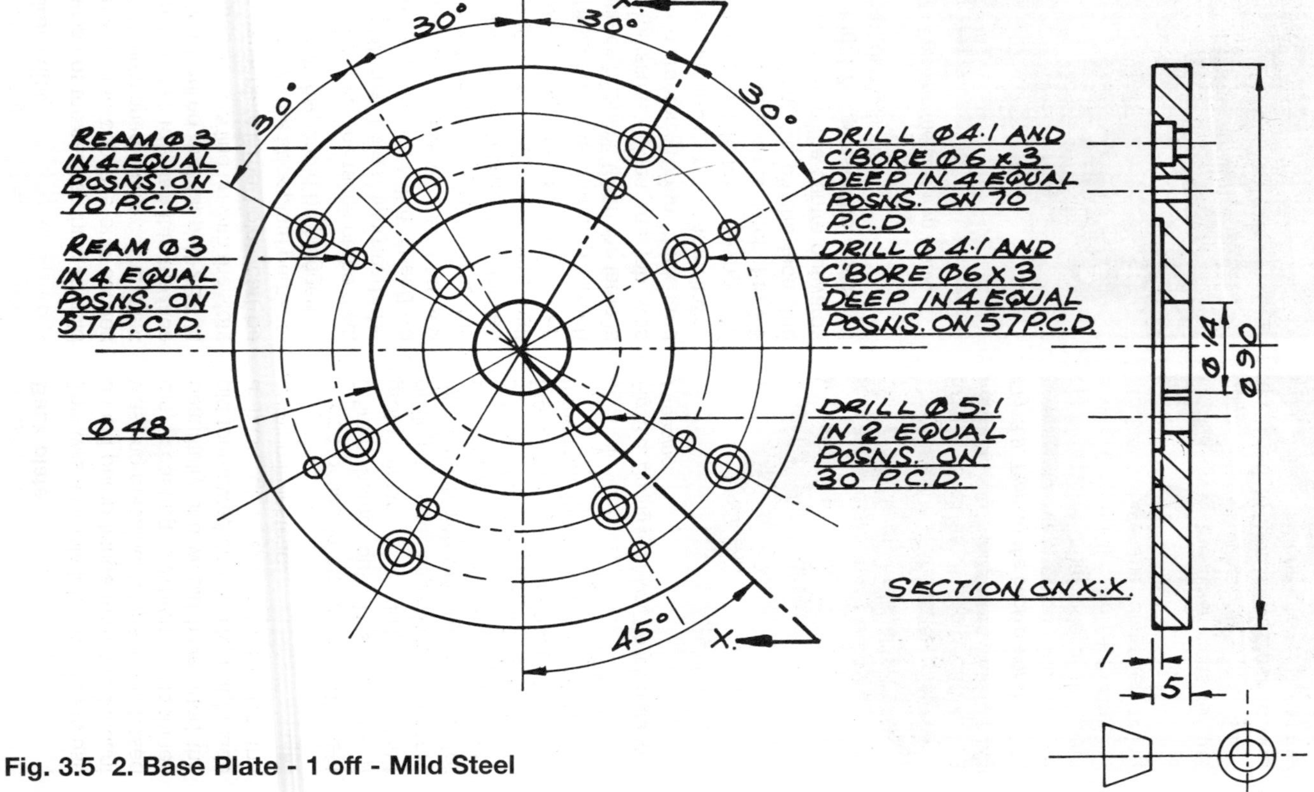

Fig. 3.5 2. Base Plate - 1 off - Mild Steel

Quadrant disc

This was not the easiest thing to hold because of the concave and convex sides I mentioned earlier. The best way to hold was to screw it to the face plate, so I drilled and tapped 2BA in three positions to line up with the slots in the face plate. The holes can be used to fasten the back plate perhaps, or if not suitable, could be plugged.

While machining the faces of the disc, I was glad that I was using carbide-tipped tools. I kept the speed to 130rpm, because there was a bit of a wobble on each side, as well as the concave/convex business. I locked the saddle for each cut and half locked the cross slide to make it a bit stiff; it stops the jumping which sometimes happens when the lathe is under pressure. When the job was 90mm diameter, 10mm thick and bored out in the centre to 14mm it was de-burred and left for finishing and cutting into quadrants later. **Fig.3.6** shows the final cut off the face, the tool cutting from the centre outwards and **Fig.3.7** gives the finished quadrant dimensions.

Fig. 3.6. Finishing the cast-iron blank.

Back plate

This was a simple job. I wanted to use an old pump flange from a redundant washing machine. It was a zinc based die casting which machines beautifully and would have fitted the old four-jawed chuck bits, but I made a hash of it and had to use the duralumin instead.

It was drilled in stages, with the last 0.5mm bored out. This corrects a grotty finish or a drill which isn't drilling to size, especially necessary when machining the core diameter for a fine thread. **Fig.3.8** shows the boring set up for the discarded one and **Fig.3.9** the thread being cut. For threading, the chuck was rotated by hand with a centre bearing in the

Fig. 3.8. Boring the Mark 1 back-plate for threading.

Fig. 3.9. Tapping the back-plate.

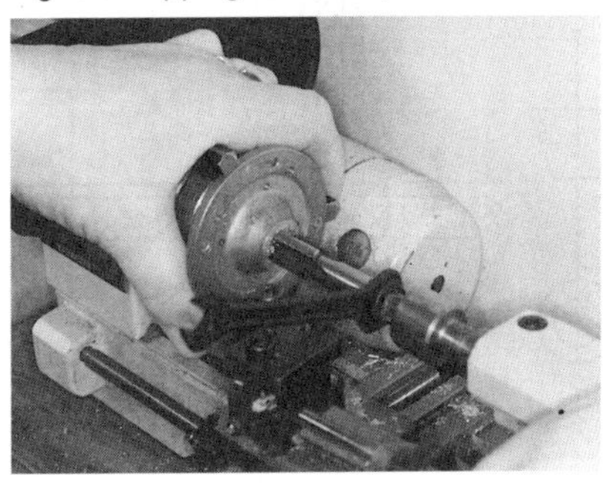

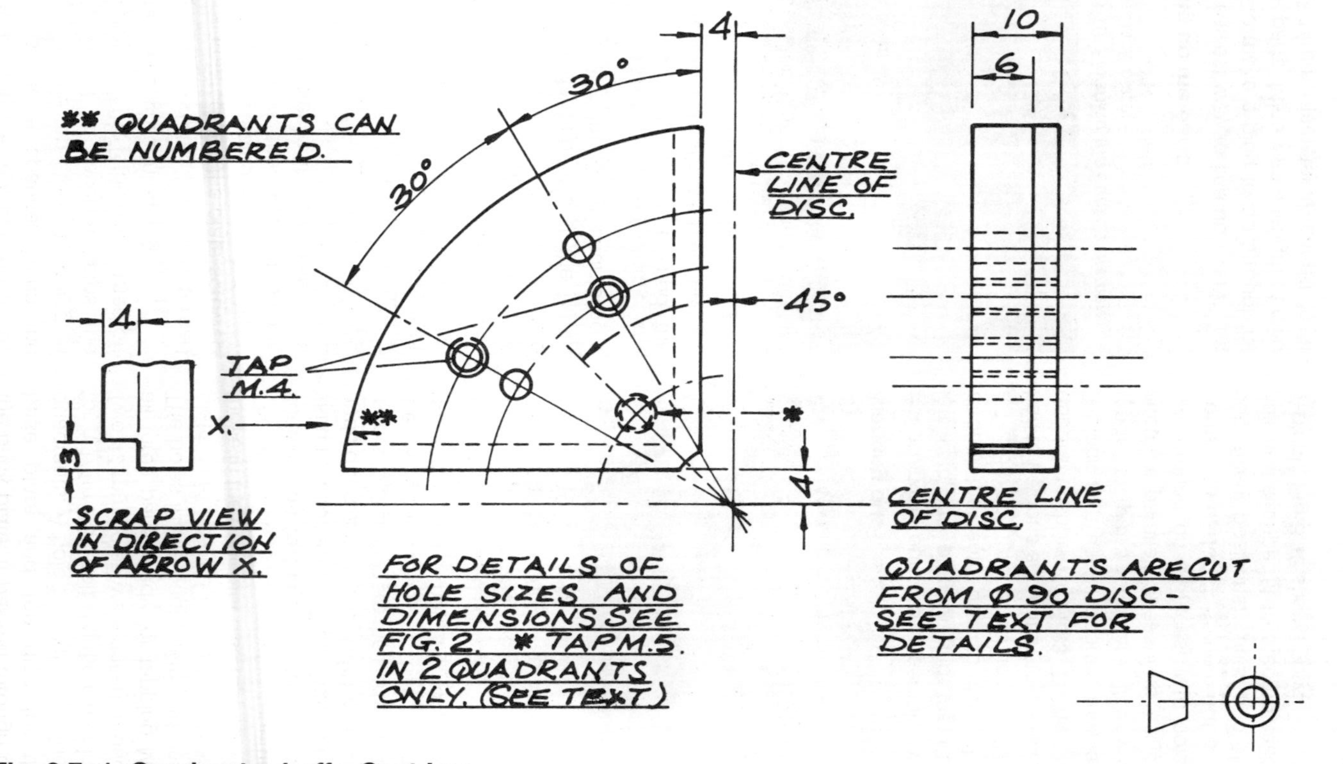
Dimensions in mm's except where stated
** QUADRANTS CAN BE NUMBERED.
30°
30°
4
CENTRE LINE OF DISC.
45°
10
6
4
TAP M.4.
X.
1**
3
SCRAP VIEW IN DIRECTION OF ARROW X.
*
4
CENTRE LINE OF DISC.
FOR DETAILS OF HOLE SIZES AND DIMENSIONS SEE FIG. 2. * TAP M.5. IN 2 QUADRANTS ONLY. (SEE TEXT)
QUADRANTS ARE CUT FROM Ø 90 DISC - SEE TEXT FOR DETAILS.

Fig. 3.7 1. Quadrant - 4 off - Cast Iron

centre hole in the tap, backed up by the tailstock. A spanner fitting the square on the tap stops it turning. A smear of oil or Vaseline helps the threading and the lathe was turned off at the mains while threading.

When threaded, the boss was turned and chamfered and the plate screwed on the lathe spindle for finishing. **Fig.3.10** shows the final cut off the 48mm diameter to fit the recess in the base plate. It needs to fit freely but with no slop. The plate can be unscrewed for checking because it will go back true every time. **Fig.3.11** gives the dimensions for the back plate. When finished the 5.1mm holes can be drilled. If any dimensions are changed to suit other materials, leave the 12mm depth of thread, the 14mm diameter and the 4mm counterbore alone.

With all the main parts machined, the drilling, reaming and tapping can be done.

Fig. 3.10. Finishing the outside diameter of the back-plate.

Lining up the parts

The easiest way to line up everything was to make a plug to go through all three parts. Mine was a length of mild steel 14mm diameter threaded to fit the back plate. It passed through the base plate and the disc for the quadrants. A hole through the middle for a 1/4in BSF bolt did the clamping. Two 4.2mm holes were drilled through all three parts ready for tapping M5. The holes in the back plate and base plate were opened out to 5.1mm and those in the quadrant disc tapped M6. The assembly was screwed together, screwed on to the lathe spindle and skimmed to level off the base plate and quadrant disc. Centre-punch marks to show where the parts line up are a good idea at this stage, preferably where they will not be too obvious.

Fig. 3.13. Marking out the quadrants.

Marking out

For marking out, the assembly was left with the plug in and the hole through the centre used to clamp it to a 1-2-3 block for the marking out. This had to be done accurately to make the quadrants shown in **Fig.3. 7**. The 1-2-3 block is a useful gadget; they are made in pairs and are like very accurate parallels, measuring 1 x 2 x 3in, ground on all faces, with holes, some threaded, some not, in convenient positions. I used one of a pair and clamped it to a combination V-block, **Fig.3.13** shows how.

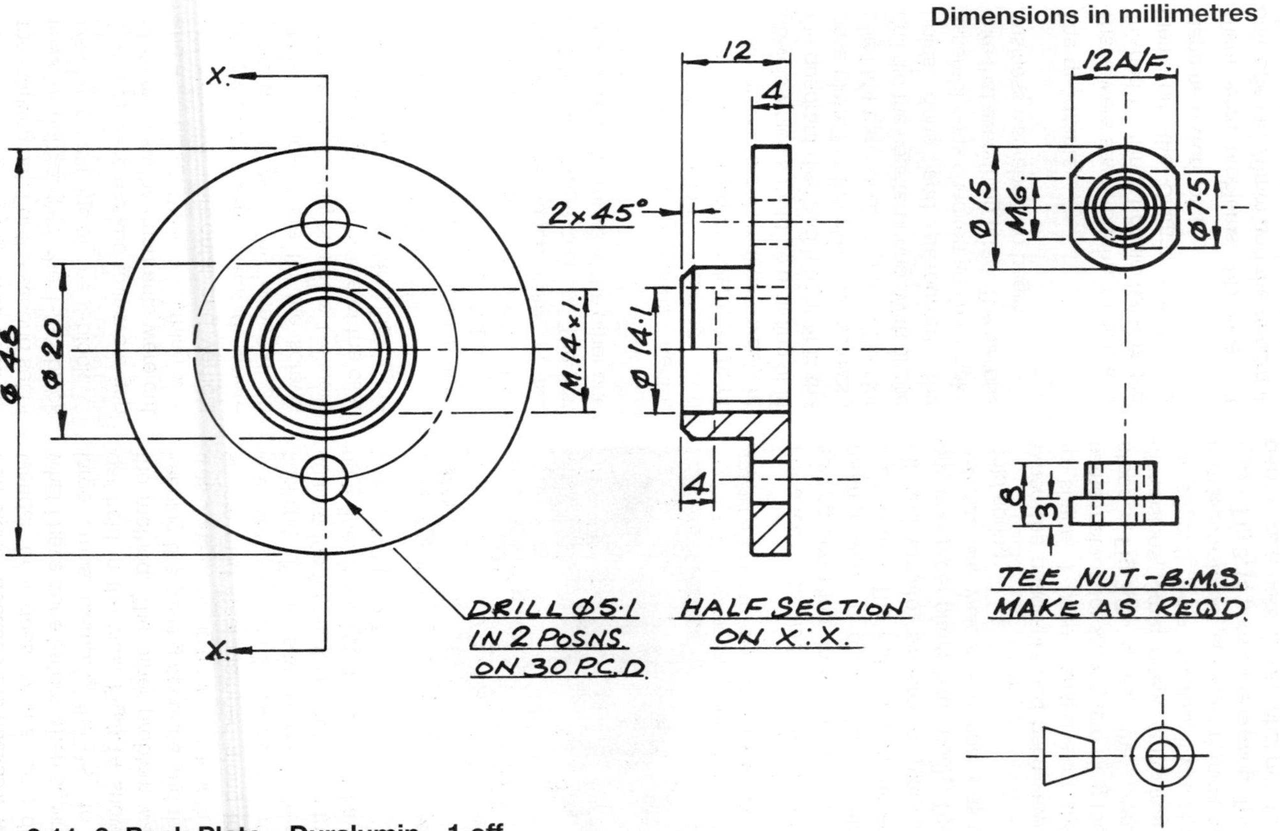

Fig. 3.11 3. Back Plate - Duralumin - 1 off

A vernier height gauge was used for the marking out. For the second set of lines, at right angles, the 1-2-3 block was put on a ledge on the V-block.

The lines were marked to leave a gap of 8mm when the quadrants were cut and assembled. While everything was still clamped, horizontal and vertical centre lines were marked where needed and also the ones at 30 degrees: those were for the screws and dowels. Lastly, numbers 1-4 were punched on the underside of the cast iron disc and the hidden side of the base plate, to identify positions.

The screw and dowel positions were stepped off with dividers. A bung in the centre hole in the quadrant disc, with a centre punch mark in the middle, located the dividers. The first setting was 28.5mm and the other one 35mm.

With the hole positions centre punched, drilling, reaming and tapping was straightforward. 3mm or 1/8in silver steel makes excellent dowels which should be a sliding fit in the quadrant disc and a tight fit in the base plate. For the clamping screws I used M4 cap heads and a 7/32in slot drill did the counterboring. With all the holes done and de-burred, the assembly was checked again to make sure that everything fitted. The serious business was about to begin.

The quadrants

These were sawn roughly to size and finished by filing. I could have milled them, but the Unimat would have made hard work of it.

There were problems. My vice will only open to 70mm and the quadrant disc was 90mm. Holding vertically is a non-starter because the hacksaw will wander, or it does for me. So I did what I have done before when sawing large lumps, clamping the disc to a bar held in the vice. **Fig.3.14** shows the method. The other problem was keeping the sawing accurate and this was done by using a fence, a length of square mild steel clamped along the line with a small allowance for finishing. If the saw blade is kept against the fence, it will cut down the right line. It works; a method I have often used before.

Fig.3.14. Cutting the quadrants, sawing against a fence to keep the cut accurate.

For once I was glad of the exertion of sawing and filing. In spring the small room I work in doubles as a cold greenhouse. The radiator was turned off and tomato, sweetcorn, marrow and cucumber plants had priority. The exercise was welcome in what was a cold spring.

When the quadrants had been sawn to shape, I used variations of the same method for sawing and filing the steps. **Fig.3.7** gives the step dimensions, 3mm deep, 4mm from the edge. It can all be filed, if you are a masochist, but is easier if most is sawn. **Fig 3.15** shows the sawing. The depth was left a bit shallow for finishing off.

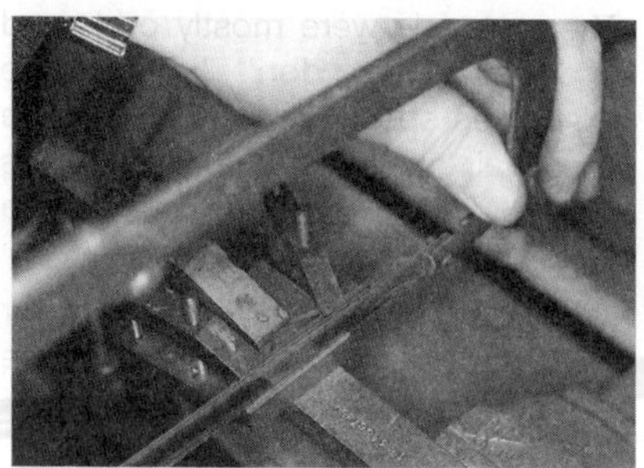

Fig. 3.15. Sawing the step in a quadrant, using the fence, note the bar in the vice for clamping large sizes.

Fig. 3.16. Filing the step in a quadrant.

To finish the steps, a piece of 6mm steel plate was clamped to the bar for the finished edge of the quadrant to butt up to; this was the vertical datum. The horizontal one was a piece of 6mm square. **Fig.3.16** shows a 4in hand file cutting away at the edge. When the one edge was almost there, the file was turned so that the safe edge was against the 6mm plate. If the safe edge is really safe, the method works well. If, when the file was made, the teeth were cut after the safe edge was made, there will be enough burr to make a mess of a filed edge, so check first. These burrs can be easily stoned off. Be careful not to use hardened steel for fences; 1/4in tool steel looks lovely but will not do file or saw teeth any good. When finished with, fence material will not be the size it started off as, so it needs keeping in a different place from stock.

Final machining

With everything checked and deburred, the face plate was assembled, screwed to the lathe spindle and the lathe turned on to make sure that all was as it should be.

The last two jobs were to chamfer the outside diameter and machine guide rings in the face at 5mm intervals. The guide rings are optional, but it finishes things nicely. If the lathe makes hard work of the rings, switch off, take the belt off and rotate the face plate by hand, feeding the tool in bit by bit. **Fig.3.17** shows it being done.

Fig. 3.17. Machining the setting rings in the faceplate surface.

Special T-nuts

The T-nut shown in **Fig.3.11** can be used in the Unimat cross slide as well as in the face plate. I prefer T-nuts to T-bolts because they will take a bolt of any length and it saves hunting for a T-bolt of the right length. If bolts are the choice, the slots will fit M8 or 5/16in with the heads faced to 3.5mm thick.

The face plate in use

Of the many uses, for me the main one is being able to use it as a drilling table. It provides plenty of room to use custom-made clamps or simple strap clamps. There is also scope for the many improvised set-ups I use and because the back of the face plate is quite flat, it will take various sizes of parallel clamps. **Fig.3.18** is one of the quadrants and **Fig.3.19** is the completed face plate.

The materials were mostly odds and ends and they don't have to be exactly as specified; if others can be used, fair enough. The same applies to the dimensions, they are only a guide.

It is a useful piece of equipment for the Unimat and, of course, can be changed to suit most small lathes.

Fig. 3.18. One of the finished quadrants.

Fig. 3.19. The finished faceplate.

Fig. 3.20. A typical job for the faceplate.

Chapter 4

An Adjustable Tool Post

I expect that there are plenty of Unimat users who, like me, use the standard toolpost. I expect that they sometimes get exasperated looking for the last piece of shim to centre the tool just right.

It is my own fault, for not making a Unimat-sized toolpost with some adjustment. There have been several designs published and I'm sure that one of them could be scaled to fit.

Unfortunately, I can always find another job which is more urgent or more attractive. I did though, sit down one day and think out a quickly-made one to tide me over till I can make a better one. It uses stock materials, except for one large piece, and the standard bolts and T-nut from the Unimat. There is some adjustment, because it is a cross between a single toolpost and an American type. American toolposts were the type we used on Southbend lathes when I was an apprentice. They had a central stem, slotted to take the tool shank. The tool sat on a rocker, which could be rocked to raise or lower the tool edge slightly to get it on centre.

There were one or two problems. Using the rocker too much could change the tool angles, and using a straight tool made cutting close to the chuck bad news for the front of the compound slide, which bore the evidence, from slight rub marks to deep gouges. We avoided knocking lumps off it by using cranked tool holders; not always convenient.

Fig.4.1 shows the assembly. **Fig.4.2** shows the completed job and **Fig.4.3**, a tool set correctly. **Figs.4.4** and **4.5** show what can happen if too much rock is used. The photos are exaggerated a little, but I have seen settings almost as bad. Different tool selection or packing pieces under the tool will put things right.

Fig. 4.2. The completed toolpost.

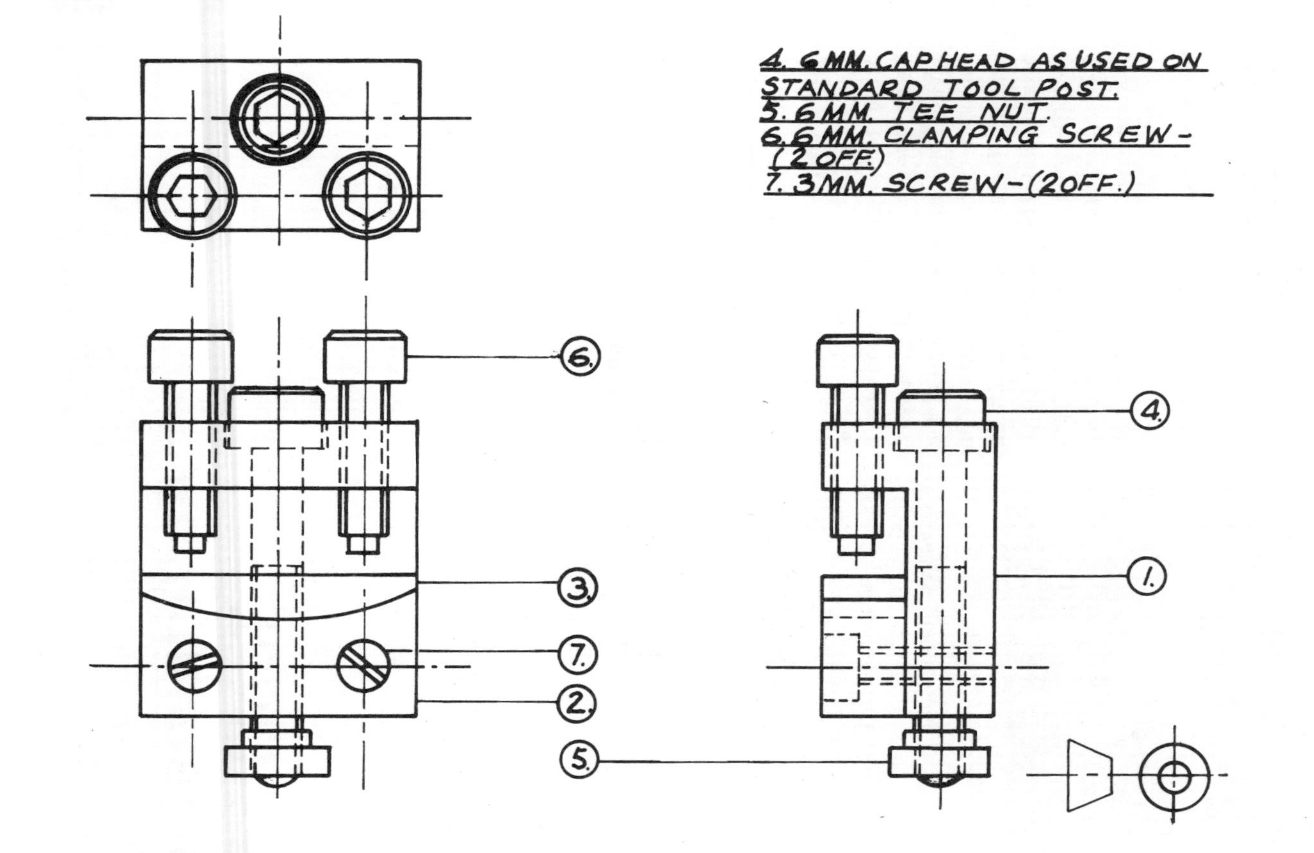

Fig. 4.1 Adjustable Tool Post

Dimensions in millimetres

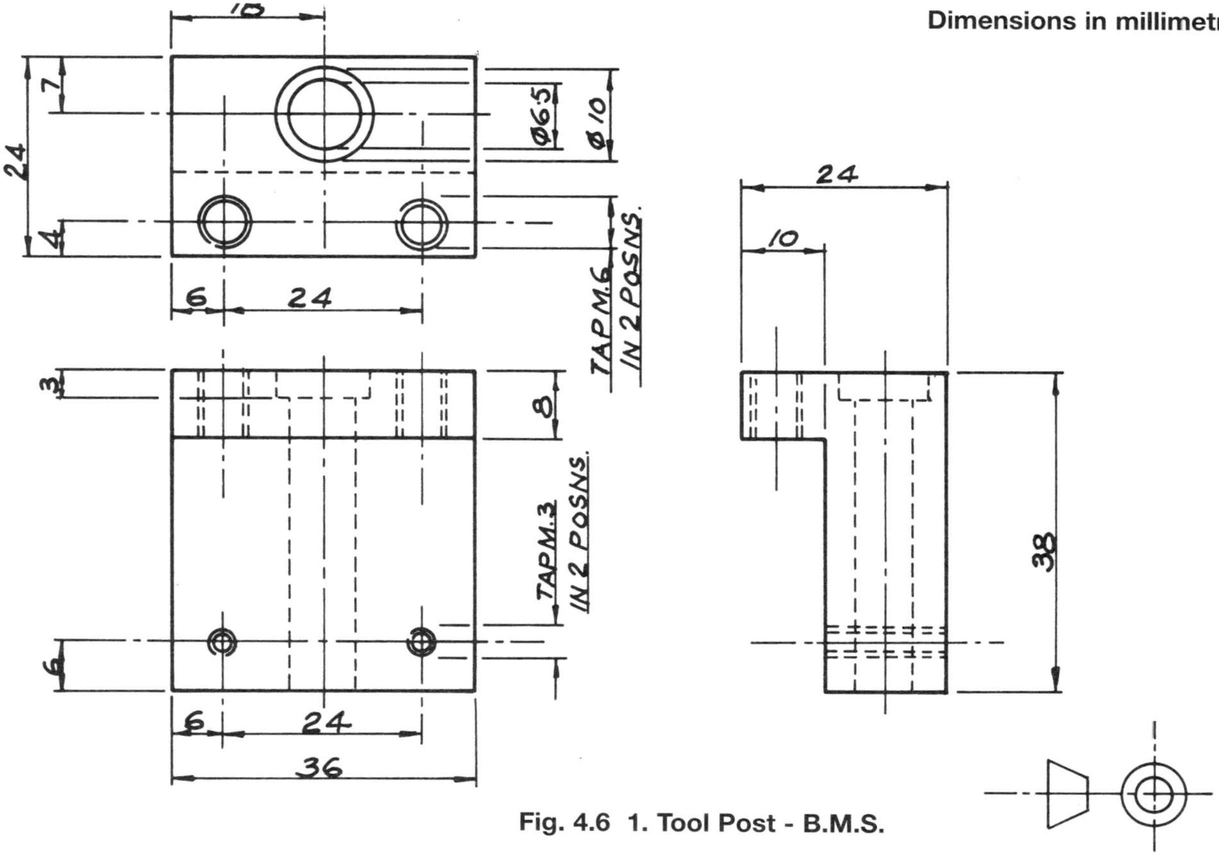

Fig. 4.6 1. Tool Post - B.M.S.

Notice that the spigots on the clamping bolts are overdue for trimming the mushrooming off. This is one of those little tasks which tends to get overlooked.

Choice of materials

It is not a difficult thing to make and mild steel does very well. I have though, a weakness for using cast iron for jobs like this and as I have several off-cuts of convenient sizes, I used one of them for the body of the toolpost shown in **Fig.4.6**. It involved a bit of hacksawing and filing, well, perhaps more than a bit, but I never mind a little hand work. It cuts the noise level down to comfortable CD listening and I had a new Goon Show to listen to. At times I laughed so much that I could hardly file straight.

Methods of trimming when too much to file

The hacksaw is the most valuable roughing tool in the box. There are times though, when the amount to be removed is too small to saw and very hard work to file. When this happens, I use the method shown in **Fig.4.7**. Sawcuts are made almost to the marked line, crossed by another set and the bits in between are chiselled off. A small chisel is just the right tool for this and does the work much faster than the coarsest file, then all that is left is the cleaning up. **Fig.4.8** shows the final flattening, using a fine small file and working on the block where the high areas were. The pressure of the fingers will pick the high spots off using short strokes. The marking out can just be seen. I always use a broad black marker pen as they last a long time.

Fig. 4.3. A tool correctly set.

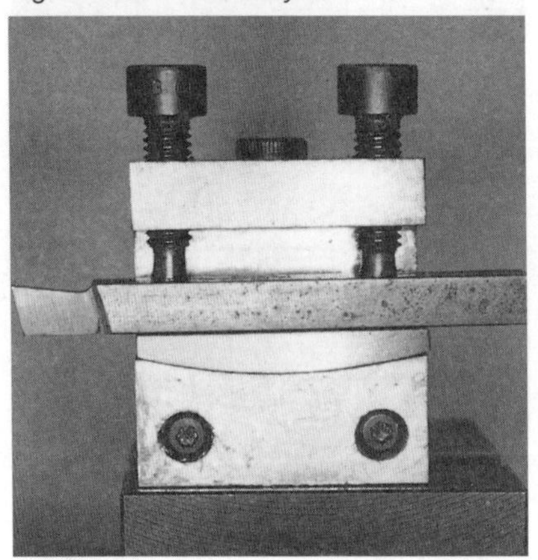

Fig. 4.4. The tool sloping down, rake decreases, clearance increases.

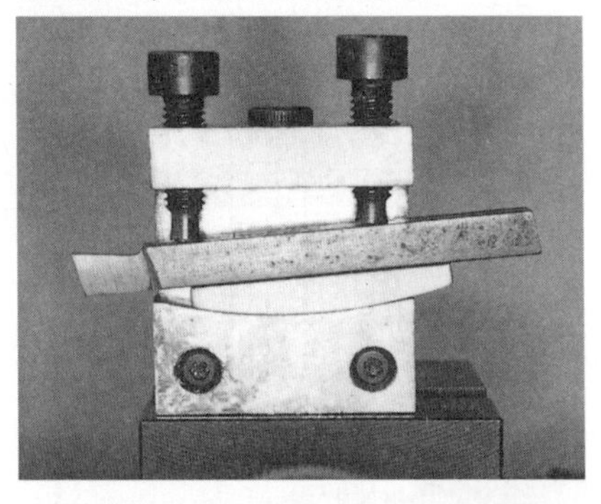

Fig. 4.5. The tool sloping up, rake increases, clearance decreases.

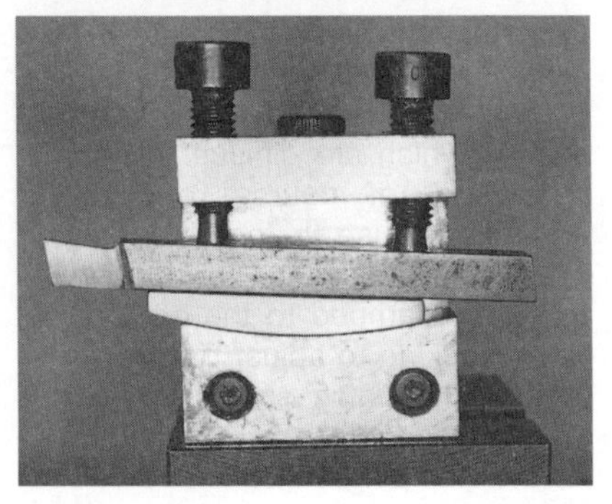

Shaping the toolpost

Whichever material is used, the final shape is an L with some holes drilled in it. There are many ways of making it, but the method described is best for the small lathe which has to do everything. It is important to make all the faces flat and square with each other. The only tiresome operation is cutting off the slice to make the long leg of the L.

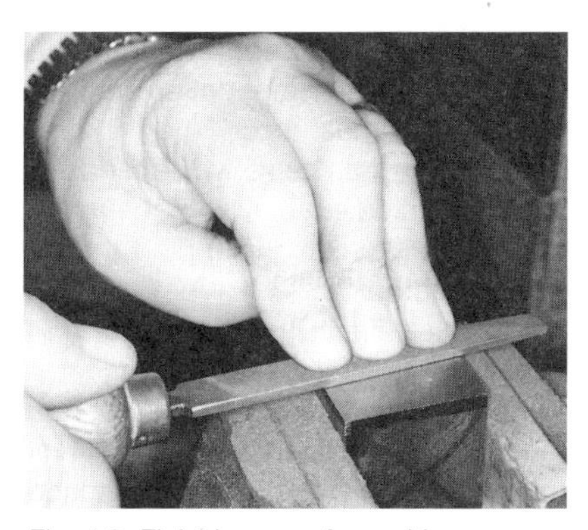

Fig. 4.8. Finishing a surface with a small fine file.

Fig. 4.7. A small chisel removes waste quickly.

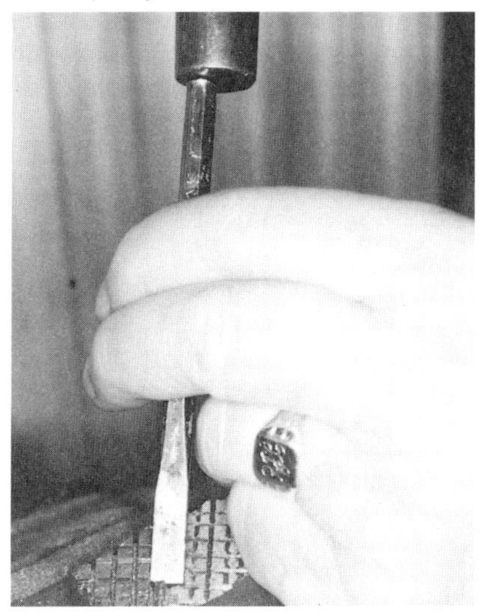

Fig. 4.9. Drilling the rocker seat.

Drilling the holes

I use the lathe for drilling in two main ways; the first uses the face plate as a drilling table, **Fig.4.9**. Awkward shapes which are difficult to hold by hand are, of course, clamped. I sometimes use a combination of methods. The second method is with the work clamped to the cross slide, using packing to adjust the height, as in **Fig.4.10** which shows the centre drilling stage of the two tapped holes for the clamping bolts.

Fig. 4.10. Centre-drilling the position for the clamping bolts.

The 6.5mm hole is a different proposition and needs drilling by stages. A series of drills with about 2mm between them is the best for deep holes. The lathe lacks the power to take large cuts. This applies to drills as well as any other cutter and it will react by stalling. The other problem is the swarf, unless it is cleared frequently it will bind in the hole and add to the tendency to stall. The counterbore for the head of the cap-head screw can be done with a slot drill or an end mill. The two small holes for the 3mm screws can be left till later.

Rocker seat

This was made from 10mm mild steel and the 70mm radius was marked out and roughly cut by sawing to almost meet the line, with cuts about 6mm apart, then a junior saw was used to follow the curve, **Fig.4.11**. Because the junior saw blade is a little flexible it will follow the curve. A bit of careful filing will nearly finish it and final finishing can be done with a piece of emery cloth stretched over a radius of the right size, **Fig.4.12**.

Fig. 4.11. Rough sawing the internal radius.

To make the seat fit right and be able to take it off without losing position, I used cap-head screws as fitted screws. At 25mm long, there is a plain length under the head which can be made to fit the holes accurately. This then combines the function of dowel to locate and screw to clamp. It can be done similarly with slotted screws such as those on the drawing.

Rocker

It is always easier to file an external radius, so the rocker didn't take long. The material was mild steel. The fit can be made by trying the rocker on the seat against the light and picking off the high spots. If the top surface is kept flat and the top and bottom square to the sides it should fit nicely.

Fig. 4.12. Finishing the internal radius.

Fig. 4.13. A bit of 'decoration'.

Dimensions in millimetres

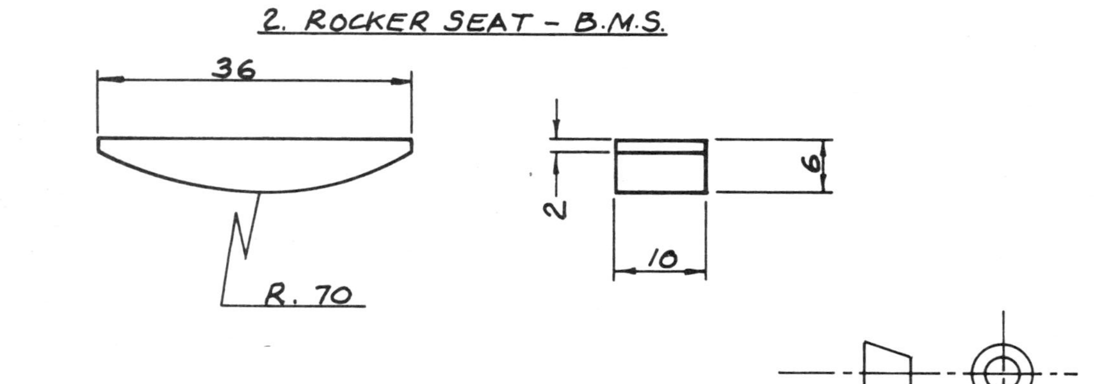

Fig. 4.6 1. Tool Post - B.M.S.

Drilling the rocker seat

When the rocker fits, the seat can be clamped to the toolpost and the holes drilled through. I found it to be a bit difficult to clamp, so I smeared some Loctite on the toolpost, clamped the seat to it and went to have a cup of tea. When I got back it was as stuck as it was going to be and it just held enough to spot through. When the holes were tapped, the only thing left was to clean up.

As I had just found my favourite scraper after it had been missing for a while, I spent some time getting it stoned to my liking, and still more time getting myself into the swing of scraping. If you haven't done any for a while it takes a bit of practice.

When I could do better than pathetic scratch marks, I scraped the surfaces where I could. I find it difficult to resist a cast iron surface if a scraper is to hand, **Fig.4.13**.

I am now the proud owner of an assortment of toolposts. There is a very tall one for when the lathe is fitted with the raising block I made, another with a larger slot for the tools which are too large to fit the standard toolpost and the original supplied with the lathe. The original is still the most used because the holders I made, to take the tungsten carbide tips I use most fit exactly. However, with the selection I have now, I should be equal to any type or shape of tool that comes my way.

Chapter 5

Inexpensive Tungsten Carbide Tooling

I first saw tungsten carbide-tipped tools demonstrated at the British Industries Fair at Castle Bromwich in, I think, 1947. I was one of a group of apprentices on the first of quite a few outings to various engineering activities. It was impressive; our eyes came out like organ stops to see some real metal cutting. We were more used to high-speed tools, often not quite sharp, used on not-quite-good machinery.

Ever since, I have been aware of the material, but not a great user of it. A few years ago I shed one or two wrong ideas. I used to think that small lathes lacked the power to use TC to its maximum and I had doubts about the sharpening. That was before I tried the small tips and found them so good. Now I use tipped tools, the throwaway ones in the small size which are made by Steliram.

Early misgivings

My first thoughts were wrong on several counts. Tips can be sharpened, both by grinding if a silicon carbide wheel is used, and by honing with a diamond hone. I use a grinding wheel to grind a small radius on the tip, which is where the tip usually gets dull or chipped. It makes a radius tool which is quite alright for normal turning, as long as no sharp corner is needed. The power business is no problem; the Unimat is quite able to machine most of the materials a model engineer will come across, as fast or faster than with other tool materials. I have found that the best way of using tungsten carbide is to keep the revs up and the cuts moderate to light.

Another of my doubts was cost; not the cost of the tips, because they last a long time. What made me wonder if it was worth investing in the tips was the cost of the holders. I was very reluctant to part with about £30 for one. Regular readers will be aware of my liking for making instead of buying. One of my philosophies has always been, 'why buy when it can be made?'. Very useful items

Given that the holders can be made quite easily, the tips are very good indeed. As the Unimat is a fairly light machine, the technique of many small cuts at high speed, rather than a smaller number of heavier cuts at slower speeds which a larger lathe would do, is the best way to shift metal. An assortment of holders can be made to cope with all the usual turning jobs. One other thing I like about using tips, is that they were originally developed for high-speed cutting without coolant. Since then, improvements in the material and modern coolants and cutting oils have changed that. To those, like me, who are able to work indoors, the ability to work without using coolant is very much appreciated.

Making the holders

There are several variations, some easier to make than others. The most awkward parts are making the register to locate the tip and a modified screw to hold it. The holders can be made from materials out of the odds-and-ends box and, although all but one of those described are for the Unimat, they can be scaled up for larger lathes. **Fig.5.1** shows a selection of home-made holders with tips. From top to bottom, a 10mm square for a larger lathe, a boring tool, a single-ended one and a double-ended one for turning and facing.

Single-ended holder

The holder shown in **Fig.5.2** is the easiest to make. It is made from a length of 6mm square mild steel, with an angled cut-out holding the tip in a position where it can turn and face on the same setting.

The cut-out must be angled at 10 degrees from the vertical so that it matches the clearance angle on the tip and fits snugly. It could be milled, but the setting up could be tiresome and involve a compound angle. I prefer to file such jobs because I find it quicker.

Fig. 5.1. A set of home-made tipped cutters.

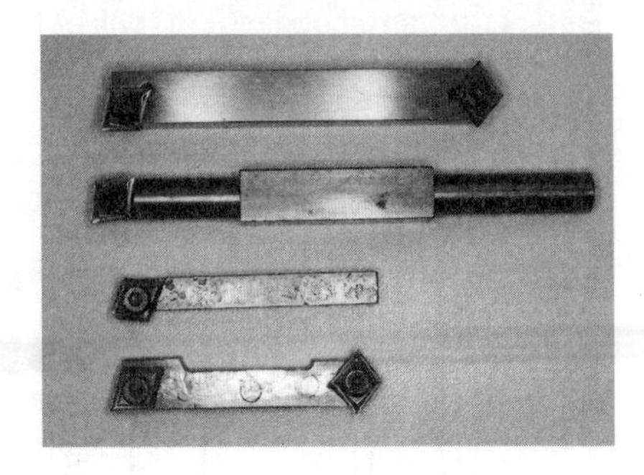

When I had fitted the tip, I clamped it lightly in position and spotted the hole through for the screw. A 4.2mm drill is the right size, or a scriber can be used to mark the outline and pick up the centre and punch it. It may sound strange to have a screw of 3mm needing a clearance hole of 4.2mm but it fits and does the job.

When the M3 thread had been drilled and tapped the holder was finished, except for the screw to hold the tip. This can be made from a cheese head turned to a countersunk shape at 60 degrees included. I made it from a cap-head screw treated the same way. Whichever screw is used, it needs to be a bit longer than the finished length, so that it can be held in a collet or chuck to turn the angle. If a cap-head is used, turn it with a tipped tool if possible, because the forming processes used in making the hexagonal socket and the straight knurl tends to work-harden the material. If high speed is used, cut the speed a little and use lighter cuts.

When finished to the dimensions in **Fig.5.2** the holder should sit nicely in the Unimat toolpost. I adjusted the one I made for height by filing the bottom of the shank till the cutting

Dimensions in millimetres

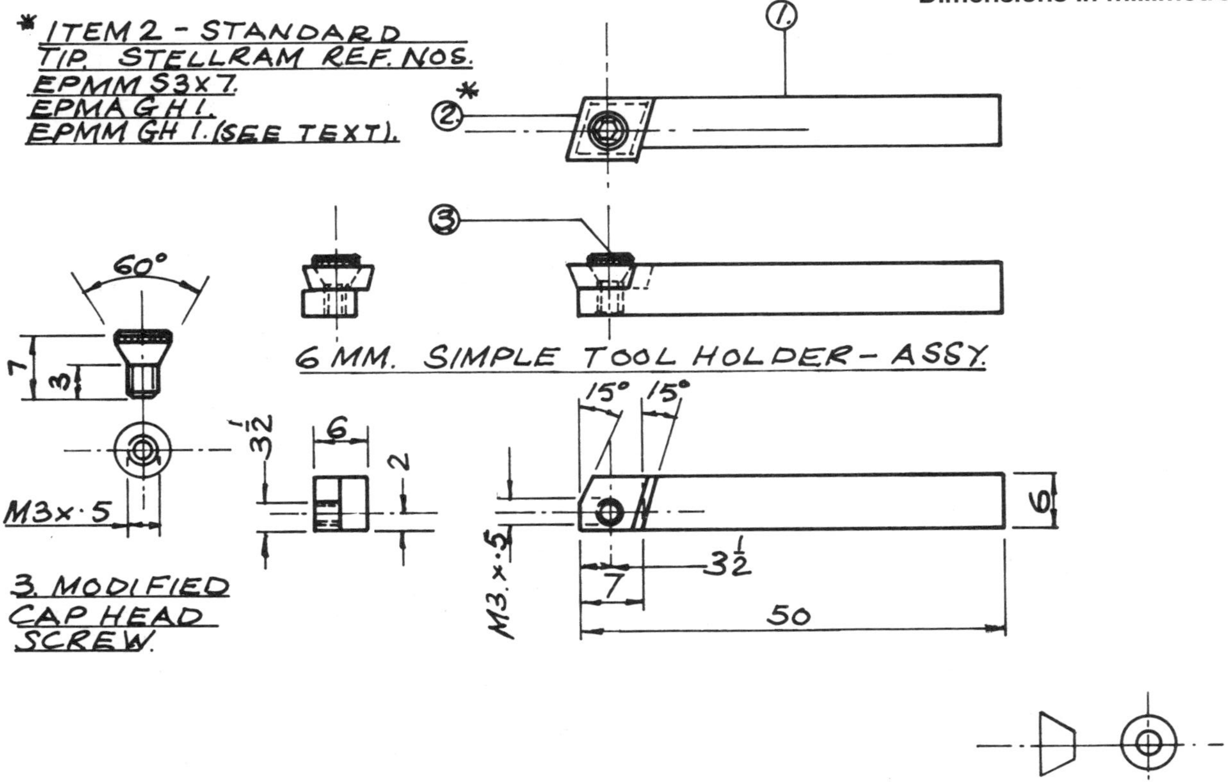
* ITEM 2 - STANDARD
TIP. STELLRAM REF. NOS.
EPMM S3x7.
EPMAGH1.
EPMM GH 1. (SEE TEXT).
1.
2. *
3
6 MM. SIMPLE TOOL HOLDER - ASSY.
60°
7
3
M3x·5
3. MODIFIED
CAP HEAD
SCREW.
$3\frac{1}{2}$
6
2
15°
15°
M3.x·5
7
$3\frac{1}{2}$
50
6

Fig. 5.2 1. Tool Holder Body - B.M.S

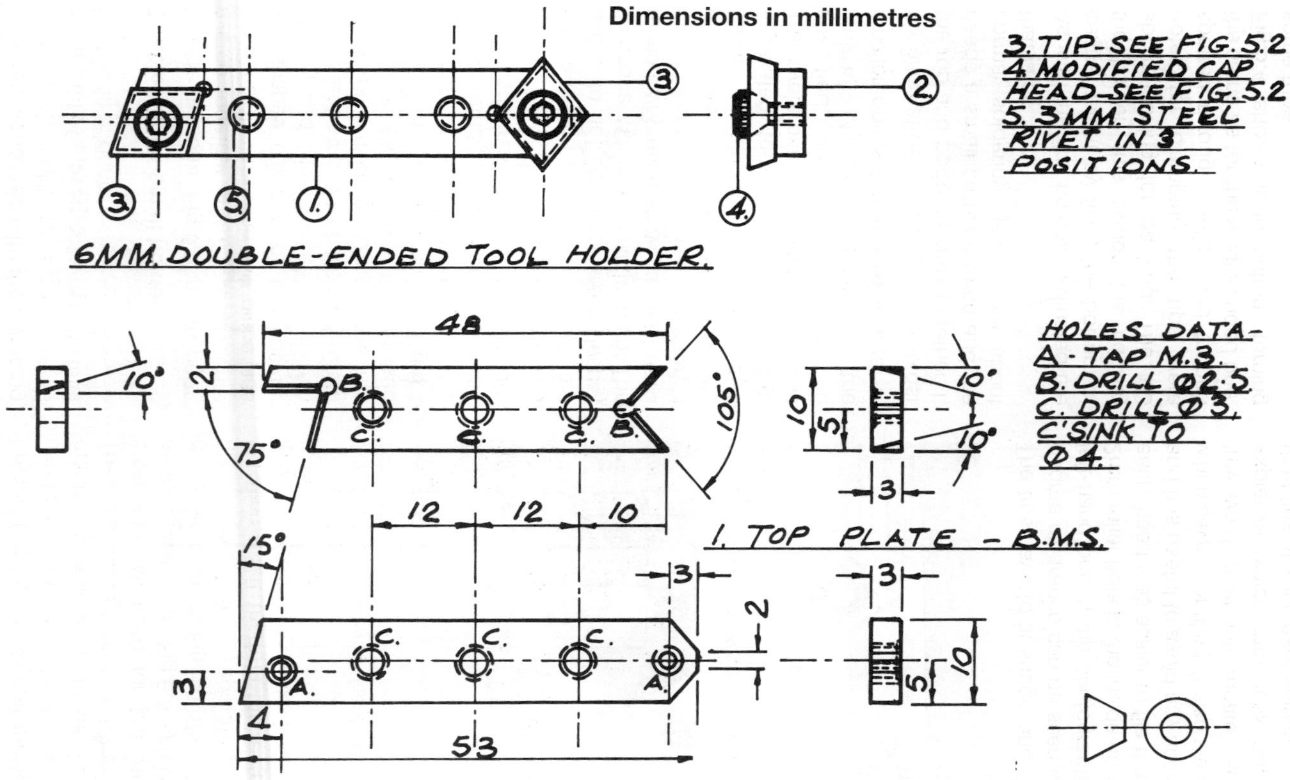

Dimensions in millimetres

3. TIP-SEE FIG. 5.2
4. MODIFIED CAP HEAD-SEE FIG. 5.2
5. 3MM. STEEL RIVET IN 3 POSITIONS.

6MM. DOUBLE-ENDED TOOL HOLDER.

HOLES DATA-
A-TAP M.3.
B. DRILL Ø2.5
C. DRILL Ø3. C'SINK TO Ø4.

1. TOP PLATE - B.M.S.

Fig. 5.3 2. Base - B.M.S.

edge was right on centre when clamped. I checked with the clamping bolts firmly tight because there is often a bit of movement when the final tightening is done.

Double-ended small holder

I made this one, **Fig.5.3** in two parts riveted together and it is a favourite for general work. The top piece has the shapes cut out for the tips by sawing and filing. I used 3 x 12mm mild steel strip and I filed to 10mm wide after riveting. Dimensions are shown in **Fig.5.3** and the finished holder is the bottom one in **Fig.5.1** The cut-out is not important and I cannot remember why I did it, I must have had a rush of blood to the head.

Notice the outlines of the rivets and take a lesson from them. If rivets are used, do not countersink too deeply, someone will have to fill them up! The reason why mine show, is that I used rivet material which was too short. I drilled for the rivets with the two halves clamped together and separated them for countersinking. The rivets can be smaller than those specified, down to 2mm but no smaller. My usual choice for the smaller jobs is 1/16in welding wire.

An alternative to riveting is to solder the top and bottom plates together. It needs a small propane torch and the normal soldering gear; more about that later.

As with the first holder, I adjusted the centre height by filing the bottom of the holder, this avoids the fiddling about looking for packing. The M3 holes for clamping the tips were spotted through, drilled and tapped the same as for the single-ended one. **Fig.5.4** shows it in action, turning some tube.

Double-ended holder

I made this holder so that those who use larger lathes may like to try it. It is made with inserts to locate the tips. They are made from 3 x 12mm mild steel strip as used for the double-ended small one. **Fig.5.5** shows the dimensions and **Fig.5.6** the inserts filed ready for separating and finishing. I left them in the length as long as possible, to make it easier to hold in the vice.

Fig. 5.4. Using the small double-ended tool holder.

Fig. 5.6. Two inserts ready to separate and finish.

The tips have to fit snugly and the 10 degree clearance can be seen on the left-hand one in the photograph. The 2mm relief hole in the inside corner of each insert was easier to file than drill and it is useful to avoid any accidents when sawing or filing. It also saves the 'my word, how unfortunate', style of expletive which may leak out from tight lips at such happenings.

The 10mm square bar which this holder is made from has 3mm steps cut into each end to take the inserts. **Fig.5.5** is not completely dimensioned, so that there can be a little latitude about the shape of the ends. As long as the inserts fit and the 68mm centres are right, all will be well. The vital thing is to avoid the tips overhanging as tungsten carbide is quite brittle and the tips need all the support they can get.

The inserts can be riveted with small rivets, or they can be soldered to the body. I chose to solder them. It has to be done with a good heat source. I used my small propane torch. The easiest way to do it is to sweat-solder the inserts to the body. If the body and insert are tinned first, the soldering is easy.

I started by making sure everything was clean, then I did the body first, heating it gently till a smear of flux on the surface of the cut-out began to spit and splutter. I dabbed it with the solder, without putting the flame on it and rubbed it with a piece of wire and some more flux till the solder spread over the cut-out. I wiped it off with a clean piece of rag and the result was a very thin coating of solder which looked like a coat of silver paint. I did both ends and put the body aside to cool off.

Fig. 5.7. An insert being tinned.

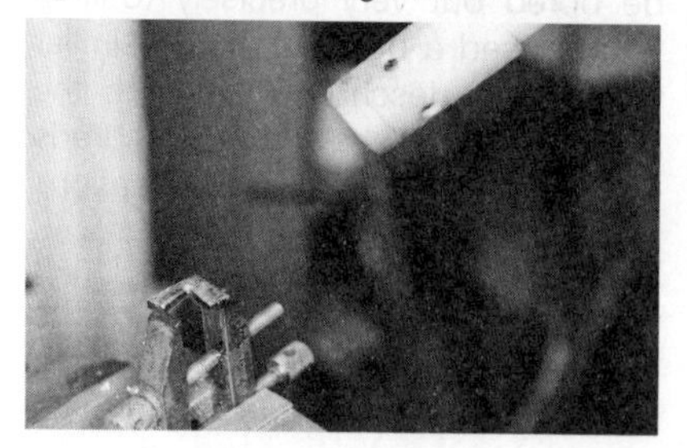

The inserts had to be held differently for tinning. I didn't want to hold them in the vice; for one thing it was a new vice and I didn't want to mess it up, also the bulk of it would act as a heat sink. I solved these difficulties by holding the inserts in a small clamp, **Fig.5.7** and holding the clamp in the vice. In the photograph, the insert has got its solder coating and just needs wiping to get rid of the excess. I used an old clamp and held the torch at about the distance it is in the photograph.

Both inserts were tinned and wiped off. I checked to make sure that they still fitted the steps in the body and filed off any little bits of solder which were in the way. I also broke the edges where they butted against the steps. I put a very light smear of flux on the steps and clamped the inserts in place, one at a time. All that is needed is a gentle warm up and capillary action does the rest. When the solder runs, a little extra can be dabbed on. The result is shown in **Fig.5.8** where the facing insert has been soldered. I cleaned off the excess, there is always some, and filed the insert flush with the body.

Fig. 5.8. An insert soldered to the 10mm square holder body.

The flux can be cleaned off with methylated spirits. It is important not to get the work too hot, it should not show tempering colours. Other fluxes could be used, but avoid the acid based types such as Baker's fluid because they are corrosive and not easy to clean off.

I didn't try getting the work hot enough with a soldering iron. I don't think even the largest iron would, so if you haven't got the tackle to do the soldering, rivet the inserts to the body.

Lastly, I clamped the tips in position and spotted through for the drilling and tapping of the M3 screws. It can be done before cutting out the step. **Fig.5.9** shows my way of drilling these holes. The face plate is used as a drilling table and I had to be careful about the clamping, hence the large strap clamp. If a drilling machine is available, it makes life a lot easier but I am so used to using the Unimat for everything that it is automatic to set up the face plate for drilling.

The tips are the ones specified in **Fig.5.2** and are common to all the holders, as are the modified M3 screws. The only difference is that the screws will be different lengths to suit the depth of the holder. For the 10mm square holder they will be between 6mm and 7mm under the head.

Tipped boring bar

A set of tools for a lathe would not be complete without a boring bar. The dimensions are shown in **Fig.5.10** and it is simple to make from 8mm diameter mild steel, quite similar to the single-ended one in **Fig.5.2** in the way the cut-out is shaped to take the tip. I know that these boring tools work alright because I used one when I worked part-time for a small company which made cleaning equipment for jet engines. Almost all the components were made from stainless steel, among them a collet which came in roughly drilled. It had to be bored out very precisely to fit a tube. I used a boring bar very similar to the one described here with the same tip. It must have done hundreds of the collets with very little attention.

The only small difficulty, once I had filed the cut-out and marked the centre for the tapped hole, was the drilling. I used a home-made crutch

Fig. 5.9. Drilling the tapping-size hole in the 10mm holder body..

Fig. 5.11. Using a crutch centre to drill the tapping-size hole in the boring bar.

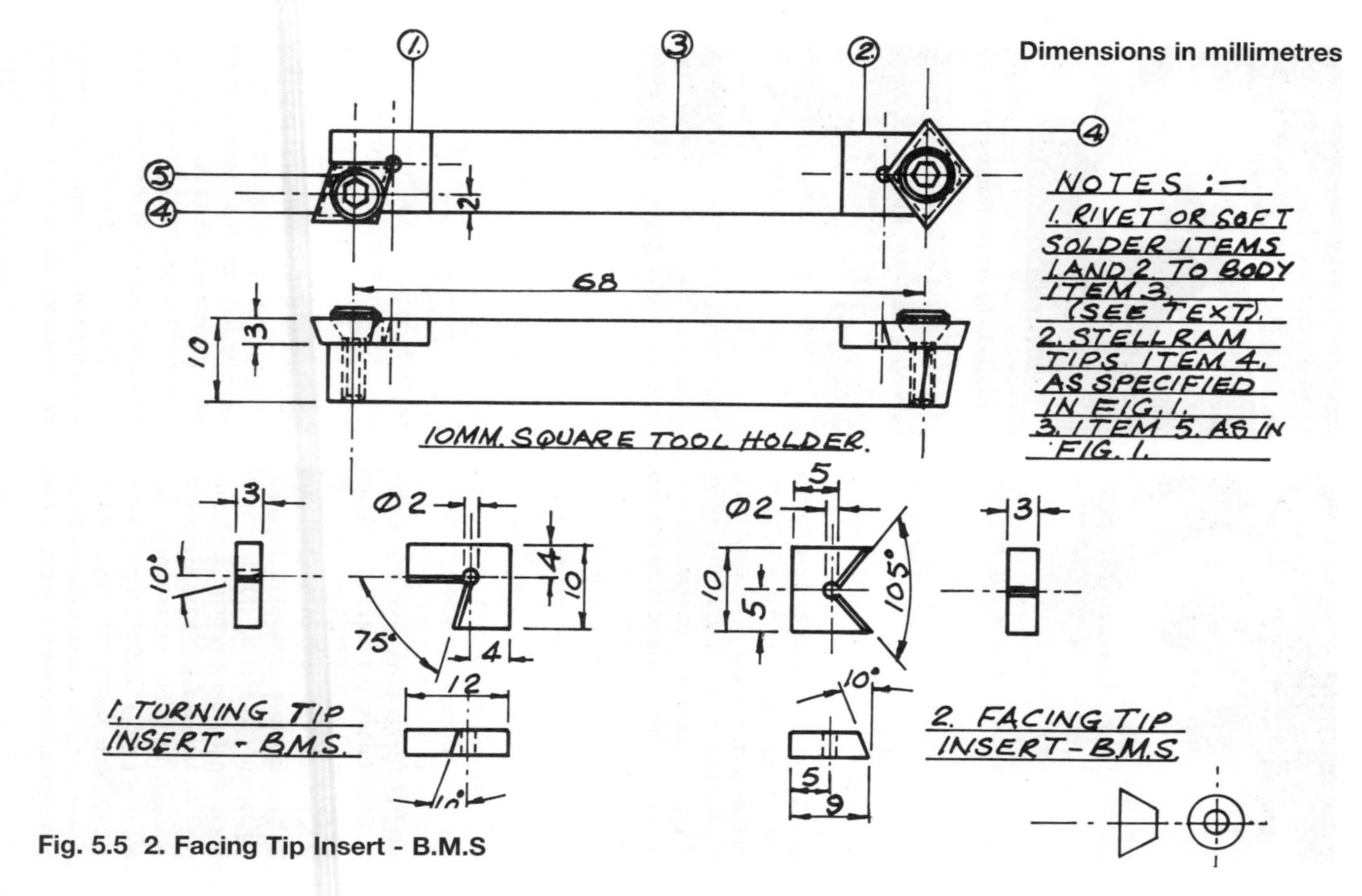

Fig. 5.5 2. Facing Tip Insert - B.M.S

centre in the Unimat tailstock, see **Fig.5.11**. It had to be clamped; I have done similar jobs before and if it is not clamped, it will try to rotate in the vee when the drill takes hold.

Another home-made accessory was used to make the split jacket which holds the boring bar. It was the four-jawed chuck I made. It is not perfect and the jaws are spread a bit, but it works and does all I want. I used a piece of 10mm square mild steel and once it was running true, and had been faced, it only needed drilling 8mm to take the bar. The drilling, as is normal on the Unimat, was done in stages, **Fig.5.12** shows it well under way. When I'd drilled right through, the jacket was reversed and the other end faced. After de-burring, I split the jacket by hacksawing, **Fig.5.13** shows this. There is no need to make a jacket, because the bar can be held on a small shallow V block if the jacket is too much trouble to make. By accident or design, I made the bar and jacket to just fit the Unimat toolpost, although when the bar is swivelled to bring the cutting edge on centre, the tool has a slight negative rake. As **Fig.5.14** shows, it doesn't seem to make any difference to the finish of the bore or the faced section of the test disc.

Fig. 5.12. Drilling the jacket for the boring bar.

Fig. 5.13. Splitting the jacket; a careful hacksaw job.

A special toolpost

I wanted to try out the 10mm square holder and it was far too big to fit in the standard toolpost, so the solution was to make an over-sized one with a larger slot to fit the tools which are a tight squeeze in the standard one or don't fit at all. **Fig.5.15** shows what I made, very quickly from a piece of cast iron. I tried out the 10mm square holder and it worked a treat. **Fig.5.16** shows the turning end and **Fig.5.17** the facing.

Fig. 5.14. The boring bar being tested.

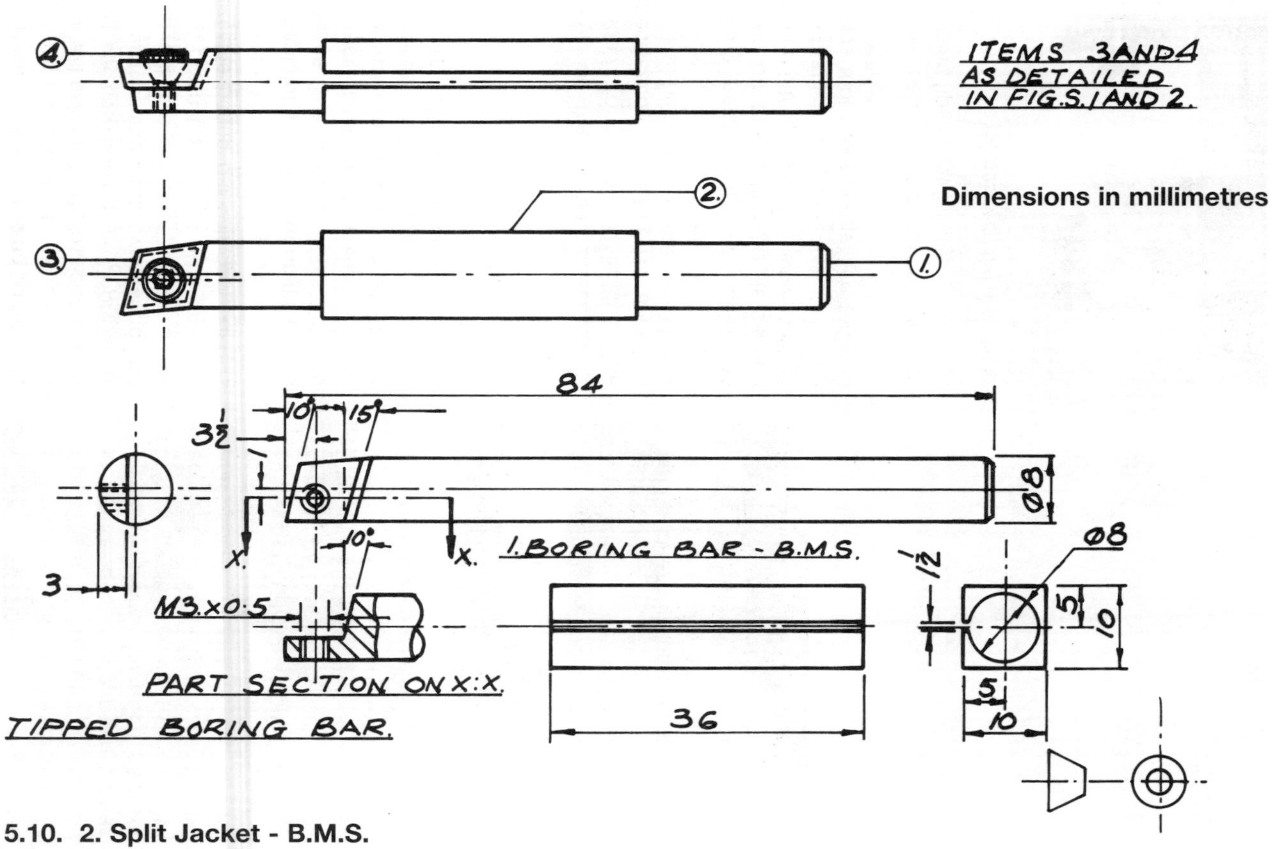

ITEMS 3 AND 4
AS DETAILED
IN FIG.S. 1 AND 2.

Dimensions in millimetres

4.

3.

2.

1.

84

3½

10°

15°

1

Ø8

10°

3

M3.×0.5

1. BORING BAR - B.M.S.

PART SECTION ON X:X.

TIPPED BORING BAR.

36

½

Ø8

5

10

5

10

Fig. 5.10. 2. Split Jacket - B.M.S.

Just one small but important point about the boring bar jacket. The place to position the clamping screws is directly over the edge where the split is. It will only pinch the bar correctly in that position. Look at any boring bar of this type in a typical workshop and you will find scars left by the bolts right down the middle. The smallest size the boring bar will cope with is about 12mm.

Except for the 10mm holder, all the holders I've described are for the Unimat or lathes of similar size, but they can be scaled up for larger machines. A selection of tips and holders will make most turning jobs easier and quicker. Grinding is not difficult; I use a silicon carbide wheel which is 125mm diameter, 13mm wide, with a bore of 12.7mm. It fits nicely on the grinding attachment I made for the Unimat. The specification is, CG-60-KV and it is stocked by many companies. When a tip no longer cuts correctly, it is usually because a small chip has come off the cutting tip. It can be ground into a radius tool which will go on churning away for some time as a radius tool has a longer life than an edged tool.

Home-made holders reduces the cost of using tips considerably.

Fig. 5.15. The toolpost with the extra large slot.

Fig. 5.16. Testing the turning end of the 10mm square holder.

Fig. 5.17. Testing the 10mm square holder for facing.

I know that we call anything which does the job a DTI or 'clock', but we only do so for the same reason that we call a vacuum cleaner a 'Hoover'. What I mean by dial gauge, is the one with the large clock face, operated by a plunger and gearing.

Things which are most difficult to do without attachments are: checking small holes and internal features, lining up shallow projections, like the

Chapter 6

Attachments For Dial Gauges

One of the most useful instruments a model engineer can have is a dial gauge. It will check a lot of things: alignment, parallelism, concentricity, roundness and squareness to name a few. It can even be used in some applications, for measuring. I am lucky to have one, given to me by a very good friend, but there is one snag, there are no accessories and without them, the usefulness is at least halved. A dial gauge when bought, or given, is usually just that, the gauge only. It takes a big pocket to equip it with all the extras. My pocket is quite small and I am reluctant to buy what I can make, so I made a set of attachments. It is best to be clear first about which instrument I mean.

I know that we call anything which does the job a DTI or 'clock', but we only do so for the same reason that we call a vacuum cleaner a 'Hoover'. What I mean by dial gauge, is the one with the large clock face, operated by a plunger and gearing.

Things which are most difficult to do without attachments are: checking small holes and internal features, lining up shallow projections, like the fences on my milling table, and setting vice jaws true. There are ways of solving these problems, but they take time and often mean hunting for bits and pieces. **Figs.6.1** and **6.2** show two examples of the attachments making life easier.

Fig. 6.1. Using the accessory for truing a bore.

Fig. 6.2. Using an accessory for setting a fence true.

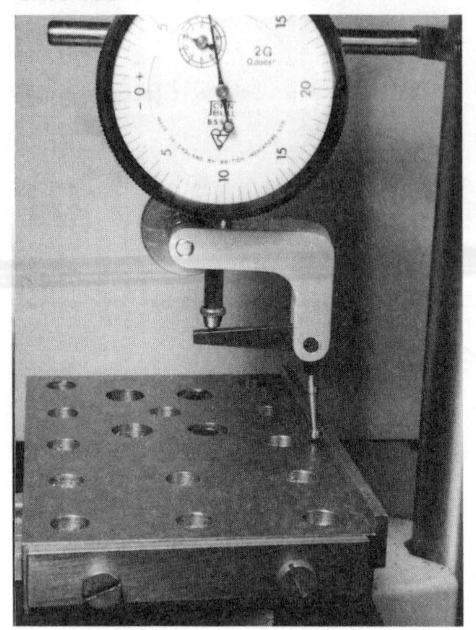

The components

All the components can be made using a small lathe, drilling machine, files, drills, taps and dies, a couple of reamers and a hacksaw. It is a useful exercise in marking out, fitting and turning. The dimensions are metric except for the 5/16in hole in the bracket, but they could be converted to imperial if more convenient. **Fig.6.3** is the assembly.

Bracket

This is the largest part, shown in Fig.6.4 which fits over the stem of the gauge, clamps it and holds the pivoting arm. I used a piece of duralumin which was close to the size I was looking for and had a hole drilled in the right place, so that I didn't have to file the internal radius. Mild steel could be used instead, but if it was, some lightening holes would be a good idea to reduce the weight. Duralumin, or a similar alloy is an easy material to use; nice and light, and easy to cut and shape. If like mine, your equipment is a bit limited, using a material which is no problem for machining is a good idea. I milled enough of the bracket to establish accurate datums and filed and hacksawed the rest. The milling and drilling were done using a home-made milling/drilling head, something I have since discarded in favour of using the lathe for all machining. The hole for the 5/16in reamer was drilled by stages to 9/32in which left enough for the reamer to take out. I reamed it by hand because a hole that size would stall the lathe motor. The 2BA tapping drill was a No.25 and the clearance 3/16in, taken about half way through. The 6BA tapping drill was No.43 and the clearance No.30, again taken half way through.

The slots were marked and cut. They can be milled, but I find it quicker to do jobs like that by hand. The slot which goes through to the 5/16in hole is only for clamping, so a nice accurate hacksaw cut is enough. My bracket has slots of the same size in both positions. I blame Mr. Puccini for that, because it was a particularly beautiful part of one of his operas that I was listening to at the time (favourite background music when I'm working but normally turned off when I have to concentrate); there must be a moral there. Luckily, the oversize slot didn't matter.

The important slot is the 3mm one and it needs a bit of care. A good way to rough it out is to put two hacksaw blades in the same frame using two

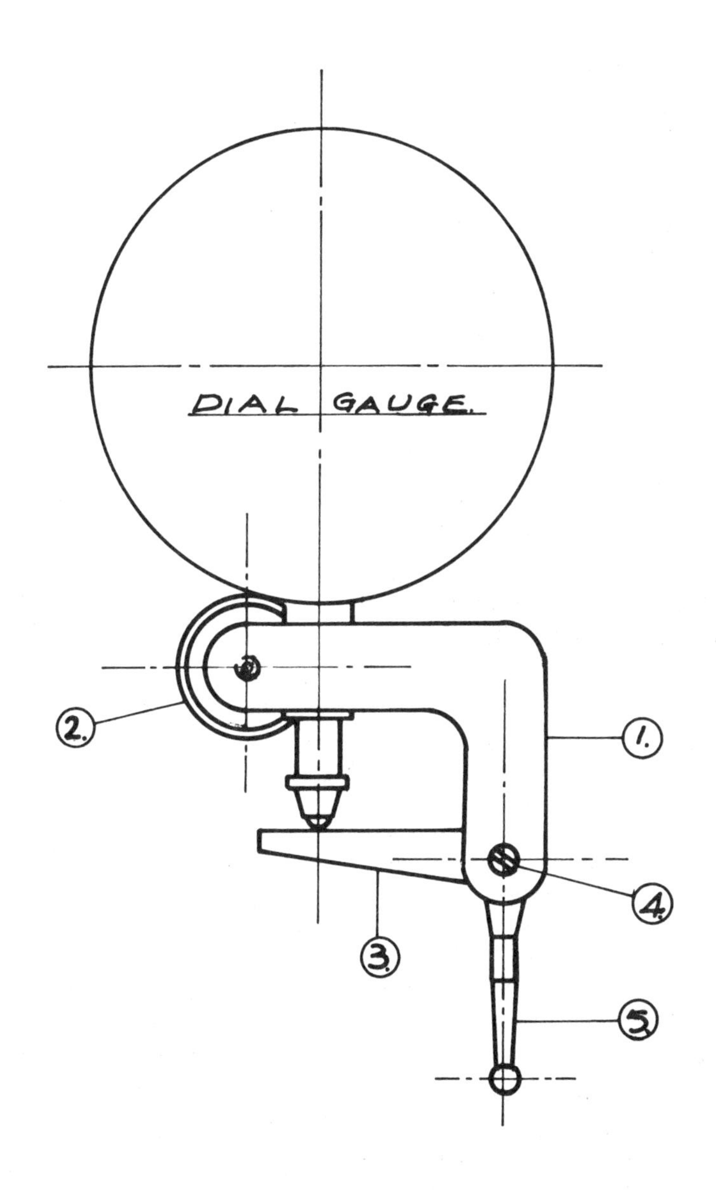

Fig. 6.3
Dial Gauge Attachments
(Fitted With 3 Angled Arm & 5. Stylus)

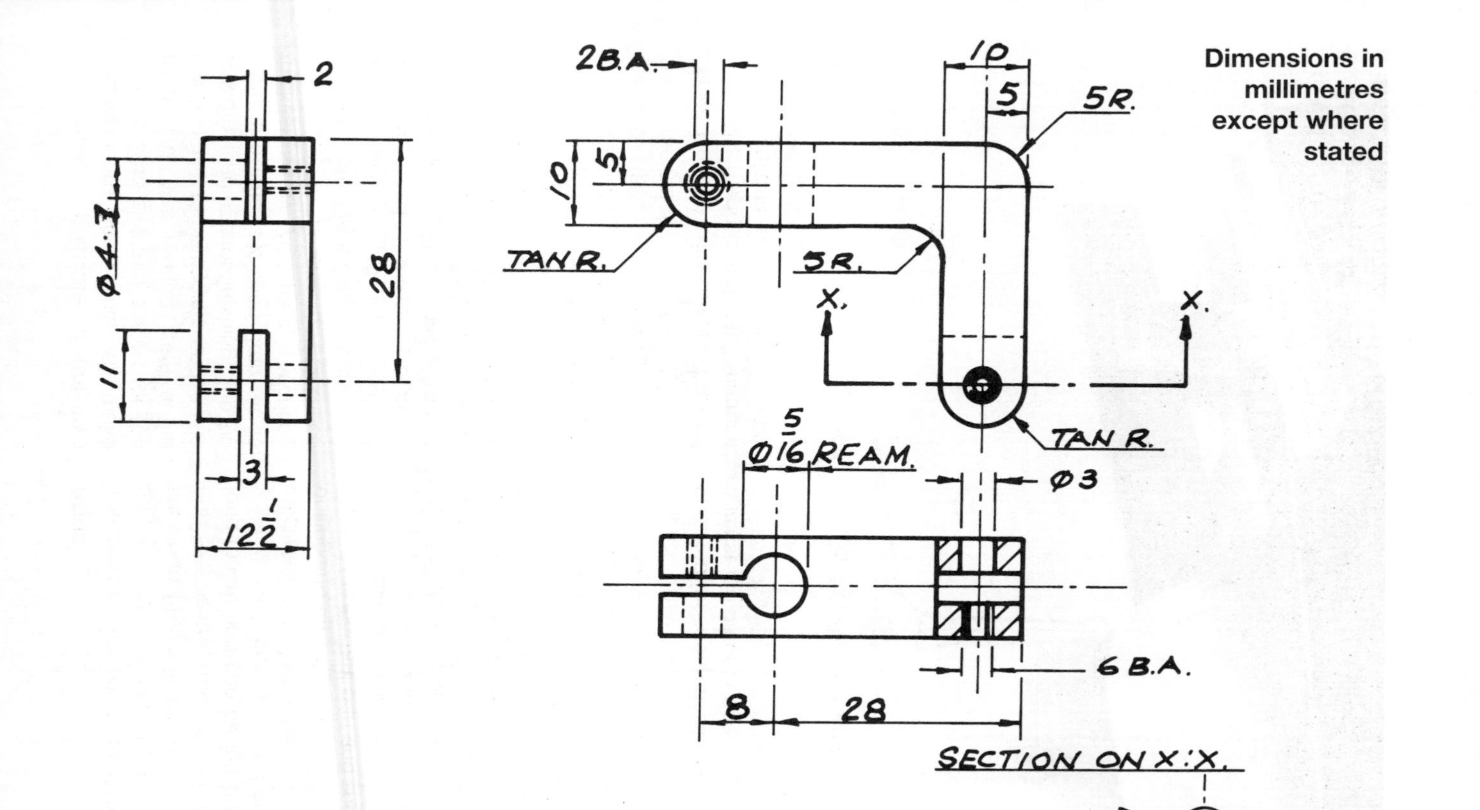

Fig. 6.4 Bracket - Duralumin

new ones if possible, if not two equally worn ones. This will make quite a wide slot and a start for the filing. The files I used were a 4in warding file for roughing and a 4in smooth hand one for finishing. The 4in hand is a little less than 3mm at its thickest, so by the time it is working freely in the slot, there won't be much to come off. **Fig.6.5** shows the slot almost done. I used a piece of the 3mm strip used for the arms to gauge it, filing gently till it was a free fit without wobble. I filed the depth to 10mm to allow the arms to tilt enough. After the slot was finished, I tapped the holes, entering the tap through the clearance holes, which helped to keep them nicely upright. I filed the radii on the ends last, then thoroughly deburred the holes,

I finish-filed the surfaces and took off all the sharp edges. It doesn't matter if all the outside edges have a small chamfer or radius.

Arms

The arms were next, three of them, an angled one and two straight ones, shown in **Figs.6.6** and **6.7**. The long one is an extra, intended for a really long reach, and can be left out if not wanted. Each one is made from 3mm mild steel strip. The marking out and drilling and tapping of the 8BA holes is the most important part and should be done before any shaping. It is easier to mark out and hold the pieces while they are still in parallel lumps. Drilling and reaming the 3mm holes is an easy job, if a 3mm reamer is not available, 1/8in will do. The 8BA holes were something else. Firstly, I made sure that the centre punching was as close to the centre of the 3mm dimension as possible, a watch maker's eye glass helped. They were drilled in a vice, checked for squareness with a square against the datum edge.

Fig. 6.5. Filing the slot to fit the arms.

Dimensions in millimetres except where stated

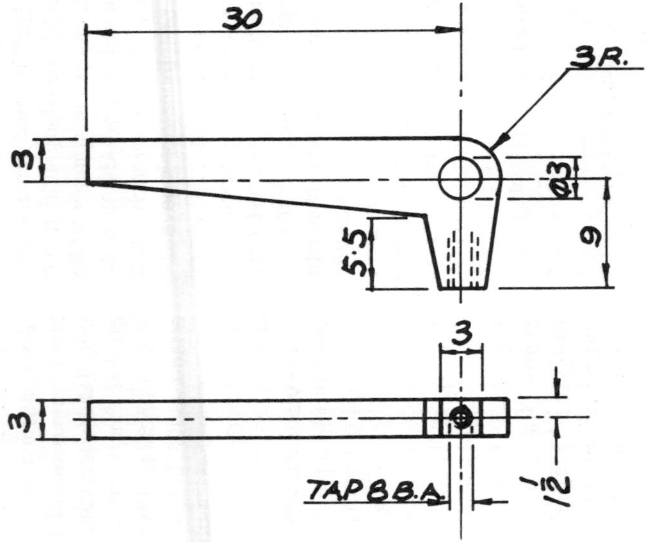

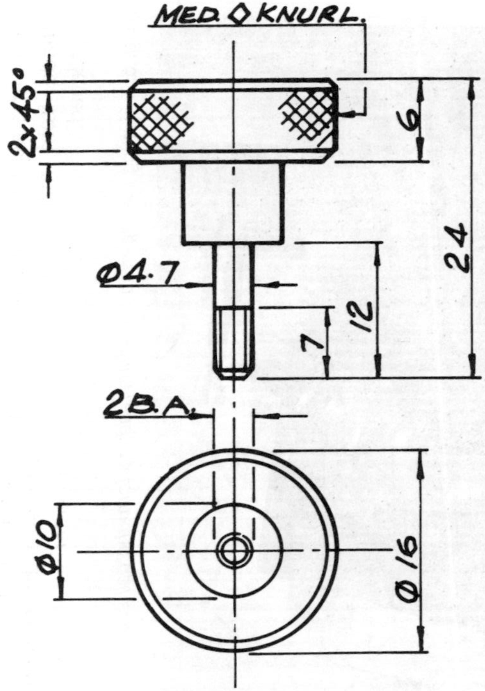

2.. Clamping Screw - Duralumin

Fig. 6.6 3. Angled Arm - B.M.S.

I started with a 3/32in drill taken 1/32in deep, followed by a No. 50 drill 3/16in deep, as shown in the scrap section in **Fig.6.6**. This makes sure that the stylus thread will fit flush and that the tapping drill is at least 1/16in deeper than the tap needs to go. I used the smallest tap wrench I had and plenty of lubrication. I gave the tapping drill a few more hundredths of a millimetre than the book said because when tapping a small blind hole, I needed all the help I could get. Two things which will break small taps are, using a tapping size too close to the core diameter and using too big a tap wrench. With all the holes tapped and de-burred, I filed the arms to shape and checked the fit in the slot. They all fitted; if they hadn't I would have worked on the arms, not the slot.

Pivot screw

The pivot screw was made from 1/8in or 3mm silver steel depending on what is available, the same with the probe and stylus, all shown in **Fig.6.8** If silver steel isn't used they can be made from mild steel and case-hardened.

Clamp screw

This component, **Fig.6.6** was another easy job because I had one which only needed a bit of modification, just the 4.7mm diameter turning down and the 2BA thread cut. Once again the chosen material was duralumin, mainly because I wanted to keep the attachments light. Mild steel could, of course, be used instead.

Styli

These were made from the same silver steel as the pivot screw. I made three styli. The turning is best done with a tool like a screw-cutting tool, a plan angle of about 30 degrees is ideal. The spherical radius was left as a short section about 3mm long, see **Fig.6.9** and filed and stoned to its final shape. The 5 degree angle was cut using the compound slide, starting at the chuck end and working back. The one shown in Fig.6.9 is ready for final shaping. When the shank and the radius had been finally polished, I cut it off at about 22mm long. Holding on the straight section, I turned the diameter for the 8BA thread a little

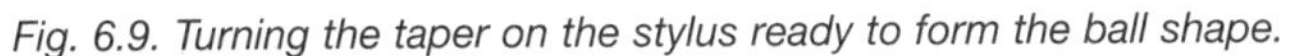
Fig. 6.9. Turning the taper on the stylus ready to form the ball shape.

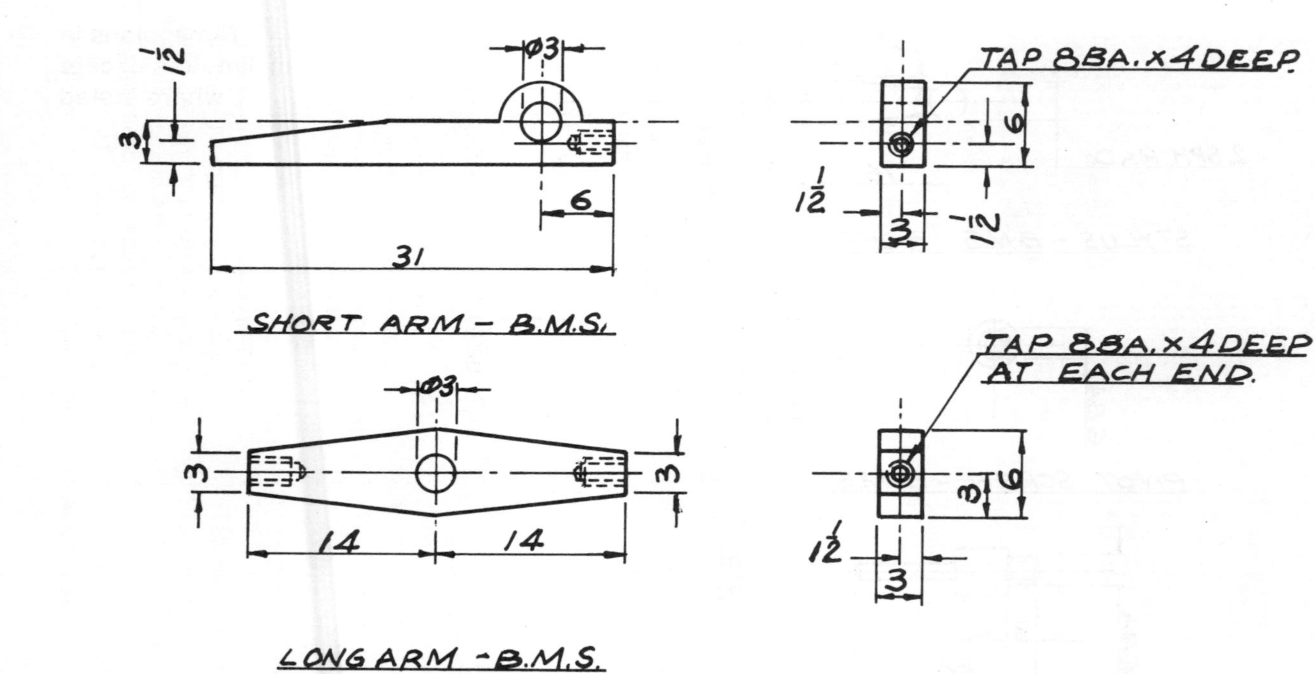

Fig. 6.7 Dimensions in millimetres except where stated

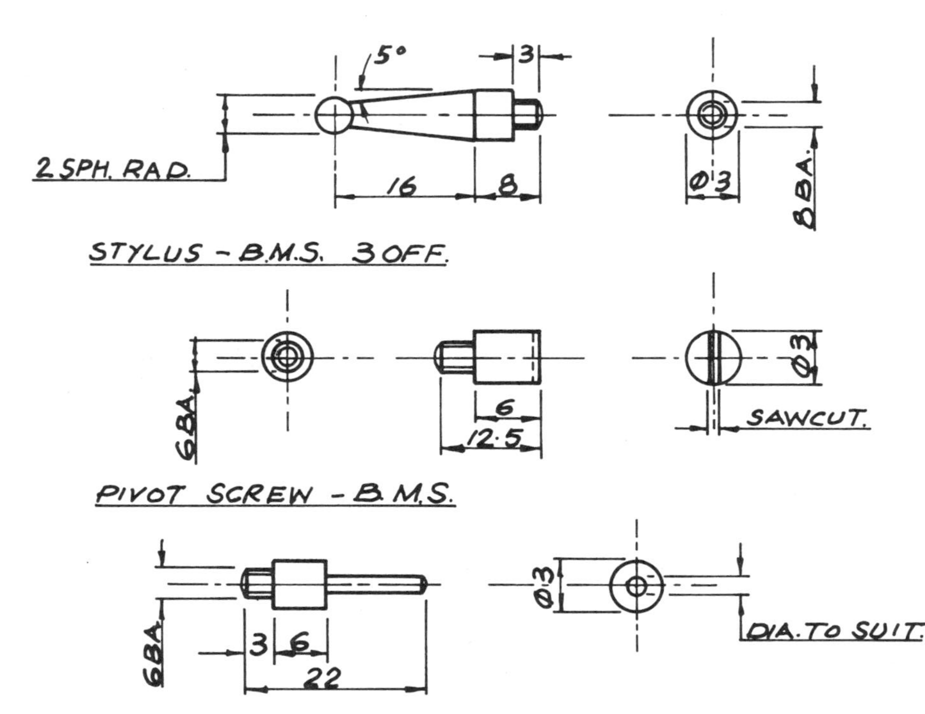

Dimensions in millimetres except where stated

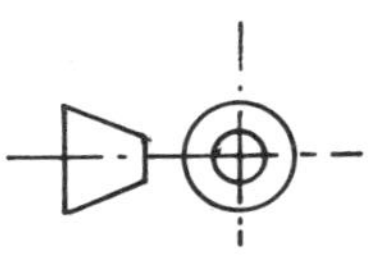

Fig. 6.8 Probe - B.M.S.

longer than needed and made the first 2mm or so 1.8mm. This gives the die a good start and because it is only cutting a trace for the first 2mm.,there is every chance that the thread will be cut truly. After all the turning and threading was done, I faced off the extra length and chamfered with a fine Swiss file. The facing should be at high speed with light cuts. All the dimensions for the styli are in **Fig.6.8**.

The styli should screw into the arms nicely and, if you have strong fingers, no more needs to be done. If you want to be certain that they go in tightly, small spanner flats can be filed on to fit a 10BA spanner or a home-made key. I did this and the slotting of the pivot screw, using a sprung thread plate, which I use a lot for holding small or awkward threaded parts. **Fig.6.10** shows one of the styli being worked on with the plate. It only needs a few light strokes on each side.

The last component, the probe, Fig.6.8 is an extra and could be left out. Its function is to replace the stylus on the end of the dial gauge plunger. Using the probe, which can be made any shape, can be useful for getting into places which would be very difficult otherwise. I have found it useful for finding the depth of square and acme threads, where the stem of other instruments is too large. The thread is 6BA and the probe is very easy to make.

When all the smaller parts were finished, I hardened the silver steel ones and oil-blacked the mild steel ones. I have a large coffee jar half full with quenching oil and the use of the gas stove; good enough for small jobs. If you do the same, choose a time when food preparation or cooking is not being done, and ask permission first. Oil-blacking makes a lot of smoke and smell.

The reason for making three styli was so that there would be one each for the angled and short arms, the ones I thought would be used most, the third one being a spare as they are very easy to lose.

As **Figs.6. 1** and **6.2** show, these attachments are well worth making and extend the range of a dial gauge no end.

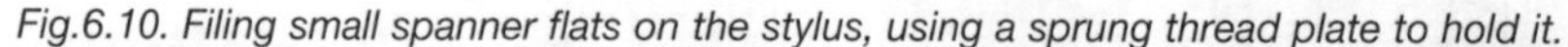

Fig.6.10. Filing small spanner flats on the stylus, using a sprung thread plate to hold it.

Chapter 7

Tailstock Supports and Accessories

In the mid 1950s, when I worked for a hearing aid company, I had to make some ear piece casings. They were pressed into a shape like a shallow top hat with a bit of an angle on the top bit and, for a reason I forget, a small amount had to be turned off the diameter after they had been formed. It was an extremely awkward shape to hold, but in the model shop/toolroom where I worked, we always pooled our knowledge and skills, and, when needed, our gadgets for making things easier. 'Jimmy the hands' lent me one of his to do the skimming of the top hats. We called him 'the hands', because they were enormous, but very highly skilled; he was one of the best craftsmen I knew.

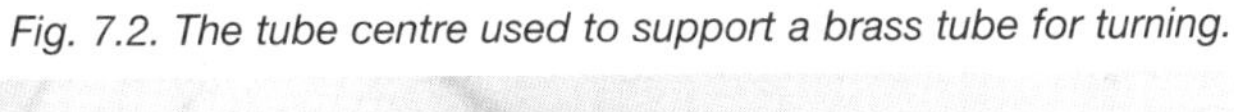

Fig. 7.2. The tube centre used to support a brass tube for turning.

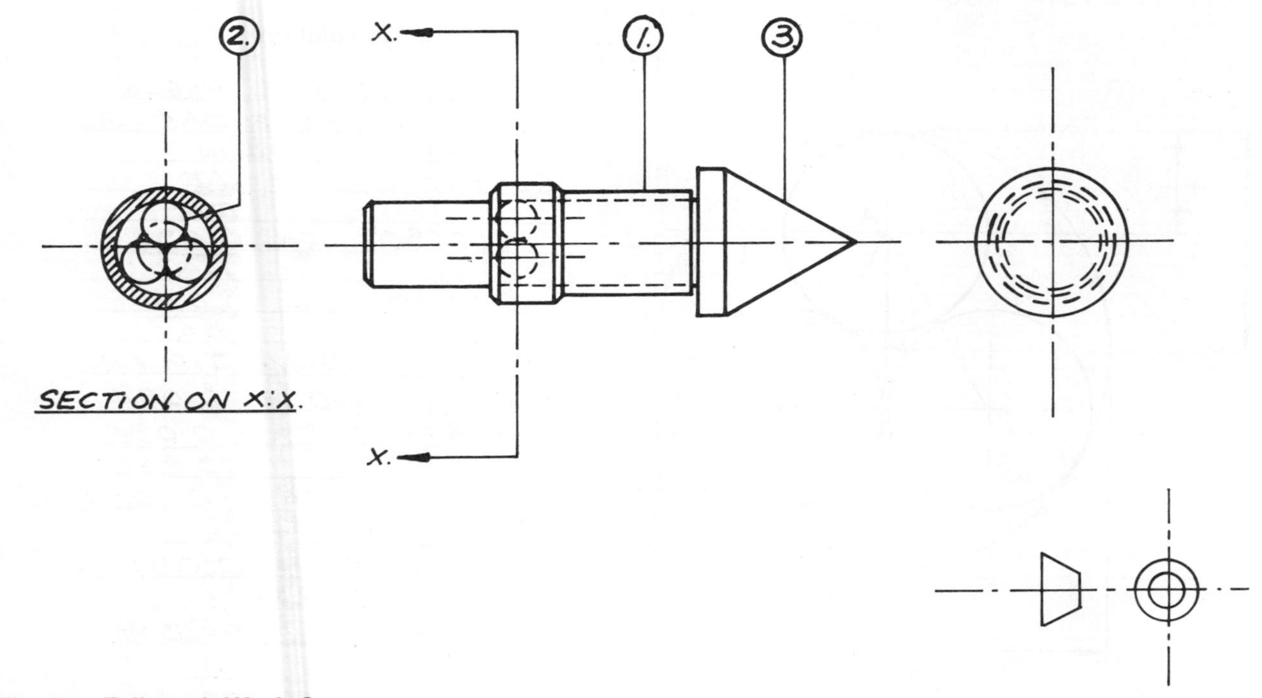

Fig. 7.1 Tailstock Work Support

Fig. 7.3

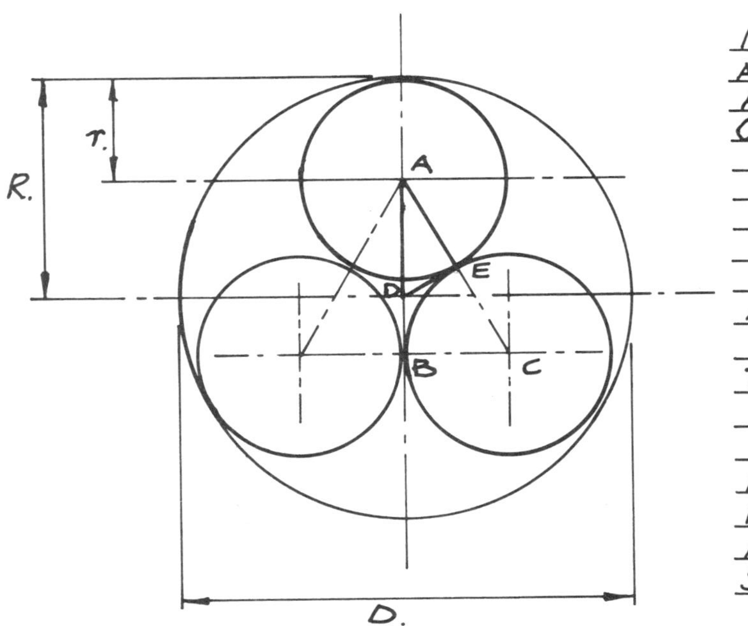

The Calculation

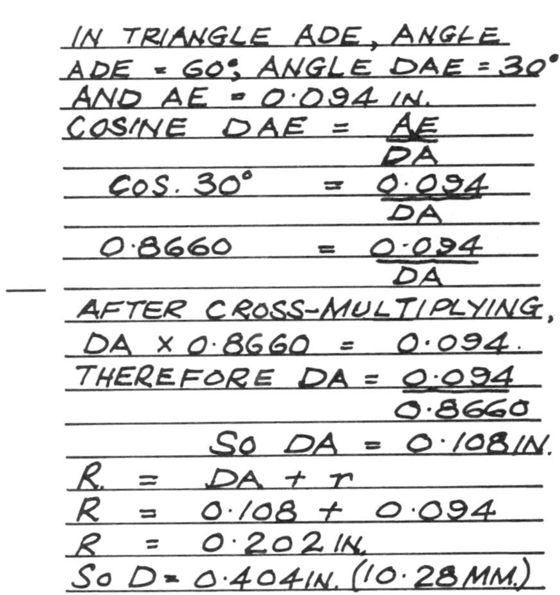
IN TRIANGLE ADE, ANGLE ADE = 60°, ANGLE DAE = 30° AND AE = 0·094 IN.

$$\text{COSINE DAE} = \frac{AE}{DA}$$

$$\text{COS. } 30° = \frac{0{\cdot}094}{DA}$$

$$0{\cdot}8660 = \frac{0{\cdot}094}{DA}$$

AFTER CROSS-MULTIPLYING,

$$DA \times 0{\cdot}8660 = 0{\cdot}094.$$

$$\text{THEREFORE } DA = \frac{0{\cdot}094}{0{\cdot}8660}$$

SO DA = 0·108 IN.

$$R = DA + r$$

$$R = 0{\cdot}108 + 0{\cdot}094$$

R = 0·202 IN.

SO D = 0·404 IN. (10·28 MM.)

Dimensions in millimetres

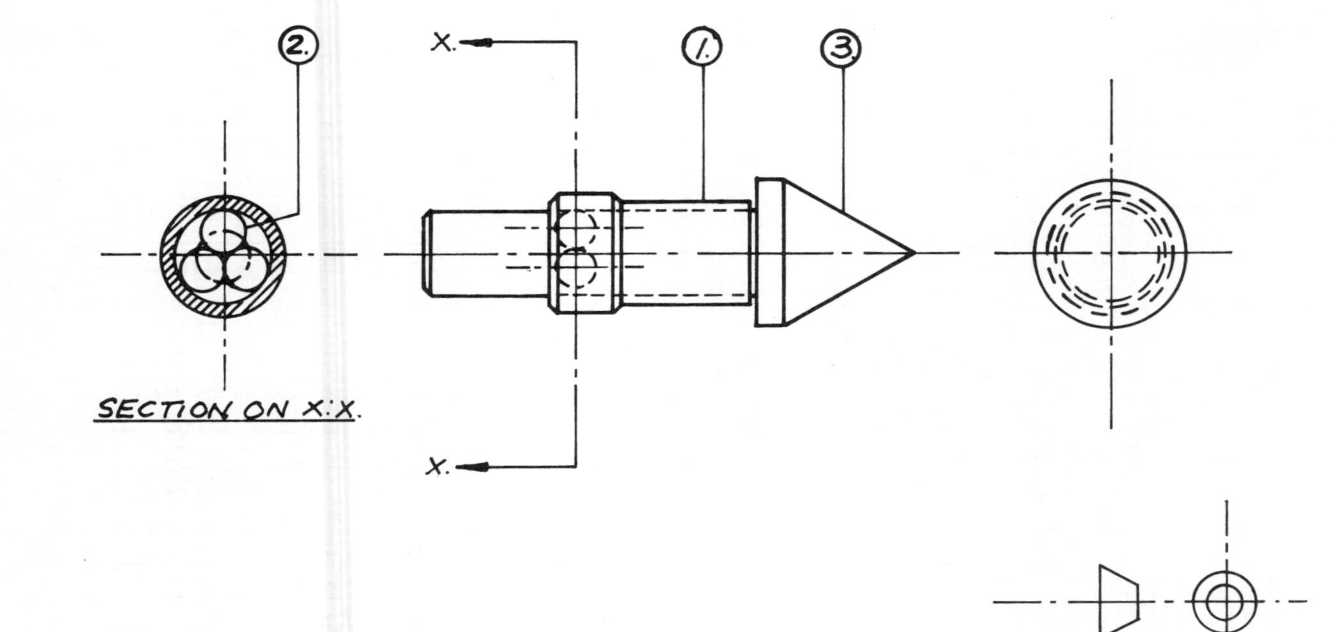

Fig. 7.4 1. Body - B.M.S.

The thing he lent me was very like a simple revolving centre with several different inserts. It could be changed to male centre, female centre, tube centre or pressure pad, depending on what was needed, by taking one out and putting another one in. As all the inserts were sliding fits, it was quick and easy. **Fig.7.1** shows my version of Jimmy's gadget and **Fig 7.2** shows it in action with a tube centre supporting the work.

I cannot remember the sizes of the original, larger than mine I should think. Mine was made for the Unimat, or similar small lathes. With the straight shank, it could be held in a Jacob's chuck for non-critical work. I made the one shown to fit the tailstock bore of the Unimat.

To finish the top hats, I used the pressure pad to push a stack of about ten of them at a time against a turned form. Using light cuts, it soon did the job. I had been going to make one for a long time and had made a start in anticipation of a job I knew would need something similar.

The essentials

Coming back to **Fig.7.1**, my design is a body fitting the tailstock with various centre inserts to fit the centres running on three steel balls which act as a simple thrust bearing. The accuracy is maintained by the inserts' close running fit in the body.

A bit of trigonometry

I chose 3/16in steel balls for the thrust bearing. I had plenty of them and they were a convenient size. They must fit the bore with enough clearance to rotate. To get things right there is a bit of maths to do.

This is laid out in **Fig.7.3** which shows the construction and the stages in the calculation. I apologise to those who can do the sums easily without guidance, but for those who need a bit of help, it is just a matter of finding, or making, the right triangle. If a different size of steel balls is used, it doesn't matter but it will change the calculation.

Fig.7.5. Rough turning the body.

Dimensions in millimetres

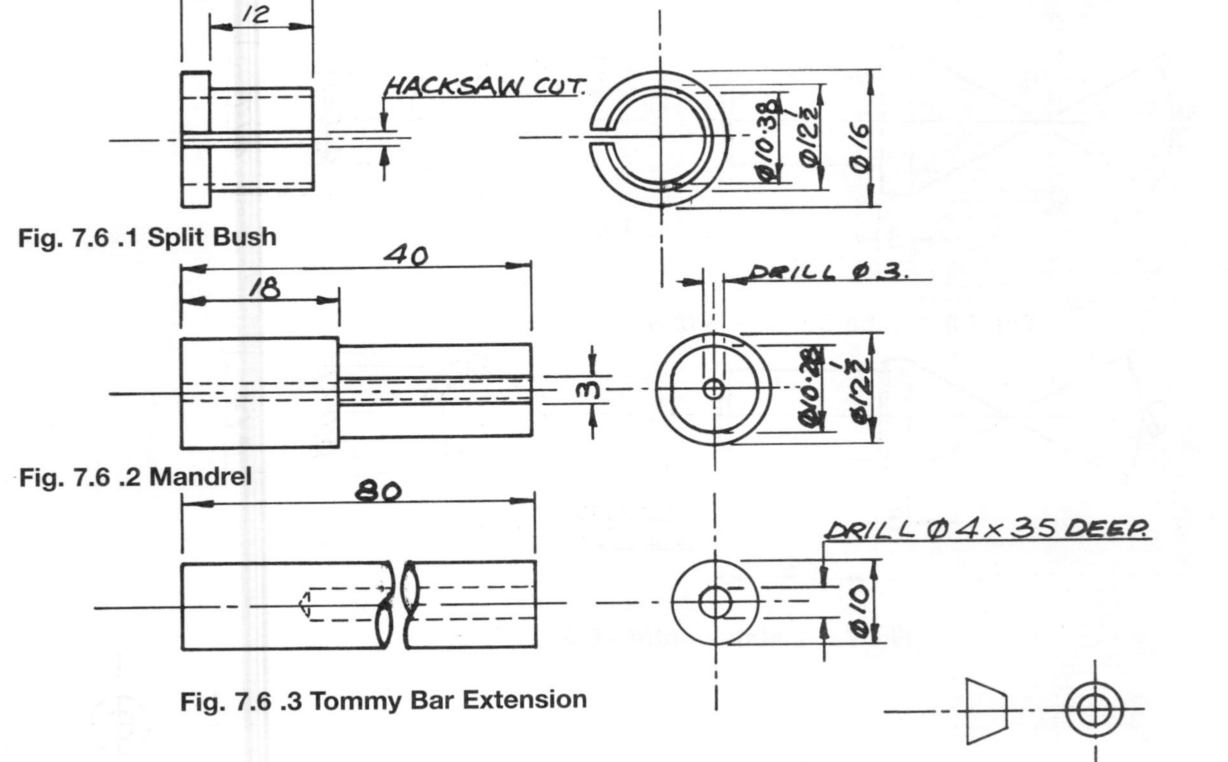

Fig. 7.6 .1 Split Bush

Fig. 7.6 .2 Mandrel

Fig. 7.6 .3 Tommy Bar Extension

Fig. 7.6

Dimensions in millimetres

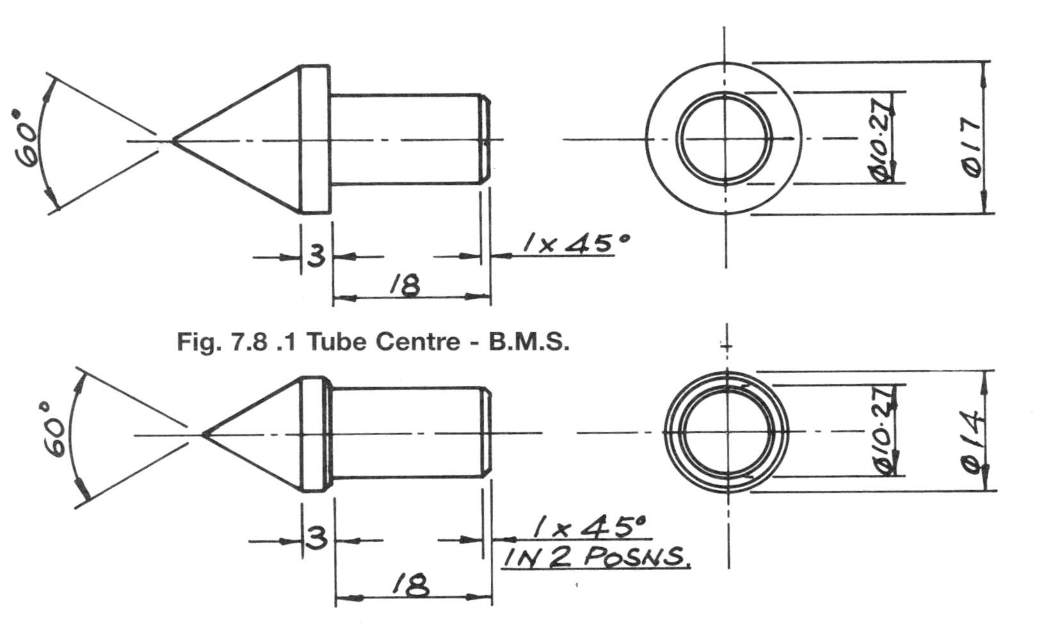

Fig. 7.8 .1 Tube Centre - B.M.S.

Fig. 7.8 .2 Male Centre - B.M.S.

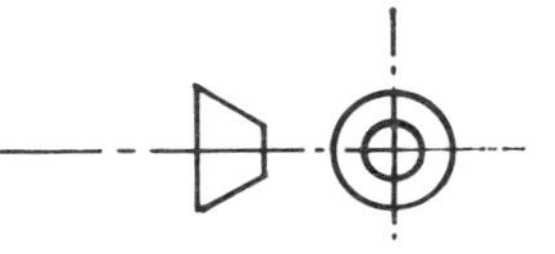

Fig. 7.8

If you don't want to fiddle about with sums, choose the size of balls you would like to use, find a washer they won't fit in, position them as in Fig.7.3 and open the washer up bit by bit till they go through with a little clearance, that will be the size of the bore in the body. If the 3/16in balls are used and the radius is taken as 0.094in there will be enough clearance, especially when machining error is added.

The body

I started by making the body, **Fig.7.4.** It was roughed out first to 0.5mm oversize, then the bore was finished. **Fig.7.5** shows an early stage in the roughing out. The bore was finished to 10.28mm as closely as possible. Most of the waste was drilled out in stages and the last 1mm or so bored. The bottom of the hole can be flattened with an end mill or slot drill. It could be bottomed out with a flat-bottomed drill or a D-bit if necessary. The boring tool was fed as slowly and steadily as possible and the depth was set by clamping a small parallel clamp to the lathe bed for a stop. The clamp was set to a little under the 22mm depth, so that, when the bore was right, the saddle was fed up to the stop, the stop taken off and the saddle indexed the amount to bring it to full depth. At the same setting, the cross slide was wound in to flatten the bore bottom. When the bore bottom and outside diameter were finished, they were chamfered where shown and the burrs taken off. The body was then turned to the 10.37mm diameter to fit the tailstock. The easiest way to do this and keep everything true is to turn the body on a mandrel.

Mandrel

This is shown in **Fig. 7.6.2** and can be made from brass or aluminium alloy. Do not make it from steel. Use of steel on steel is unwise as the parts can become stuck. I used a piece of duralumin about 35mm long and 12.5mm diameter. A 3mm hole drilled through was for a piece of 3mm brass rod to punch the finished work off the mandrel.

The fit is critical and the best way of getting it right, is to aim for a hundredth of a millimetre or so

Fig.7.7. Using a piece of tube to push the body on to the mandrel.

oversize and rub the rest down with emery cloth. Ideally, the body should slide on nicely till the last 4mm and then tighten up. Before final sizing, I filed the 3mm flat shown in **Fig.7.6.2**, it lets the air out and stops the hydraulic effect that a smear of oil or grease can sometimes cause.

When the mandrel was finished, the body was pressed on using a piece of tube, **Fig.7.7**. It should be done in the lathe and carefully enough not to move the mandrel, so for this operation, hide the chuck key! A smear of oil or grease, I used Vaseline, will help to get the body seated on the mandrel. Turning to size was quite easy, just a matter of making the body the same size as the lathe centre diameter. When they matched, I'd won. As an additional check, when the fit is right, it will make a cork-pulling noise when it comes out of the tailstock.

With the machining finished, the mandrel was held in the vice by the 12.5mm diameter and the body tapped off with a piece of 3mm brass rod so that it did no harm. It came off nicely.

The male centres

There are two of these, **Fig.7.8.1** and **7.8.2**, one made large to use as a tube centre. The only complication was making the points concentric with the shanks. I wasted some time fiddling about with a special carrier which involved some four-jawed chuck work, **Fig.7.9**. The carrier scheme didn't look as if it would work, so I used another way and put the carrier away to use on another part of the job.

The easiest way of getting points true with shanks was to use a split bush, like the one in **Fig.7.6.1**.

The split bush

This was a piece of brass made to the dimensions in **Fig.7.6.1**. I turned the 12.5mm diameter first, then drilled 10mm. It was taken out of the chuck, the saw cut sawed, then put back in the chuck tight enough to hold, but so that it could be tightened some more. It was then bored out till the finished centres shanks just slid in without any play. The first one to be machined was put in and the extension tommy bar used to tighten up. I made this extension because the tommy bars

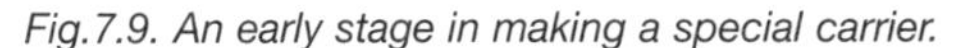
Fig.7.9. An early stage in making a special carrier.

supplied with the lathe aren't sensitive enough to be able to slacken off and still have the bush gripped. As soon as one centre was machined, it was gently slid out and the other one put in.

The bush must not be taken out of the chuck till it is finished with.

If it is, the accuracy will be gone. When turning the points, I used high speed and light cuts, it gives a good finish and doesn't put too much strain on the holding power of the bush.

Female centre

This one, **Fig.7.10.1** was made the same as the male ones but while in the bush for finishing, was centre drilled as shown in the scrap section. The centre drill was a BS2. This has a body diameter of 4.8mm and a pilot diameter of about 1.6mm. As the pilot is the part which does most of the drilling, the drilling speed must be set to suit it. Even rounding it up to 2.0mm and using an average cutting speed for mild steel, it will work out to well over 5,000rpm, so use maximum speed unless you have a high-speed machine. More centre drills are broken by using too slow a speed than any other cause. **Fig.7.11** shows the female centre being turned and gives an idea of the depth of cut.

Pressure pad

Fig.7.10.2 shows the pressure pad. It can be turned from solid or made in two parts. I made mine in two parts. Diameter 'A' is a spigot on the end of the shank and diameter 'B' a hole in the disc. 'B' is drilled first and 'A' turned to be a slight interference fit in it. The disc is pressed on in the vice and the excess turned off, **Fig.7.12.**

Fig.7.13. shows the range of inserts I made - enough for most jobs.

Further thoughts

There is no reason why the parts shouldn't be made from silver steel and hardened, or they could be case hardened. Case hardening would probably be the best option because it would be less likely to distort anything. Thinking back, and it was a long time ago, Jimmy's probably was hardened. If the parts are made from mild steel and left soft, the balls will, in

Fig.7.11. Finishing a female centre held in a split bush.

Dimensions in millimetres

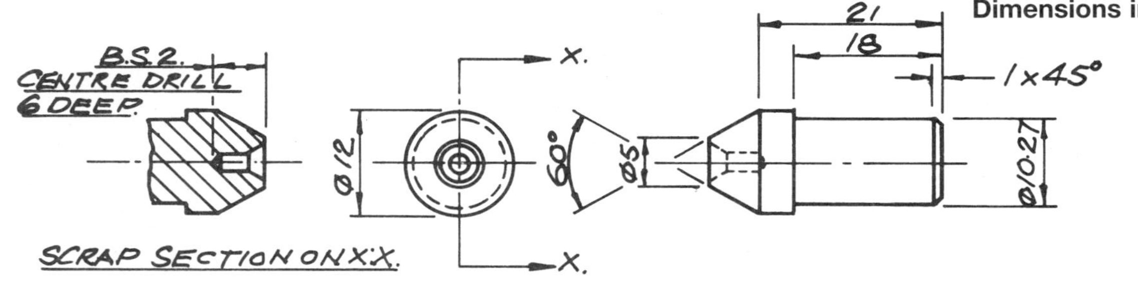

Fig. 7.10 .1 Female Centre - B.M.S.

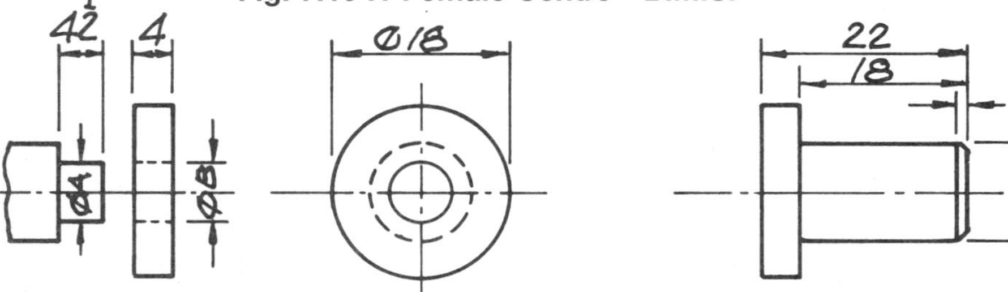

Fig. 7.10 .2 Pressure Pad - B.M.S.

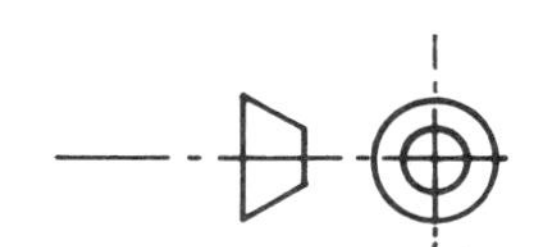

Fig. 7.10

time, wear tracks in the ends of the shanks and at the bottom of the bore in the body. This may reduce the gap between the flange of the centres and the end of the bore. A fine facing cut will put it right, the gap should be about 0.5mm. All the shanks can have the centre holes in them left, as long as they are not too large.

In use, the gadget will run quite sweetly with a smear of grease round the balls. I prefer grease because when an insert is taken out, the balls are more likely to stick to one part or the other. Remember Sod's law and, when taking one out, have a hand underneath. If the balls escape, they will roll about the floor till they find the most inaccessible crevice.

The tension on the inserts when they are used should be no more than enough to make them rotate, as with a running centre. If the pressure pad doesn't do what it should, the cut is probably too heavy or the feed too coarse. The friction can sometimes be increased by a piece of hard rubber, cut to fit, between the pad and the work.

Remember, it is only a light-duty accessory, not intended for heavy work.

Problems with centres

While I was making the parts, I found that I badly needed a half centre so I made one. Without this, it was very difficult to turn a small diameter with a centre in it, unless some very peculiarly shaped tools were used.

The half centre was made to the same dimensions as the ones supplied with the Unimat 3 then cut and filed almost half away, leaving enough of the point to register the hole made by a BS3 centre drill at half way up the angle. Making it reminded me of another thing I lacked, a soft head centre. Those with the lathe are hardened, alright most of the time, but can be a nuisance. There are times when the tailstock centre could be soft too. This would avoid some grief when heavy cuts or coarse feeds generate a lot of heat. The work expands and gets tighter and tighter on the centres. The only warning the turner gets is a wisp of blue smoke as the lubrication vaporises, then a high-pitched scream, followed by a bang.

The result of this mini 'son et lumiere' is, quite often, the end of the centre friction-welded to the centre hole in the work. That is why I like to use soft centres whenever possible or a revolving centre in the tailstock. As for the live centre, which goes in the headstock, that should always be soft, so that it can be trued to 60 degrees every time it is used for accurate work.

This is less of a problem when the lathe spindle has an internal morse taper. The Unimat, however, has no taper and relies for the accuracy of the centre, on the fit. Even the best of fits can wear. There are ways of getting round the problem, putting a short piece of bar in the chuck and turning it to a 60 degree angle, for instance. That means improvising a carrier, like the one in **Fig.7.17** and driving off the chuck jaws. I prefer one which I made, a locking centre for the headstock.

Locking head centre

Fig.7.15 shows the assembly of the locking centre which only needs three components. The one not drawn is a catch plate which can be made from any suitable disc which can be tapped M14 and screwed up to the shoulder on the headstock. It can be slotted to take a carrier with an angled tail or have a pin to drive a straight carrier. As long as there is a gap so that the nut, **Fig.7.16.2** doesn't tighten on it, the thickness is not that important.

The centre

The centre, **Fig.7.16.1** is made from mild steel and like the other centres, must have shank and point true with each other. When I'd roughed out, I finished the point angle and 10mm diameter and set the job between a female centre drilled into a piece of bar in the chuck, and the half centre I had made earlier. **Fig.7.17** shows this somewhat Heath Robinson set-up.

Screw cap

The cap, **Fig.7.16.2** locks the centre and is easily made from a piece of 18mm diameter steel or larger. I had an M14 tapped hole in a piece of 20mm diameter which I had rejected because it was a 'drunken' thread, screwed it on to the M14 tap, held the tap in the chuck, and skimmed it true.

Fig.7.12. Trimming the excess off the pressure pad.

Fig.7.13. From left to right, tube centre, male centre, female centre and pressure pad.

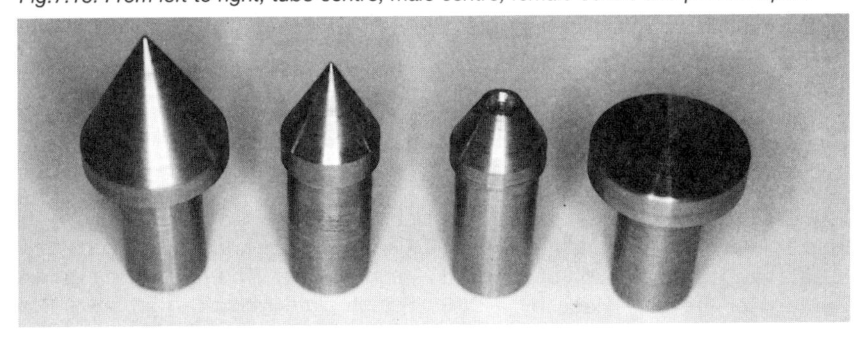

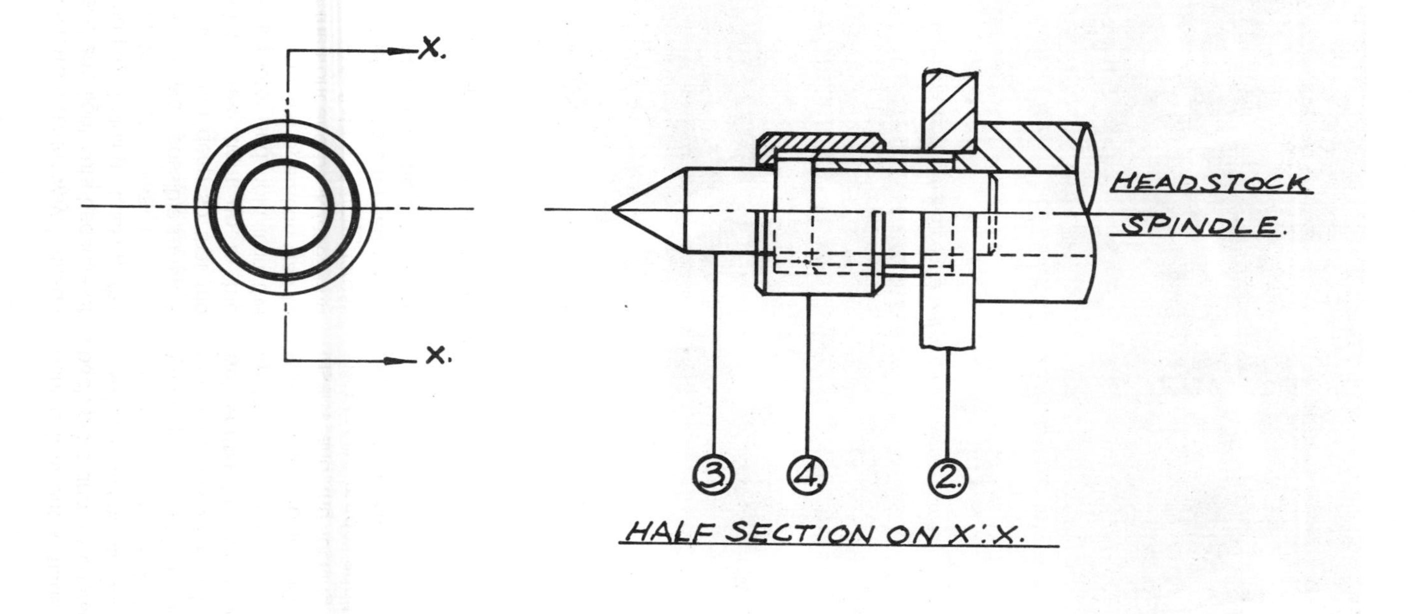

Fig. 7.15 Locking Centre Assembly

Fig.7.18 shows it under way. It needs high speed and light cuts because of the method of holding. Luckily, the tapping in the reject was not right through and it was possible to leave the face at 12mm deep so that the cap would screw tight up to the 12.5mm diameter and hold it in the headstock. The last operation was to chamfer the front and back faces and file the spanner flats at 14mm across flats. **Fig.7.19** shows the head centre being skimmed true. The catch plate behind it is one I made from an old back plate and, of course, would not need so many holes. Once locked, the centre cannot move and if it has been skimmed, it must be accurate. The skimming takes very little time and is well worth it to have an accurate head centre.

Both the tailstock work support and inserts and the locking head centre are easily made additions to the Unimat 3 tool set.

Fig.7.17. A half centre, used with an improvised carrier.

Fig.7.20. Using the locking head centre with a conventional carrier.

Dimensions in millimetres

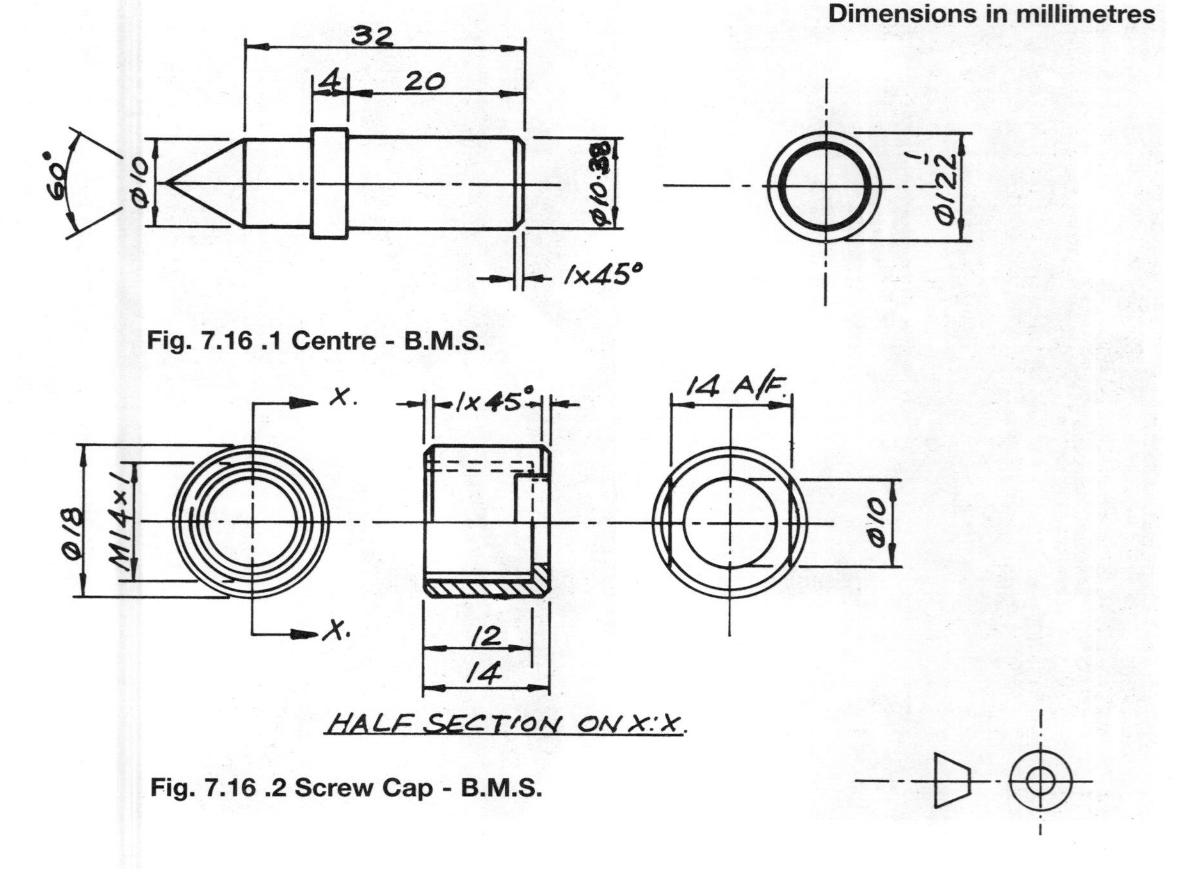

Fig. 7.16 .1 Centre - B.M.S.

Fig. 7.16 .2 Screw Cap - B.M.S.

Fig. 7.16

Fig.7.19. Truing the locking head centre.

Fig.7.18. Truing the nut.

Chapter 8

Punches

Model engineers use punches a lot, they are one of the small tools which are forgotten till wanted and sometimes, when they cannot be found, because they aren't all that noticeable, other things are substituted, like nails, round toolbits and other unsuitable objects. Given a reasonable selection of punches, the unsuitable can be left in peace. **Fig.8.1** are a few of my own, most of them home-made. That third from the right, which looks as if it had no business to be there, is an example of the longevity of some tools. I made it when I was in the training workshop, some 50 odd years ago. I include it for sentimental reasons. It started life

Fig. 8.1. A selection of punches. From left to right, spotting, riveting, special long spotting, case-hardened for seed boxes, 2 pin punches, 2 centre punches and 2 handbag punches.

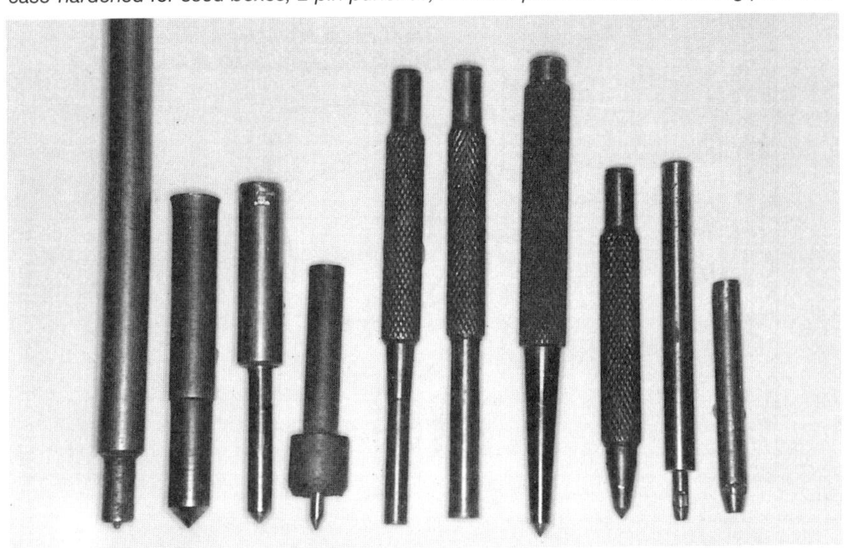

Dimensions in millimetres

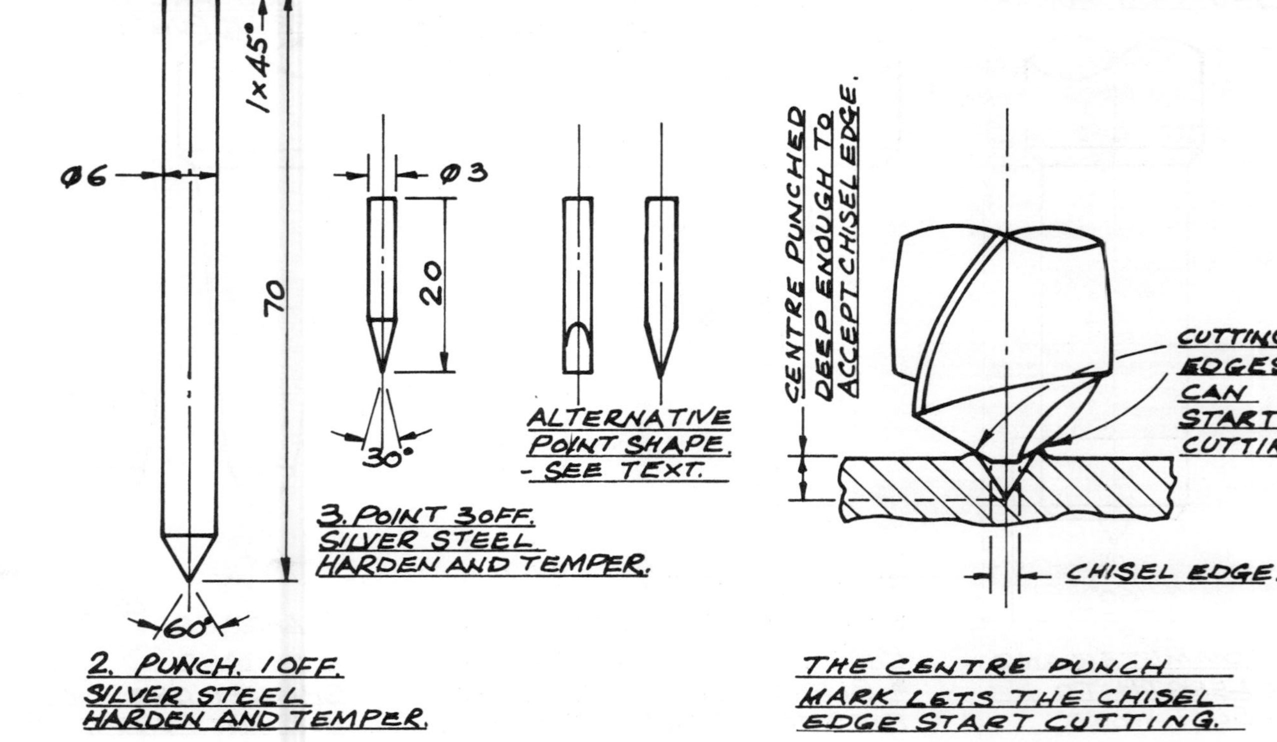

Fig. 8.11

Fig. 8.2

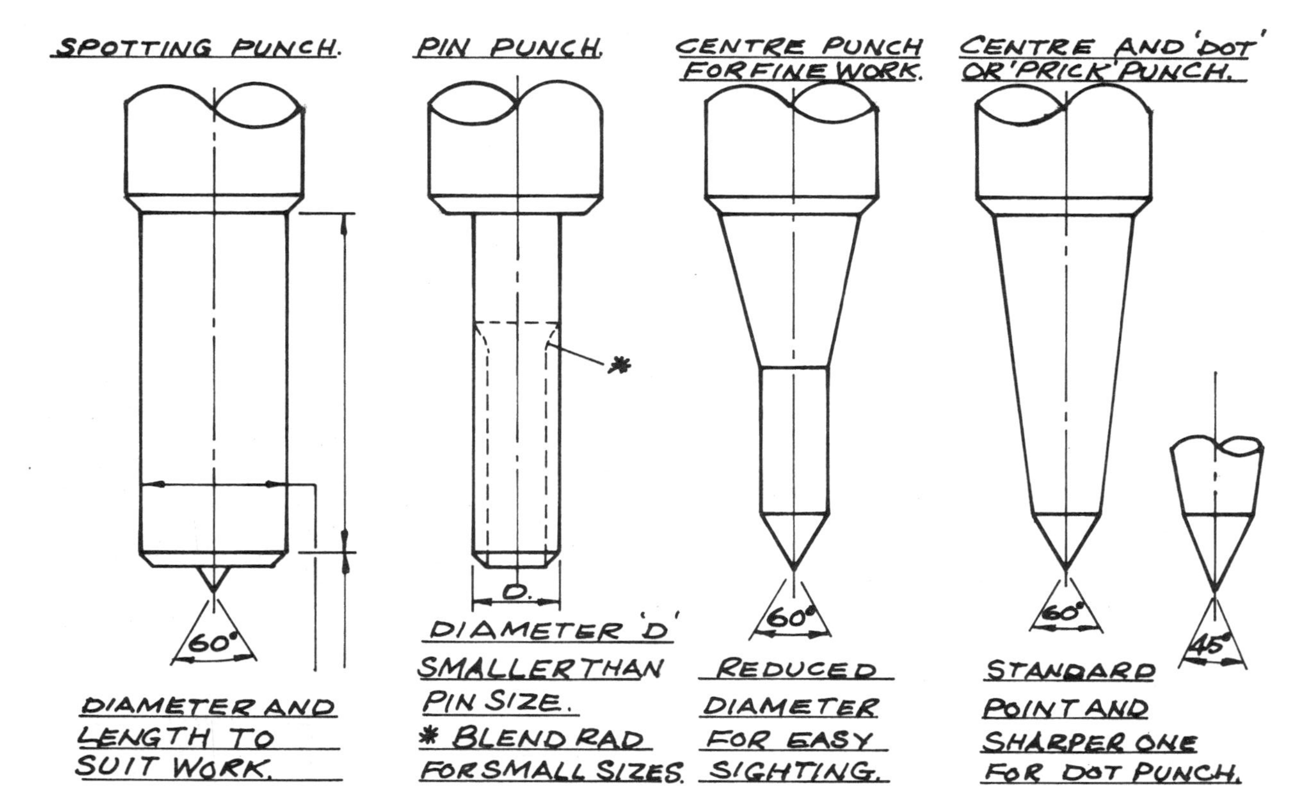
SPOTTING PUNCH.
60°
DIAMETER AND
LENGTH TO
SUIT WORK.
PIN PUNCH.
*
D.
DIAMETER 'D'
SMALLER THAN
PIN SIZE.
* BLEND RAD
FOR SMALL SIZES.
CENTRE PUNCH
FOR FINE WORK.
60°
REDUCED
DIAMETER
FOR EASY
SIGHTING.
CENTRE AND 'DOT'
OR 'PRICK' PUNCH.
60°
45°
STANDARD
POINT AND
SHARPER ONE
FOR DOT PUNCH.

Fig. 8.3 Some Types of Punches

almost as long as the one on its left and has survived many re-grinds and re-hardenings.

Without a set of punches, we would have nothing to mark centres for drilling or radii, nothing to knock pins out with, or to mark letters or numbers, nothing to cut holes in soft materials, spread hollow rivets and many other vital tasks.

Centre punches

These are the punches used most and there are one or two variations. Their main use is to make a dent in material to start a drill cutting. **Fig.8.2** shows the way in which the punch mark allows the drill to start cutting. I know that some small drills would start without, but it is still needed to make a location for the drill point. Try starting a drill of 12mm or over without a punch mark and judge for yourself.

Centre punches are also used to make small dot marks to accept divider or trammel points for marking radii. Made with a finer point, like the dot punch in **Fig.8.3** it will make a much smaller and finer mark, which will be more accurate and take less filing out afterwards. The angle can be finer than the 45 degrees shown, but beware of mistaking it for a normal centre punch; one good clout could damage the point.

Another useful variation is the one in **Fig.8.3** with the reduced diameter. I use this one when it is vital to be accurate. An ordinary one, especially one with a big point, has to be tilted quite a bit to see the place to be marked. A reduced diameter makes it easier to sight and the small dot it makes can be enlarged with another more substantial punch. Both this one and the dot punch should not be used for heavy work; they are not strong enough.

Fig.8.4. Grooves instead of knurling can give an equally good grip.

Other variations

Two more very useful shapes are the spotting punch in **Fig.8.3** and the riveting punch in **Fig.8.1** second from the left.

The spotting or transfer punch is for marking a hole position from a cover plate, cylinder head, or other application where holes have to line up. The diameter and 60 degree point have to be machined true and can have a set of bushes to extend the range of sizes. They are used in production workshops and can be bought in standard sets, expanding ones are also available.

The riveting punch is for spreading hollow rivets; the included angle is usually 90 degrees, but can be larger. Another type of punch which is used for rivets is the rivet snap, which is one with a hemispherical depression in the end. One way of making these is to drill a shallow pilot hole in the tip of a suitable blank and heat it to red heat, then drive it on to a steel ball of the radius to suit the rivet. When the shape is right , the punch can be hardened and tempered.

Pin punches

A set of pin punches is almost as important as centre punches. They can be bought in standard sizes and also as a body with interchangeable inserts in various sizes. It is more fun to make your own but there is one feature which needs watching. It is the diameter which does the job. It must be smaller than the nominal diameter of the pin it is intended for. For example, if the pin size is 6mm the punch diameter should be at least 0.10mm less. This will make sure that there will be clearance, essential when the punch has been used a bit, because it will tend to spread a little under the pressure of hammering. I learned this when I was an apprentice. I had made a set of pin punches, all beautifully knurled and finished, and dead accurate to the pin diameters. I was very proud of them and the first time I used one, I got it badly stuck, the unsticking completely ruined it. There are two in the middle of **Fig.8.1**. For small diameters they need careful making so that the small diameter blends into a larger one for strength.

Make your own

Commercially made punches are knurled, sometimes have square heads and are nicely tapered and finished. Very nice too, but it is easy to make one from a length of silver steel 10mm or so in diameter and about 100mm long. A simple centre punch needs a reduction at the head end and a taper to the point. It doesn't have to be knurled; just as well for those of us who haven't got a knurling tool or a lathe which will put up with the pressure of knurling. One or two

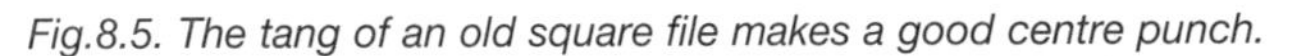

Fig.8.5. The tang of an old square file makes a good centre punch.

grooves with a 90 degree V-tool will make quite an acceptable grip. It could be made smooth, after all, my favourite fountain pen is smooth and polished and I have no trouble holding that. **Fig.8.4** shows the grooves being machined in the body of a punch. The tool used can be used to turn the head because it chamfers as it turns. Slow the speed for the grooving if you use this method.

Recycling

A good source of useful material is old files. I was lucky to be in the right place once when a batch of assorted files was thrown away. I rescued several of them and softened them. Since then I have not wanted for carbon tool steel in various shapes. I used a square one from my stock to make a centre punch from the tang end. **Fig.8.5** shows what I started with, it makes up easily and is great to hold and use. Round or three square ones would be just as good and less trouble to hold in a three-jawed chuck, not that holding the square one was any problem. It is not always necessary to use a four-jawed chuck to hold square material. **Fig.8.6** shows the solution and an easy one it is. A bush is made with the bore equal to, or a bit smaller than the diagonal of the square to be held. The bush is split and the job gently tapped in. It can then be held and machined normally in a three-jawed chuck. The only problem when using this method on a small lathe like the Unimat, is when the work will not pass up the lathe spindle. To support the head end it is as well to use a centre, as I did in **Fig.8.6**. The centre hole is no trouble when using the finished punch, especially if it is small.

For those with larger lathes, the work can be held further in the chuck. Turning the long taper needs support too. When making punches with a taper, I always turn the point first because there is plenty of material for

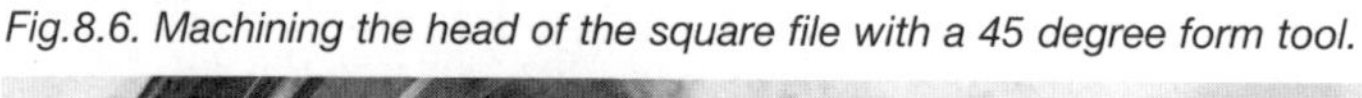

Fig.8.6. Machining the head of the square file with a 45 degree form tool.

support and it saves the point waving about while turning the last little bit. With the one made from the file tang, it wasn't easy because of the existing taper, as can be seen in **Fig.8.7**. I got over it by shaping the point by filing and then using an improvised double centre. In the photograph the long taper is being machined, very carefully and with light cuts because of the long overhang.

Everything worked and the result is in **Fig.8.8**. The angle of the long taper for the centre punch is about 4 degrees, 3/4 of a division on the scale of a Unimat compound slide. The angle of the other punch, a fine one for accurate sighting, is a bit more. Both of them work very well.

Chisel steel

Another excellent material for all sorts of punches, especially for larger ones, is chisel steel. The octagonal section can be held in a three-jawed chuck in the same way as the square. Because of the shape, it needs no knurling or other decoration, merely shaping at head and point ends. This steel has just the right composition for the job.

Special punches

Among the odds and ends I have accumulated over the years, there are several specials; the two on the right-hand end of **Fig.8.1** are examples. I call them 'handbag' punches, because among other things they are used to cut holes in handbag straps and other leather work. My wife has trouble with straps being too long, or holes in the wrong place, so I have several of these hollow punches of different sizes. They are quick to make, a short length of steel with a hole drilled in the end, tapered off to a cutting edge. An extraction slot is filed a little way back from the cutting edge so that the slug of material can be poked out. If this is not done, the punch soon gets blocked.

I use a similar but larger punch for putting drainage holes in yoghurt pots which I use for raising plants. One of these is in **Fig.8.1**. It is a piloted one, made from mild steel and case-hardened. I use a plain one made the same for making the holes in ice cream boxes for seed trays. Both have been punching holes for years with no signs of wear.

Fig.8.7. Turning the taper on the square file with a bush in the chuck and a double centre at the tailstock.

Commercially, soft materials like gaskets and similar things, are punched with 'bucket' punches, that's what I have always called them, because they are shaped like a bucket, the rim of the bucket is the bit which does the cutting and the handle is where the hammer strikes.

Of the other specials, a set of number punches is ideal and essential for marking the jaws of a chuck, or numbering an indexing dial. They need a simple jig for holding them straight and in line when they are used. Do not use them free-hand, it rarely works and the result can look very unsightly. To make sure that there is a clean and consistent profile, it helps to hit the punch several times, tilting it from side to side and top to bottom. A dummy run helps to get it right and this is where a jig works wonders by stopping the punch from moving about too much.

An ambitious project

The most difficult punch I have ever made was one for hallmarking. A friend's wife does silver work and she needed a punch made to identify her work. It was not elaborate, merely three initials enclosed in a cartouche. The cartouche, a flattened oval shape, measured 7mm long and just over 2mm high. I opened my mouth before the implications of the task had gone through my brain. Luckily I had access to an engraving machine and by making a pattern from wood with 25mm high letters and using the maximum reduction, I managed to make a reasonable punch. It was a reverse of the normal engraving process, cutting away the waste from around the letters. I had a lot of luck and the third or fourth attempt was good enough. I lost count of the number of regrinds of the cutter and the number of times I said, 'my word, how unfortunate', or words to that effect. **Fig.8.9** shows it.

Accuracy when punching

Making punches is one thing, using them another, especially getting a centre punch dot in exactly the right place. It isn't easy to pick up the intersection of two scribed lines. In theory, if the punch is drawn along one line till it meets the other, it should drop into the right place.

Fig.8.8. The finished file/centre punch and a fine pointed dot punch.

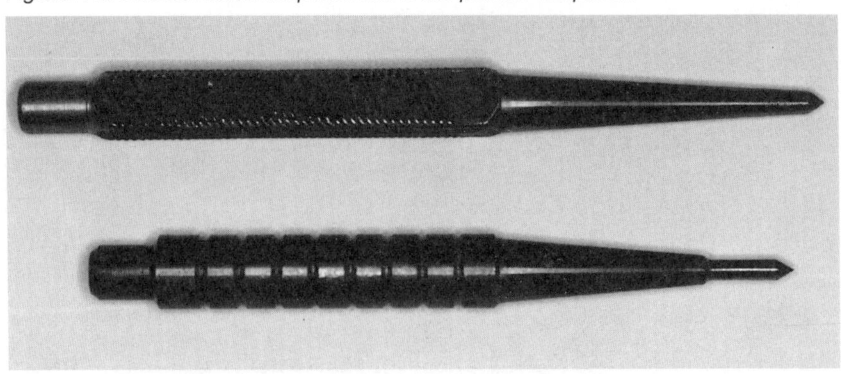

It only works occasionally for me, so I dot the work lightly for starters and correct by drawing the dot over till I have got it right. If the work has to be very accurate, I use an eye glass or a scale reader to check. I also rotate the punch while tapping it, in case there are any irregularities in the point.

Centring aids

There are gadgets to make accurate punching easier. Some have a magnifying lens which lines up a cross graticule with the scribed lines. When lined up, the lens is replaced with a punch of the same diameter, the lens is cylindrical in shape. They are excellent and do the job with very little fiddling about, but they are expensive.

A home-made aid

A fairly simple device which takes some of the problems out of centre punching, is shown in **Figs. 8.10** and **8.11**. It isn't hard to make as long as the parts are accurate and it guides the central hole over a marked cross line, much the same as the one with the lens in it. A punch is put into the hole and tapped, the mark made being deepened by a bigger punch if necessary.

The guiding is done by the three points shown in the assembly drawing. Two of the points are in line with the central hole, the third at right angles to it. The points have to be very finely pointed and finished, so that they will locate in a scribed line. They must also stick out the same amount. The technique is to locate the two in-line points in one scribed line, draw the device towards the other line, with the third point trailing along the work surface till it drops into the second line. When it does, which can be felt, the hole is in the right place and the punch can be put into the hole and tapped.

The device will only work when lines can be firmly scribed. The finished guide is shown in **Fig.8.12**.

There is no lack of advice in books and magazines about the hardening and tempering of punches, so the only advice I'll offer is that of my old friend, 'Steamboat', the blacksmith, long dead now, but a fount of wisdom in his time. 'You only 'ots the bit you wants to work on', was one of his favourite sayings. Translated, it means that the only part of a punch which needs to be hard is the first 10mm or

Fig.8.9. The hall-marking punch.

Dimensions in millimetres

Fig. 8.12 Centre Punch Guide

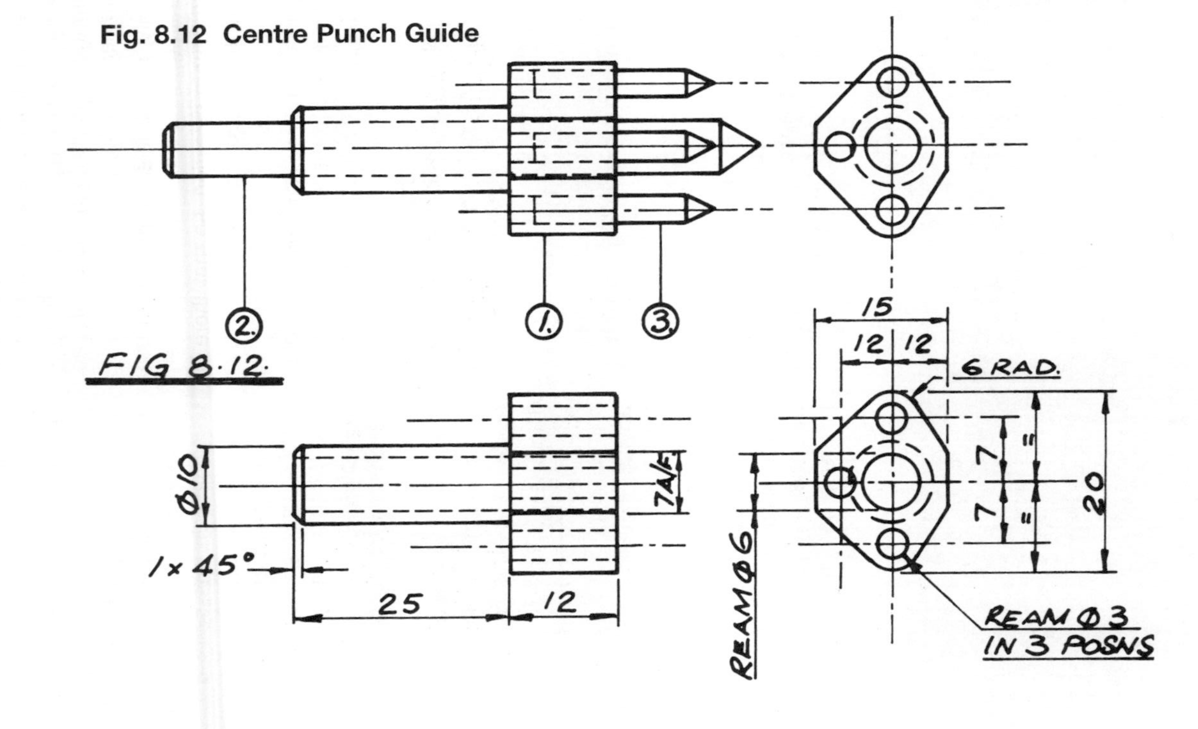

Fig. 8.10 1. Guide Body - Mild Steel

so. Also, the tempering should be started well back towards the shank, so that the hardness gradually increases towards the point. Do not harden the head end of a punch, it will damage the striking face of the hammer.

Finally, even it is a temptation to use the first punch which is handy, resist, and have a selection, so that there is one for each job.

Fig.8.12. The centre punch guide.

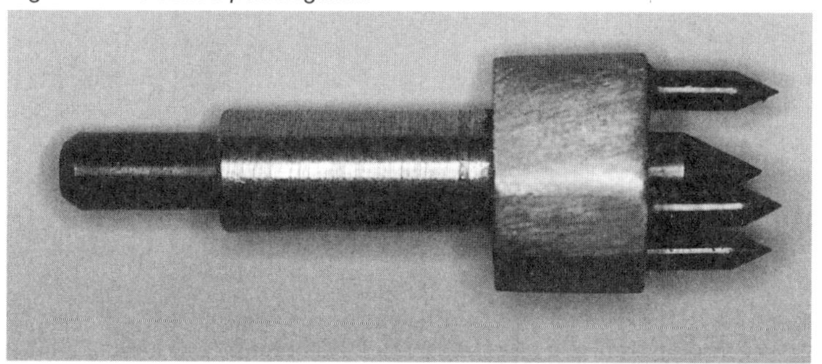

Chapter 9

An Off-hand Grinding Attachment For The Unimat

A while ago, I made a grinding attachment for the Unimat 3. For a long time I had been using a home-made grinder for sharpening tools and cutters. It wasn't much good and a rag bag of improvisation: the motor from an old washing machine, the wheel guard a part of a fly fishing reel and the eye shield the lid off an old cassette case. The wheel was a Black and Decker of 3in diameter and when I bought a 5in wheel, there was no way it would fit, so I made an attachment to fit the Unimat.

Fig. 9.1. The original somewhat over-engineered attachment.

The best thing to have, of course, is a commercial double-ended type, but I couldn't justify the expense, a common excuse for those who like making their own things.

The manufacturer's version is another option and I considered it. There were one or two features I did not like though, one of which being that it was fitted in front of the headstock. There are two snags to this, firstly, the machine cannot be used for anything else while it is fitted; secondly, I don't care how good the guards are, some abrasive and grinding dust will get where it shouldn't.

I decided to put it at the back end of the machine out of the way. It could be left in position, except when I'd have to push very long work up the spindle, or set up my primitive screwcutting tackle.

It was a limited success and did its job well but was over-engineered, a common mistake when designing from scratch. **Fig.9.1** shows it in position.

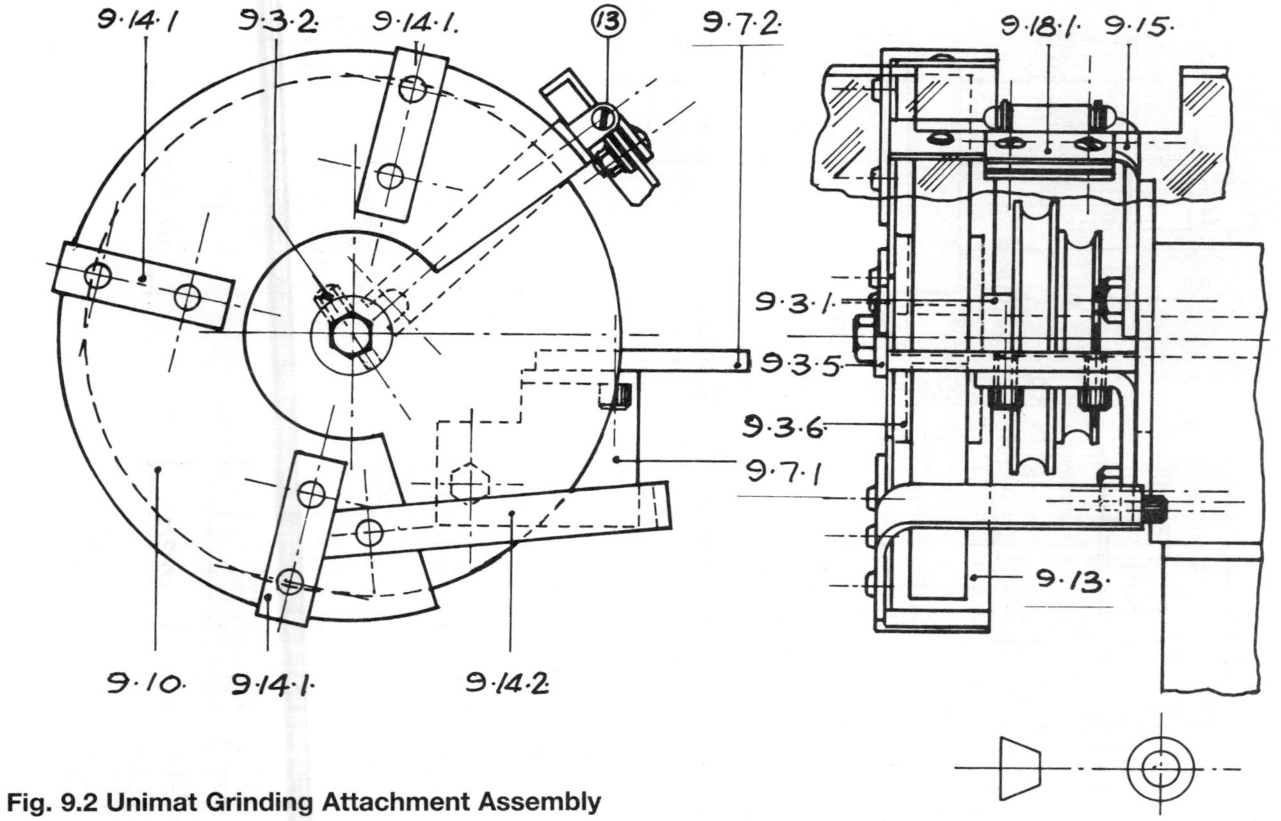

Fig. 9.2 Unimat Grinding Attachment Assembly

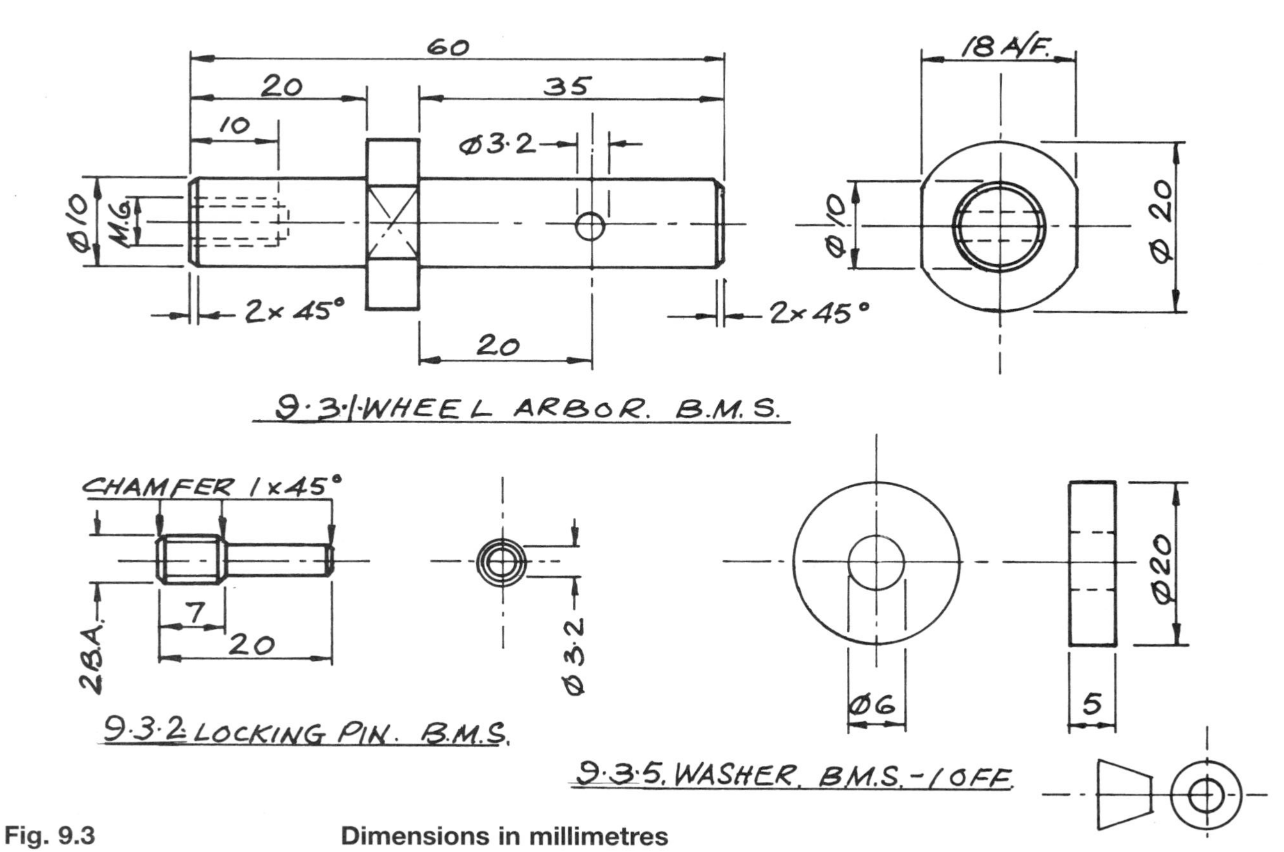

Fig. 9.3 Dimensions in millimetres

Second thoughts

I then made a Mark 2 version which is less elaborate, easier to fit and is much easier to make. It uses holes and features for clamping which are already part of the machine, except for one tapped hole mentioned later. **Fig.9.2** shows the assembly.

Wheel arbor

This is the foundation of the attachment and needs a little care in the making. The best way to make it, **Fig.9.3.1** is to rough out the smaller diameters to about 1mm oversize and finish by turning between centres. **Figs.9.4** and **9.5** shows the turning. **Fig.9.4** shows an improvised carrier used, while the other diameter is being turned with a more conventional one.

The 10mm diameter which fits the lathe spindle must be a good fit with no slop. The width of the collar section is not critical but should stand the wheel clear of the motor pulley when fitted. The other diameter, where the wheel fits, can be made to fit the wheel bore, or to fit a bush which goes in the wheel bore. I did this to allow for the bit of wear which happens when the wheel is slid on and off the arbor. It may be an unnecessary precaution, so if you don't want to make it , it is no big deal.

The 3.2mm hole cross drilled in the arbor was marked by pushing it in to the lathe spindle from the back, up to the shoulder and twiddling a 3.2mm or 1/8in drill through the tommy bar hole. It was lucky that there was a tommy bar hole in a convenient position. The mark made by the drill was centre punched, then checked by putting the arbor in again and adjusting if necessary. It was also a way of checking the fit of the arbor in the spindle, because if the fit is right, the centre punch mark will be enough to stop the arbor from fitting. File off the

Fig.9.4. Turning one end of the arbor with an improvised carrier.

raised burr round the mark and everything will fit. That is how it should be.

When the mark was as close as I could get it to the right position, I clamped the arbor to a crutch centre and drilled it. **Fig.9.6** shows the process. A crutch centre is an infallible way of cross drilling in the lathe, as long as the work is clamped but if it is not, the drill will wander.

The last job was to file the spanner flats on the collar, the dimension across the flats can be anything which is reasonable and in proportion.

When the arbor was finished, the tommy bar hole was tapped 2BA. I used this size because the hole is very close to 4mm which is the tapping size for 2BA. That was the only bit of disfigurement I did to the lathe, unlike that which I did when making the Mark 1. For that I drilled two holes in the headstock casting.

Locking pin

This is a small but very essential item, **Fig.9.3.2**. I made it from a 2BA cap-head screw with the head cut off. I used a cap-head because they are made from a nice tough grade of steel. The length of the plain diameter allows it to go through the arbor and into the opposite hole.

If it needs it, a thin locking nut will make sure it doesn't move, but the normal errors which creep in during marking and cross drilling will be enough to make it fit firmly. The turning is easy and the finished pin had a screwdriver slot, cut by a hacksaw. If it doesn't line up, the collar of the arbor can be skimmed, or a shim washer fitted between the collar and the lathe pulleys.

Wheel bush

This can be left out, as mentioned before, but if it is made, concentricity between the bore and the outside

Fig.9.5. Finishing the arbor with a proper carrier.

diameter is important. Turn them on the same setting and don't be tempted to use a piece of stock 12mm. Make it slightly shorter than the wheel thickness. **Fig.9.3.4** gives the nominal dimensions.

Washer

The washer, **Fig.9.3.5** is merely a thicker-than-standard one so that it will resist clamping pressures better. None of the dimensions is very critical, as long as the sides are parallel.

Flanges

These are the same as the ones I used on the Mark 1 so I was saved from making another set. **Fig.9.3.6** shows them. They were made from 3mm or 1/8in. mild steel, cut roughly circular and put on a mandrel to skim the outside diameters. Reverse jaws were used to hold them in a three-jawed chuck to turn the recesses. Both the outside diameters and the recesses must be the same, then they will exert an equal pressure on the wheel.

The toolrest was made in two pieces to simplify things. **Fig.9.7.1** and **9.7.2** shows the two pieces.

Toolrest bracket

This was made from mild steel angle. The dimensions given are approximate because I used 1-1/2 x 1/8in and some of the metric dimensions would be a bit adrift. It could be made from thicker material, but no thinner. **Fig.9.8** shows the 6.5mm hole being drilled in the bracket. Notice that it is still in one piece and not cleaned up at this stage. It is always best to wait till all the machining has been done before cutting to length or shape, then there is plenty of material for clamping and marking out.

The bracket has a cut-out to clear the motor mounting plate and the 5.1mm clearance holes are slotted to give some adjustment. **Fig.9.9** shows these holes being slotted with a 4in round file. If the bracket is made to the dimensions in **Fig.9.7.1** it will butt up against the bottom of the motor mounting plate, which will help to locate it.

Tool rest

This part, which the tool rests on for grinding, is a piece of 50 x 5mm mild steel 58mm long. It has the 17 x 19mm cut-out for the wheel and two M5 tapped holes. I used M5 cap-heads to clamp the two parts together, adjusting the length so that the screw ends were just under flush when tight, so that there would be no obstruction to anything during grinding.

Wheel cover plate

Although I have specified 2mm mild steel sheet for this part, 16 SWG would do just as well. In fact, when I looked for what material I had, all I could find was some tin plate. It was 18 SWG. and really too thin, but it makes no difference to the dimensions in **Fig.9.10**. It was what I had, so I used it and it didn't seem to make any problems, although it is better to use the thicker material.

The first thing to find a way round was the lack of tin snips or shears for cutting the shape, so it was improvisation time again. I clamped a large piece of bar in the vice and fastened the tin plate to it with a large parallel clamp. A junior hacksaw did the cutting, its fine teeth and the oblique angle I sawed at did the job. It took a while and needed the outline cleaned up. **Fig.9.11** shows the last cut and **Fig.9.12** the filing to finish the shape.

The 110 degree segment was cut using the same method, sawing till the saw cuts met in the middle. The 50mm hole in the centre was cut out with a fine abrafile and the metal sandwiched between pieces of wood in the vice because it reduces the overhang and the vibration. Remember that the burrs on this part, or any other in thin metal, will be extremely sharp and bad news for fingers, so remove burrs generously. When the cover was de-burred, it was put to one side and the drilling was left till later.

Wheel cover

As I had a reflector from an old lamp which was near enough the shape and size I needed, it was very little effort, just a bit more cutting with the junior saw. For those starting from cold, it is quite easy to bend some 25mm x 16 SWG to the shape in **Fig.9.13**. Leave the drilling of the four holes till later as it is far easier to drill them when assembling cover and cover plate.

The next job was to join cover and cover plate together. Of the many ways of doing this, the easiest with limited facilities like mine, is brackets and rivets.

Short brackets

Three short brackets, **Fig.9.14.1** fasten the cover to the cover plate. They can be made from mild steel or aluminium alloy. I opted for aluminium because it is easy to bend, file and drill and doesn't corrode as much as

Fig.9.6. Drilling the cross-hole in the arbor.

Dimensions in millimetres

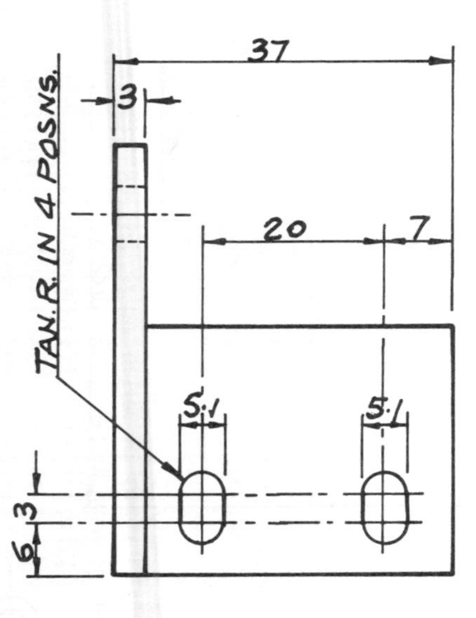

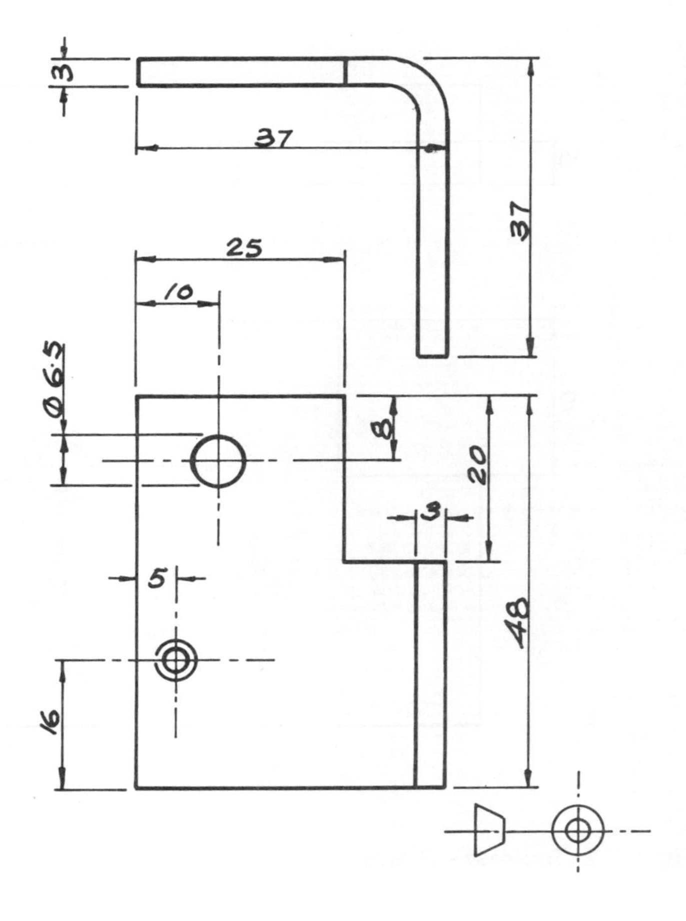

Fig. 9.7.1 Toolrest Bracket - B.M.S.

Dimensions in millimetres

58

5

20 10

19

18

50

M.5. M.5.

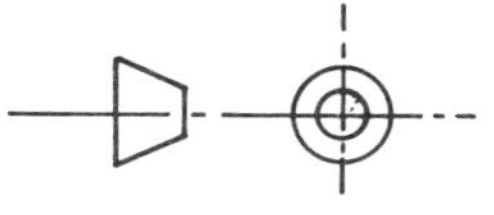

Fig. 9.7.2 Toolrest - B.M.S.

steel. All three brackets were drilled, clamped together once they had been marked out and cut to size. Marking out was done in pencil; it cleans off easily and won't make a stress raiser if bends have to be marked. The total length was about 64mm with due allowance so that I could trim them on assembly. They were bent over a small block with a radius filed on one edge. I haven't given a size for the radius but it can be as small as possible if it can be bent without damage. Once all the brackets were finished the next task was to rivet them to the cover plate.

Riveting

I chose 1/8in rivets because I had lots of aluminium rivets of all sorts and lengths. The only head shape I hadn't got was pan head and, as they would look right I made some by filing down some snap heads. I put them into a 1/8in hole and filed till they looked as if they would knock down alright. The result is shown in **Fig.9.16** and they don't look unsightly. All the knocking down was done from the inside.

The holes for the rivets were drilled by clamping the brackets to the cover plate and drilling through with a 1/8in drill. Once again I had to clamp the cover plate to the block in the vice. By doing this, I could use my Black and Decker drill. It is vital that work of this type is securely clamped because drilling thin materials is extremely dangerous, or can be if it spins. Spinning thin work will cut anything which gets in the way. So clamp the work and save yourself some grief.

Riveting the brackets to the cover plate was just a two-handed job; they closed down nicely and spread enough to hold the parts together

Fig.9.8. Drilling the toolrest bracket.

well. Riveting the wheel cover to the cover plate was a different thing and needed three hands, because the rivets had to be closed with a flat-ended punch on the inside where I couldn't get a hammer in. It was only possible with my wife's help. She is very good at being my third hand and often called on for awkward holding jobs. The only condition is that I don't beat her fingers with the hammer.

Toolrest support bracket

This one, **Fig.9.14.2** was made from 10 x 2mm aluminium alloy but could, like all the others, be mild steel. To get the dimensions right as close as I could, I made a pattern out of thick card and used it to get the inside right. With my bending equipment, a trial run is always a good idea. The pattern gave an inside dimension of 61mm so I found a combination of blocks and strips to make up that size and bent the strip round it. The holes were drilled after bending because I wasn't sure exactly where they would go. The drilled bracket was screwed to the toolrest and the angled line at the long end marked and cut. **Fig.9.2** shows how it butts against the bottom short bracket, positioning the guard assembly and making sure that the grinding wheel is free to rotate. It may need a bit of cut-and-try to get it quite right.

Eye shield support bracket

This was a simple right-angled one, the only complication was that it had to have a 'tweak' of 5 degrees to line it up, see **Fig.9.15**. Before I forget, if the material used for the brackets is an aluminium alloy, make sure that it will bend without breaking. Some duralumin especially, can be brittle and need annealing. The only way to be certain is to try bending a piece. If there is any doubt, anneal it. It is an easy process, just soap the hands as

Fig.9.9. Slotting the holes in the toolrest.

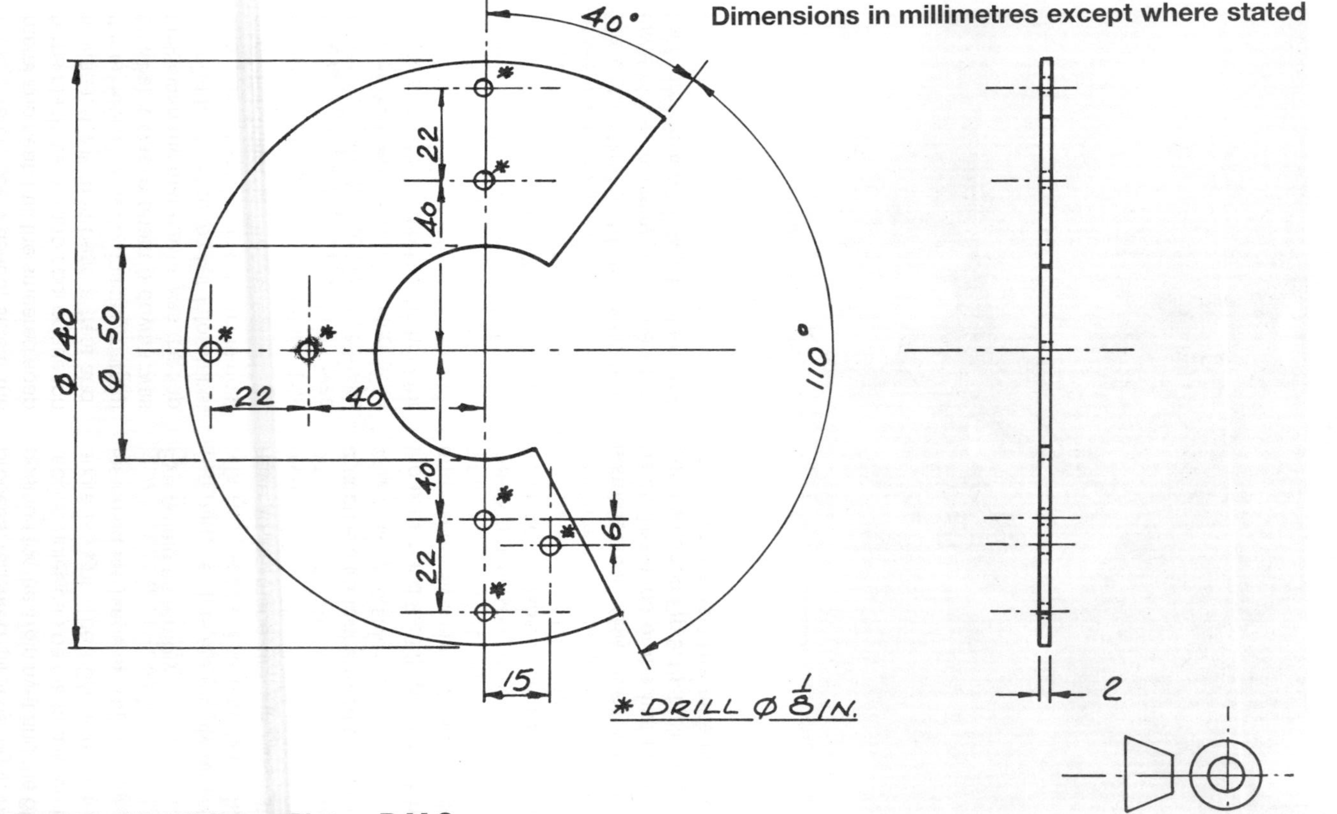

Fig. 9.10 Wheel Cover Plate - B.M.S.

if they were to be washed, smear the metal and heat it till the smeared soap turns black. Leave it to cool or quench in water, it will then bend a treat and, if it is duralumin, automatically harden to what it was in about 5 days. I was lucky with my material, it was the flap off a letter box cover cut into strips. The way it bent, I think it was almost pure aluminium.

Back to the job in question, this bracket, the eye shield one, was clamped by the M6 bolt which fastens the front of the motor mounting plate to the headstock. I slotted the hole for the bolt first, then did the bending. Once it has been clamped, the amount of 'tweak' can be judged; a large parallel clamp will give enough leverage, even if the bracket is of mild steel. One half of the bracket is held in the vice, close up to the bend. The large clamp is clamped to the other half and given a twist, then the bracket is offered up again and the process repeated till it is right. The position for the 1/8in rivet and the 6BA tapped holes can be marked when the angle is right. The 6BA holes are for fastening the hinge swivel.

Eye shield assembly

The parts for this are mostly recycled bits and pieces. The only two which have to be made are the hinge and hinge swivel. The shield is the cover off a CD case but avoid the ones with a circular clip in the middle, they will only make one shield.

Fig.**9.18.1** and **9.18.2** shows the hinge and hinge swivel. The swivel is a simple bit of filing, drilling and bending. The hinge is half of a 1-1/4in butt hinge which can be bought at any hardware shop. The pin was removed and the hole through it tapped a suitable size, 4BA fitted the one I used. The ends of the half hinge are **cut away, see Fig.9.18.1**, till it fits into the hinge swivel. The assembly was

Fig.9.11. Cutting the wheel cover plate.

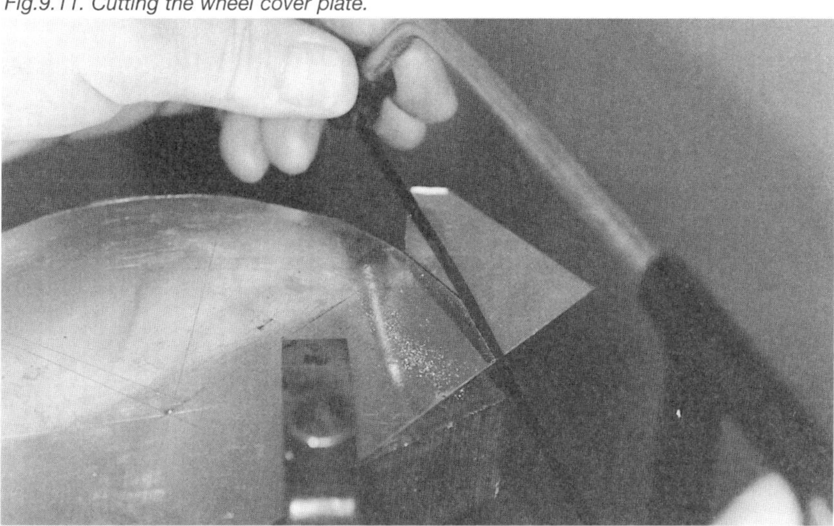

completed by 2 x 4BA round-headed screws holding the hinge and hinge swivel together. I used shakeproof washers under the screw heads so that they could be done up firmly, but still let the shield move without going slack. The hinge assembly can be screwed to the shield by any convenient screws. I used 6BA because a small hole is easier to put through the shield. It was left as it was when it was a CD cover, with just enough cut out to clear the hinge. The shape it has been moulded to is stronger than it would be filed flush.

Cutting and drilling are both a bit fraught because polystyrene is a very brittle material and will split if you look at it cross-eyed. I held it between pieces of wood in the vice to do the cutting and clamped the overhang as well, see **Fig.9.19**. It is also good practice at filing gently.

Drilling poses the same problem, so the best way of dealing with it is to forget drilling and use another method. Because polystyrene is a thermoplastic and softens with heat, the holes for the screws can be burned through or, more correctly, melted through. If a suitable sized pin, nail or other similar object, not a favourite scriber or punch, is heated to red heat, it will melt a nice neat hole in the shield. A small round file will finish it to the correct size if needed.

For the same reasons, the screwing of the hinge to the shield can be the cause of splits. I avoided this by putting a packer of thick card on each side of the shield and a thin plate on the underside instead of washers, to spread the clamping pressure.

With the shield made and fitted and last minute cleaning up done, it was time to try it out. The complete attachment was quick and easy to set up and take down. I haven't come across any snags yet; no doubt there will be one or two but small ones I

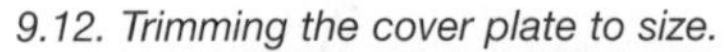

9.12. Trimming the cover plate to size.

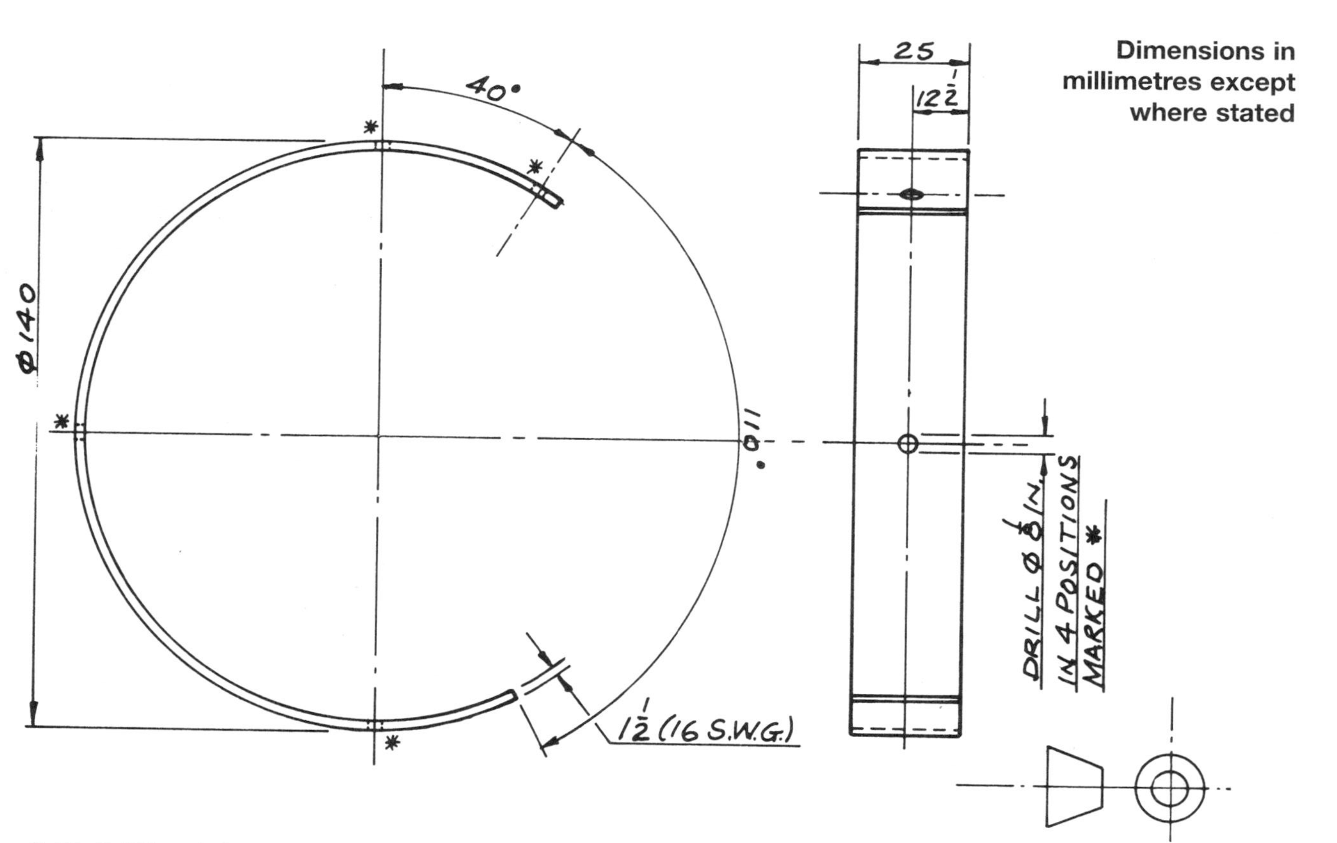

Fig. 9.13 2. Wheel Cover - B.M.S.

Dimensions in millimetres except
where stated

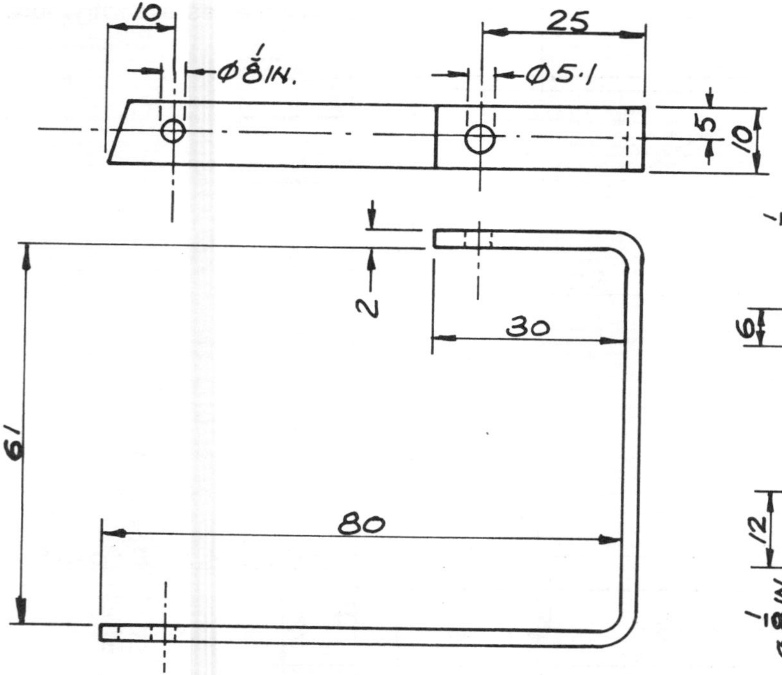
10
⌀ 1/8 IN.
25
⌀ 5.1
5
10
2
30
61
80

9.14 Tool Rest Support Bracket - B.M.S.* - 1 off

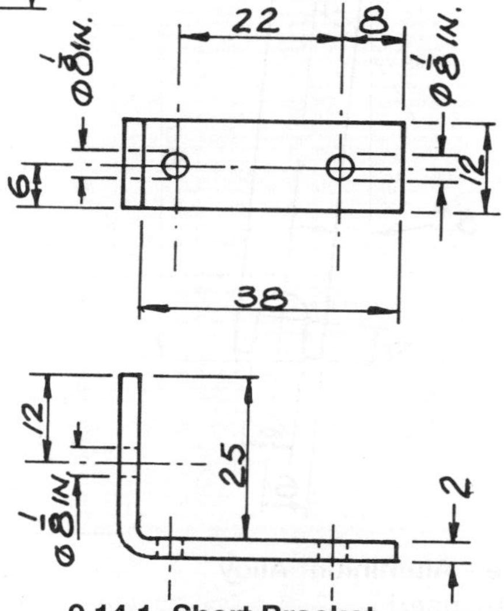
22
8
⌀ 1/8 IN.
⌀ 1/8 IN.
6
12
38
12
25
⌀ 1/8 IN.
2

9.14.1 Short Bracket
- B.M.S.* - 3 off

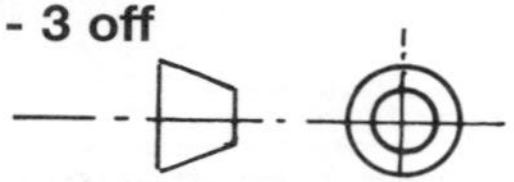

Fig. 9.14 .2

*Note - Aluminium Alloy may be used

Dimensions in millimetres except where stated

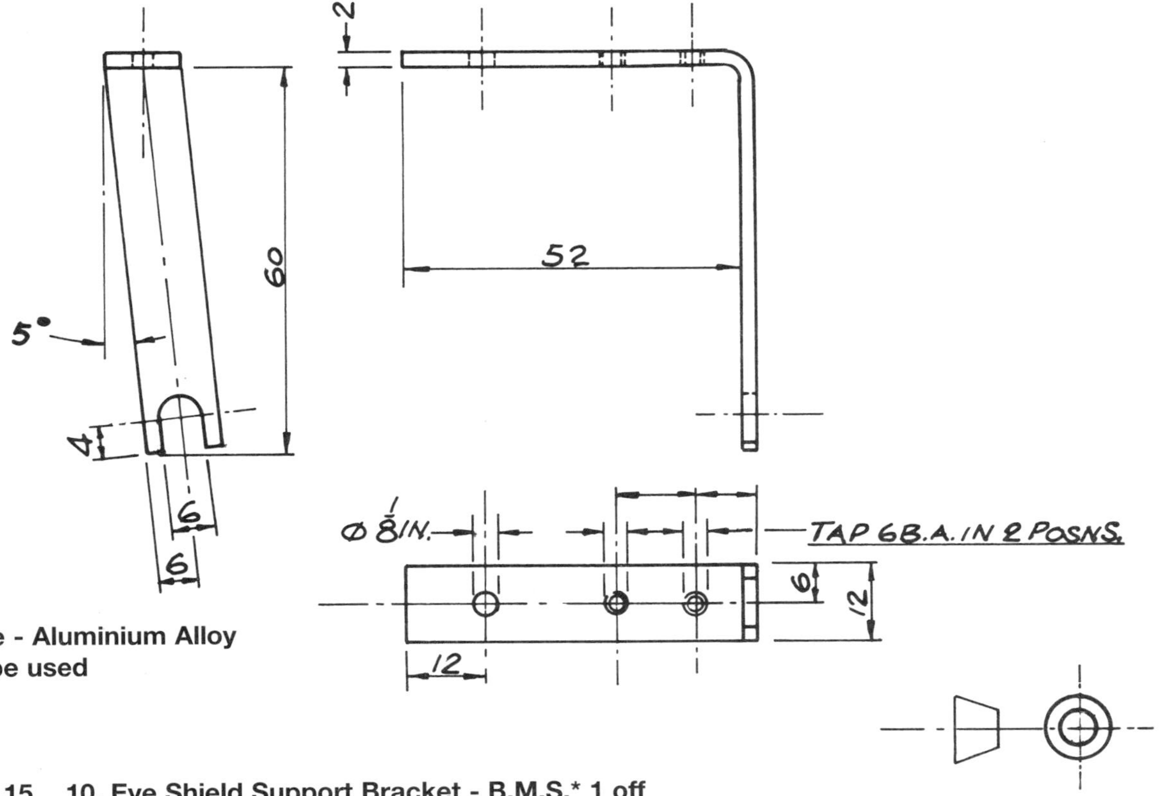

* Note - Aluminium Alloy
may be used

Fig. 9.15 10. Eye Shield Support Bracket - B.M.S.* 1 off

hope. The eye shield may be a bit too close to the tool rest for those with large hands, but that could be fixed by standing the hinge assembly off a bit higher.

My wife had the last word. She looked at the Mark 1 then the new one, hummed and hawed a bit, then said that the new one wasn't as pretty as the Mark 1 - more functional. Exactly the result I had aimed for!

Fig.9.16 The finished rivets don't look unsightly.

Fig.9.19. Filing the eye shield to shape, it needs plenty of support to stop it splitting.

Dimensions in millimetres
except where stated

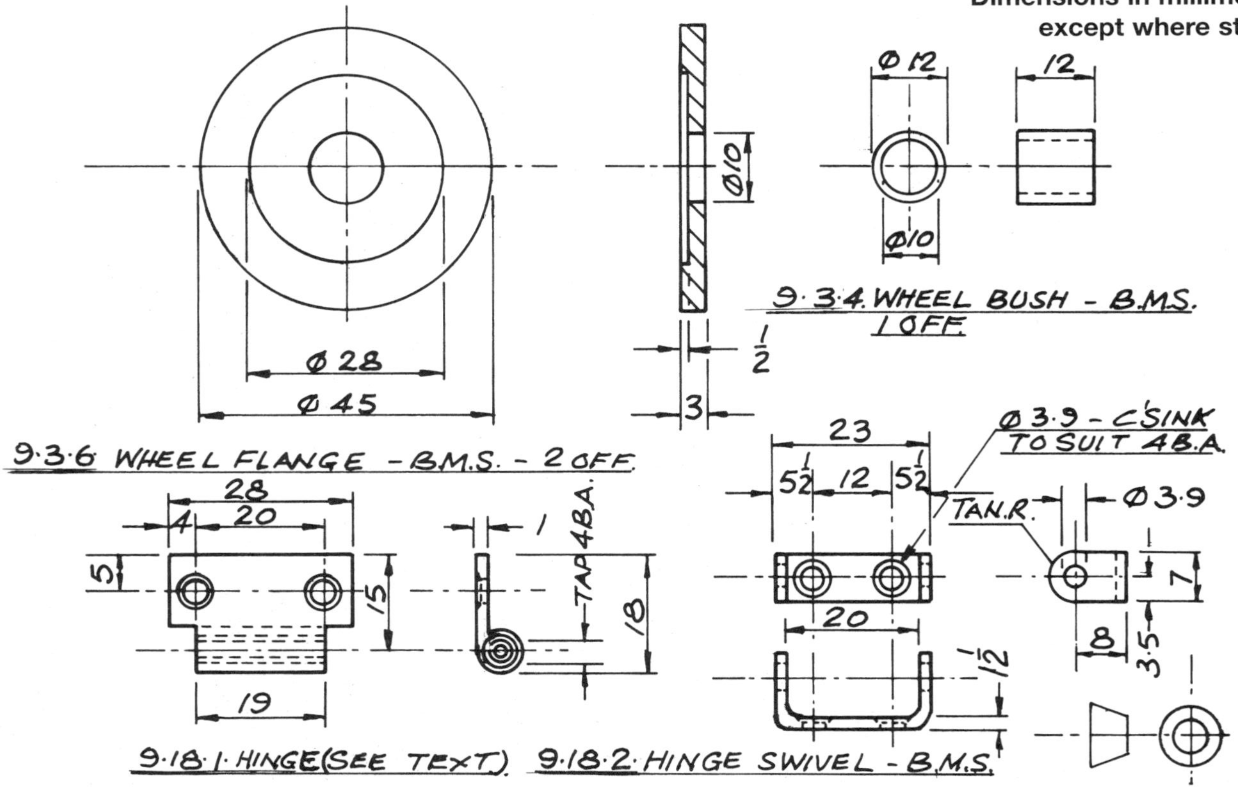

Ø 28
Ø 45
9·3·6 WHEEL FLANGE - B.M.S. - 2 OFF
Ø10
1/2
3
Ø 12
Ø10
12
9·3·4. WHEEL BUSH - B.M.S. 1 OFF
28
20
4
5
15
19
1
TAP 4BA.
18
9·18·1· HINGE (SEE TEXT)
23
5 1/2
12
5 1/2
Ø 3·9 - C'SINK TO SUIT 4B.A.
TAN.R.
Ø 3·9
7
8
3·5
20
1/2
9·18·2· HINGE SWIVEL - B.M.S.

Fig. 9.18

Chapter 10

A Simple Indexing Set-Up For The Unimat

I don't need to use an indexing device that often, but they are useful and the sort of thing which is difficult to improvise. I made one for the Unimat which does the job. It is not difficult to make and takes hardly any time or trouble, except for the index plate but more about that later.

A primitive experiment

Previously, my indexing had been a bit primitive. The first effort was a result of my clumsiness when soldering a connection in the innards of an N-gauge locomotive. I got the iron too close to the driving gear, which was made from a thermoplastic material,

Fig. 10.1. An early simple indexing method.

and melted part of it. I replaced it with one made from duralumin, the cutting of which is shown in **Fig.10.1**. I was lucky to have a gear of the right number of teeth, which I mounted behind the blank. A plunger engaging the gear teeth did the indexing, it was fastened to the lathe bed and sprung to hold it in the teeth. With a form tool, filed to shape and hardened and tempered, it did what I wanted. The method is fine if there is a full set of gears, but can be a fiddle to set up and even a full set of gears will not always give the one wanted.

With these things in mind I made an index plate which fitted on the back of the lathe spindle, so that all I had to do to fix it up was remove the driving pulley and replace it with the plate. There is an M6 tapped hole in the Unimat headstock which is in the ideal position for clamping the link and plunger which operates the indexing, see **Fig.10.2**.

The index plate

Making index plates is always the most tricky part. I decided on hole circles of 60 and 40 to begin with. I had gears of those numbers of teeth and thought I could find some way of transferring them to a blank of 70mm diameter.

The 60 was easy and **Fig.10.3** shows it under way. The plate was on top of the gear and fastened to the machine table by a bolt which was a good fit in the gear bore and allowed the assembly to rotate for positioning.

The plunger was a slotted piece of strip with a gear tooth profile filed into it. It was held in position by the block next to it and locked by the knurled screw, when located in the tooth. Once set up it was just a matter of centre drilling 60 times and opening up the holes to 2mm afterwards.

That was the easy part. The 40-hole circle was done in a different fashion.

Fig. 10.2. The indexing set-up in position.

I had a 20 DP gear and found a drill which would fit in the space made by the flanks of the gear teeth and a piece of bar held against the outside diameter. A No. 44 drill made the three-point contact with no shake. **Fig.10.4** is of this peculiar method. It worked.

By a coincidence the finished plate has a 48-hole circle as well. My daughter and son-in-law were having a clear out before moving, and one of the articles they cleared out was a 24 hour-timer, the gadget which turns lights and other circuits on and off to kid the ungodly that there is someone in the house. The piece which does most of the work is a moulded section with 96 holes in it, see **Fig.10.5**. So 48 holes was easy. I clamped the plate to the 96-hole section, making sure that the two were concentric, and drilled alternate holes. A careful look at the photograph will give the game away; some holes in the outer ring are larger where they have been drilled slightly bigger. **Fig.10.12** is a complete plate.

Apart from the plate, the rest of the attachment is simple. **Fig.10.6** is the assembly and **10.7** the components.

Link

This is made from mild steel, 10 x 8mm and about 45mm long, drilled and tapped as shown in **Fig.10.7.1**. The dimensions can be varied to suit which material is to hand, but the tapped hole must match the thread in the plunger. **Fig.10.8** shows it being finished by draw filing.

Plunger

There is no need to make a fuss of the plunger and the modified cap-head screw will be quite good enough. The small taper is to allow for any slight variations there may be in the accuracy of the hole circles. I used the M6 shown in **Fig.10.7.3** but 1/4in BSF would do just as well.

Fig.10.3. Centre drilling the 60-hole circle.

The length isn't critical, as long as it is long enough to handle comfortably.

Nut

This was made from a 1/2in BSF nut, skimmed down to the 4mm thickness shown in **Fig.10.7.2** It was drilled or bored out and tapped M14 x 1. using the tap I bought for the Unimat headstock thread, something I have found infinitely useful.

The nut could be made from scratch, but if there is one which can be modified, why bother? It only has to clamp lightly.

Fig.10.4. Drilling the 40-hole circle.

Setting up

Setting up is quick and easy. The driving pulley is taken off the back of the lathe spindle and replaced with the indexing plate, washer and nut. The washer I used was a large one, about 25mm diameter. The link is held by an M6 bolt 40mm long. A nut locks the bolt to the headstock and another nut locks the link. When the link is slackened off, it can be swung about to line up with any of the hole circles.

Another use

The index plate can be used at the other end of the lathe by putting it at the back of the chuck as in **Fig.10.9**. I hadn't made anything to hold and locate the plunger so the set-up was a bit of a problem. A U-shaped bracket was clamped to the motor mounting plate and the plunger and link clamped to the other leg of the bracket. The job was to drill 30 holes in a tufnol disc; the drilling was done by a small 12-volt drilling machine clamped to the machine table.

Making index plates

This is where the fun really starts. Some are easier to make than others, it all depends on the number of holes. The easy ones are multiples of 6 or 12. **Fig.10.10** gives the details. Once the circle has been marked, 6 equal positions can be set out by setting dividers to the radius. The 6 can be made into 12 by bisecting the angle made by two of the 6 points. If the process is repeated and the 12 divisions bisected it will make 24, then 48 and so on. The only limit is the diameter of the plate, 96 is as many holes as will fit on a plate with a pitch circle of 80mm and the holes would have to be tiny at that size of plate.

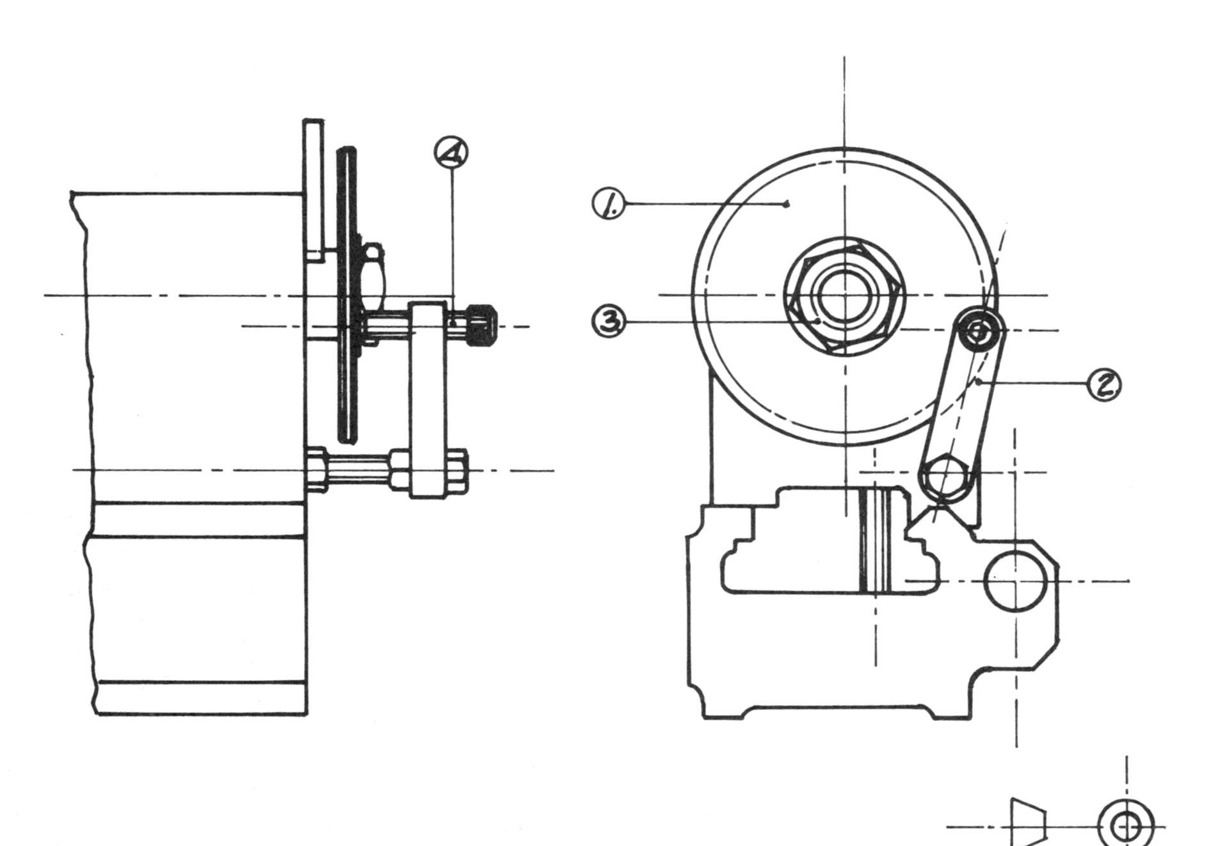

Fig. 10.6 Unimat 3 Indexing Fixture - Assembly

Of course, the hole circle wanted is always the one you have no pattern for, no gear to index from or disc to spot from, Murphy's law sees to that. When this happens there are ways to deal with it. One is to use the perforations in 35mm film. Wrapped round a suitable former, with a shaped plunger to fit the perforations, it is extremely accurate. The diameter of the former has to be worked out and accurately made. On a 24-exposure film, the length is about 45in or 114cm enough to make a circle of well over 200 holes and measuring as accurately as I could, the pitch between the perforations was 4.75mm.

A method using a jig

If you fancy that you can work accurately, there is a simple jig which can be made quite quickly. The jig and the sum needed to work it out are shown in **Fig.10.11**. I used it when I wanted to make a circle of 50 holes. The calculation uses the sine formula to work out the pitch between two of the 50 holes. For the diameter I wanted the pitch worked out to be 4.929mm. Any figures beyond the third place of decimals in imperial units and the second in metric ones can be forgotten, because they will get lost in the machining, unless you have very accurate machinery. Remember that this is written with small lathe owners in mind. So the figure I worked out as 4.929mm was rounded up to 4.93mm.

The jig was made from a piece of mild steel strip, 3 x 15mm, 50mm long. In ideal circumstances the drilling should be done on a milling machine or a lathe with a milling attachment. If this is possible, the jig is clamped to the table and centred with the pivot hole in the theoretical machine centre. One slide is then off-set exactly the radius of the pitch circle. The other slide is then set in the middle of the jig, moved to half of the pitch and the

Fig.10.5. The timing disc, used to spot the 48-hole circle.

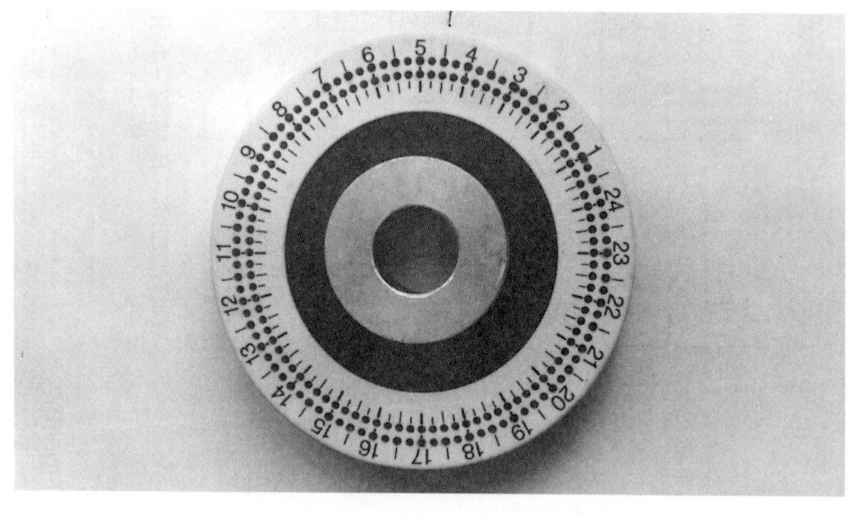

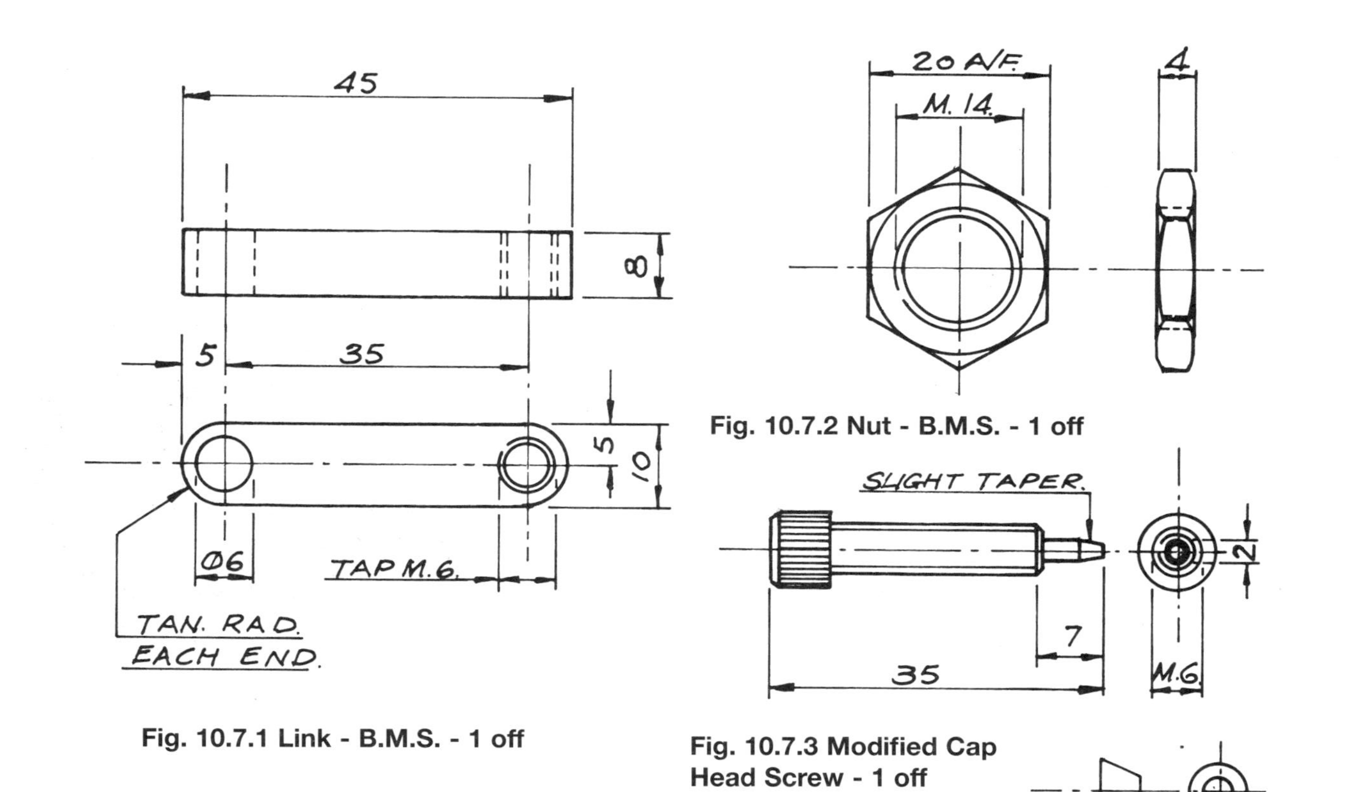

Fig. 10.7.1 Link - B.M.S. - 1 off

Fig. 10.7.2 Nut - B.M.S. - 1 off

Fig. 10.7.3 Modified Cap Head Screw - 1 off

Fig. 10.7

backlash taken out. One of the holes is drilled, then the slide is moved to the whole pitch and the other hole drilled.

So much for ideal conditions, mine were a bit different. I clamped the jig to my 3in angle plate on the cross slide of the Unimat and squared it up from the bed so that it was vertical. I have a ground point which is accurate enough to pick up a scribed line when it is held in the chuck. The scribed line was the 39.25 radius, marked as accurately as I could with dividers. The cross slide was positioned so that the point located the centre of the 15mm dimension. Then it was moved to the first hole centre and the backlash taken out. The first hole was drilled, centre drill first, then drill No. 36 then a 1/8in reamer. The cross slide was moved the pitch of 4.93 as accurately as possible and the drilling and reaming repeated. I used 1/8in dowels for the positioning, but they could be any convenient size.

Using the jig is simple; a hole is drilled and reamed in the pivot position, so that it will rotate but not flop about when a pin is put in. The disc to be drilled is dowelled to the jig by the 1/8in pin, with the jig on the top. The jig is lightly clamped and the first hole drilled and reamed. All the burrs are taken off and a dowel pushed through the first hole in jig and disc. This positions the jig for the second hole. The rest is repetition, with pauses for de-burring.

Make a pattern first

There is no point in starting off with the actual disc to be done, a piece of plastic card of the right size was my first effort. It was between 1.5 and 2mm out when I came to the last hole.

I made another jig, it doesn't take long and when I had a complete hole circle, it was good enough to use. The second pattern was a disc of plywood and the holes were transferred by spotting through and drilling 2mm to fit the plunger.

Fig.10.8. Finishing the link.

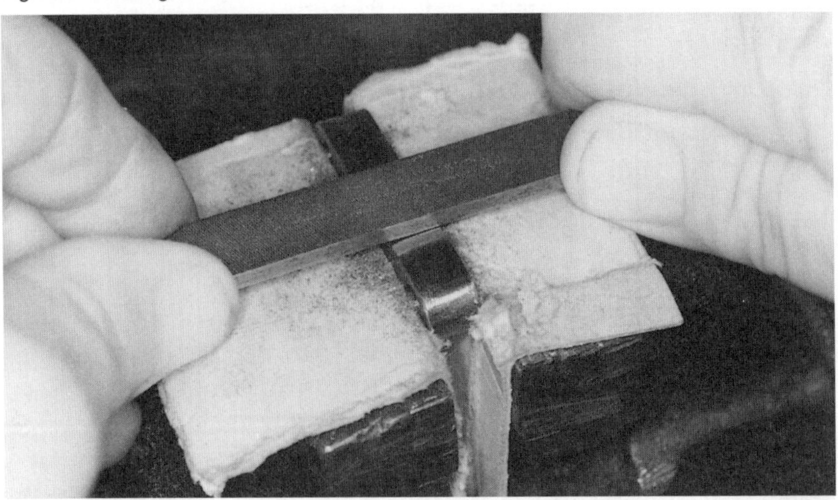

Drilling the 50 holes was tedious and I used the time to play some tapes. 50 holes took one side of my favourite opera highlights and a Goon Show, so the time was well spent.

There are many other ways of making index plates, they can even be bought ready made but that isn't as much fun as making your own and the sense of achievement when it works.

I remember once, when I ran a training workshop, we were faced with making an index plate of an unusual number of holes. I cannot remember the number, but I do remember the youth who had the task of making it by moving a circular table so many degrees, minutes and seconds for each hole. The table was one of those which had a vernier scale as well as the usual dividing plates and the circle came out right. A football team manager would have said, 'the boy done good'.

My method has been chosen to suit small lathe owners, especially Unimat lathes. It can be changed to suit what is available, so have a go. It can be done, even with the simplest machinery and a few bits and pieces.

Fig. 10.9. Using the index plate behind the chuck.

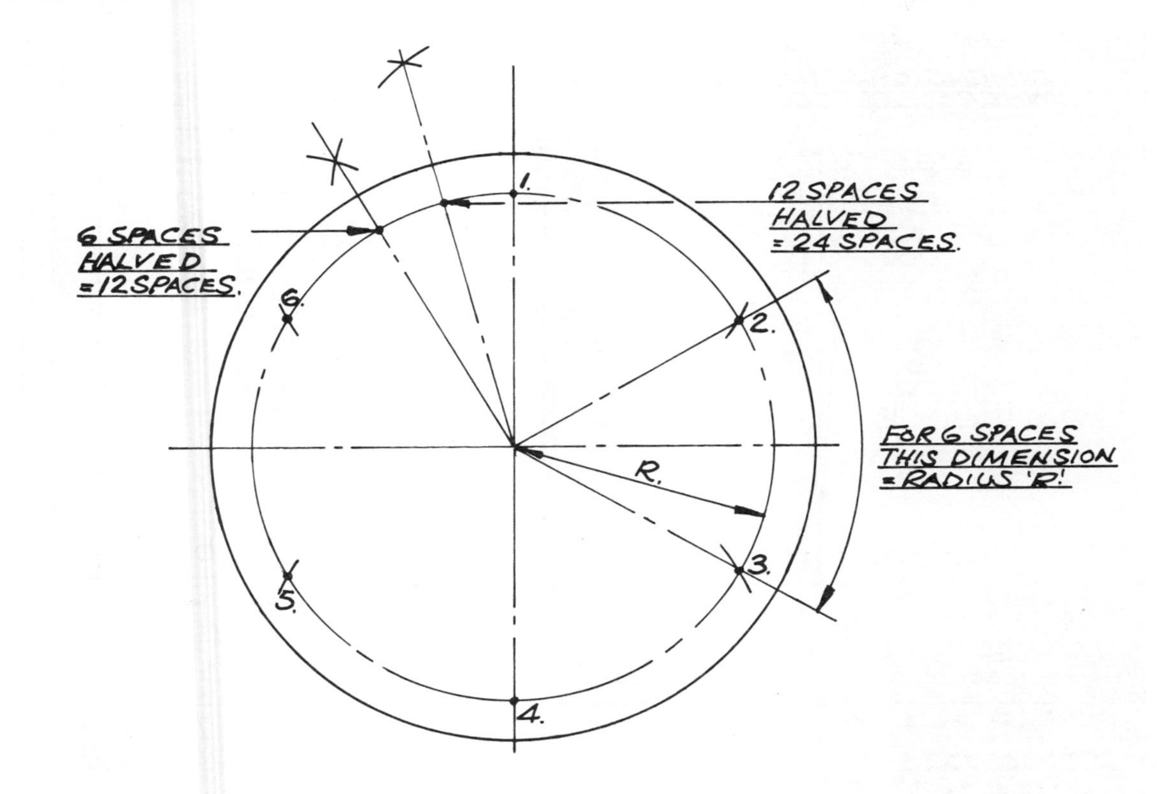

Fig. 10.10 Dividing an Index Plate in multiples of 12

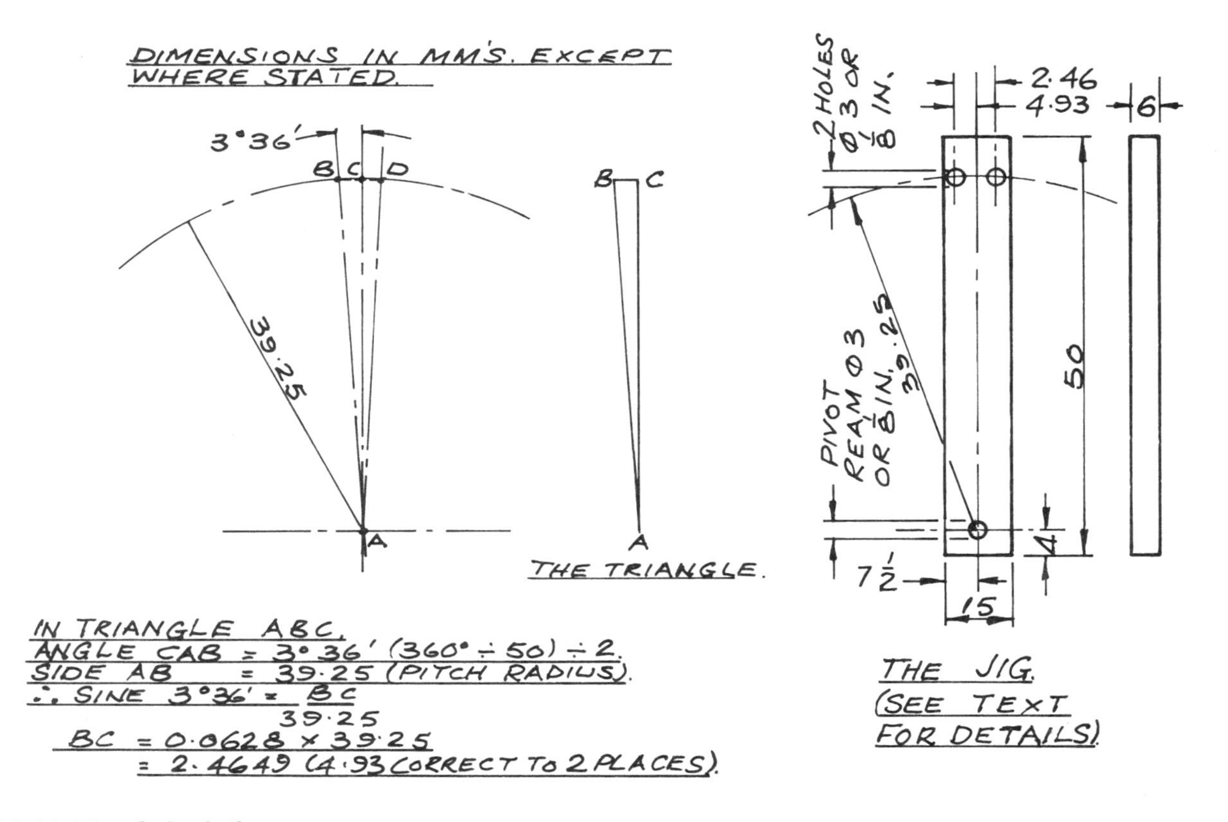
DIMENSIONS IN MM'S. EXCEPT WHERE STATED.
3°36'
B
C
D
39·25
A
B
C
A
THE TRIANGLE.
IN TRIANGLE ABC.
ANGLE CAB = 3° 36' (360° ÷ 50) ÷ 2.
SIDE AB = 39·25 (PITCH RADIUS).
∴ SINE 3°36' = BC / 39·25
BC = 0·0628 × 39·25
= 2·4649 (4·93 CORRECT TO 2 PLACES).
2 HOLES Ø 3 OR 1/8 IN.
2·46
4·93
6
PIVOT REAM Ø 3 OR 1/8 IN.
39·25
50
4
7 1/2
15
THE JIG.
(SEE TEXT FOR DETAILS)

Fig. 10.11 The Calculation

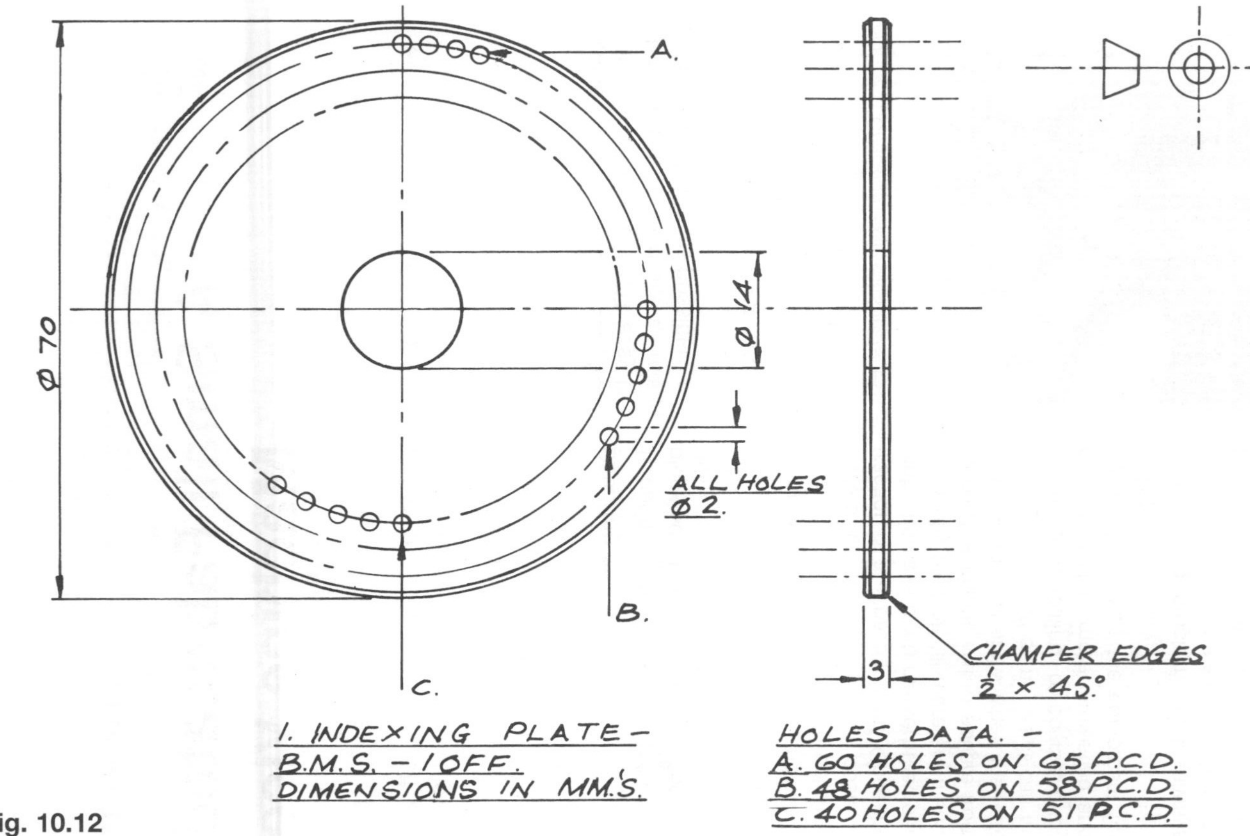
A.
B.
C.
Ø 70
Ø 14
ALL HOLES
Ø 2.
3
CHAMFER EDGES
½ × 45°
1. INDEXING PLATE -
B.M.S. - 1 OFF.
DIMENSIONS IN MM'S.
HOLES DATA. -
A. 60 HOLES ON 65 P.C.D.
B. 48 HOLES ON 58 P.C.D.
C. 40 HOLES ON 51 P.C.D.

Fig. 10.12

Chapter 11

A Small Fabricated Machine Vice

I once made a vice by using the machine table and bolting jaws and other components to it. Because of the size of the table, it came out a bit on the large size and when being used, meant that the table couldn't be.

I decided to scale it down, start from scratch and make a small easy-to-make one which could use as many standard-sized parts as possible.

The scaled down sizes were, 100 x 40 x 10mm for the base, with 20mm square jaws and a thrust block of 20 x 10mm. I had stock mild steel of all those sizes and all it needed was cutting to length, squaring off and drilling some holes, tapping some and reaming others. There were some other components but nothing very complicated. **Fig.11.1** is the assembly.

Fig. 11.2. Checking a jaw for squareness.

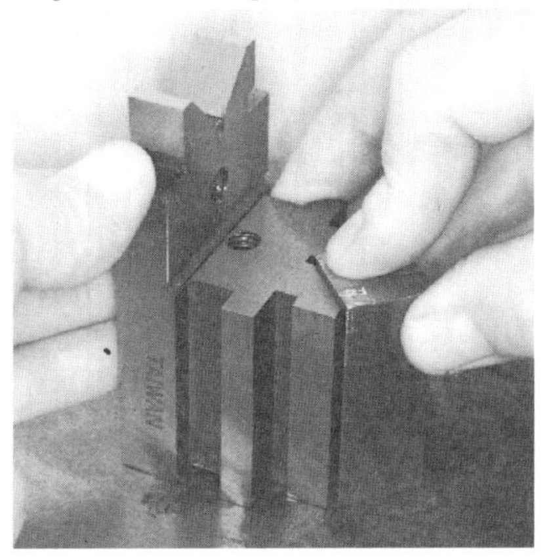

Squaring off

To get the ends of the jaws and thrust block accurate, I filed them, checking them by holding them in the vee of a V-block and rubbing gently on a blued surface plate. **Fig.11.2** shows one of them being checked. My engineer's blue is my wife's navy shoe polish, it makes excellent blue and costs a fraction of the 'proper' stuff. Once the high bits have been marked they can be gently filed off till there are marks all over. A check with a square from time to time will show when they are getting near. The same result can be achieved by milling, of course, but I often find filing more interesting and not everyone has the equipment for milling.

When using stock material, always check to see if there are any bumps or blemishes. There was a fault in the piece I was using for the base which needed some attention; it probably

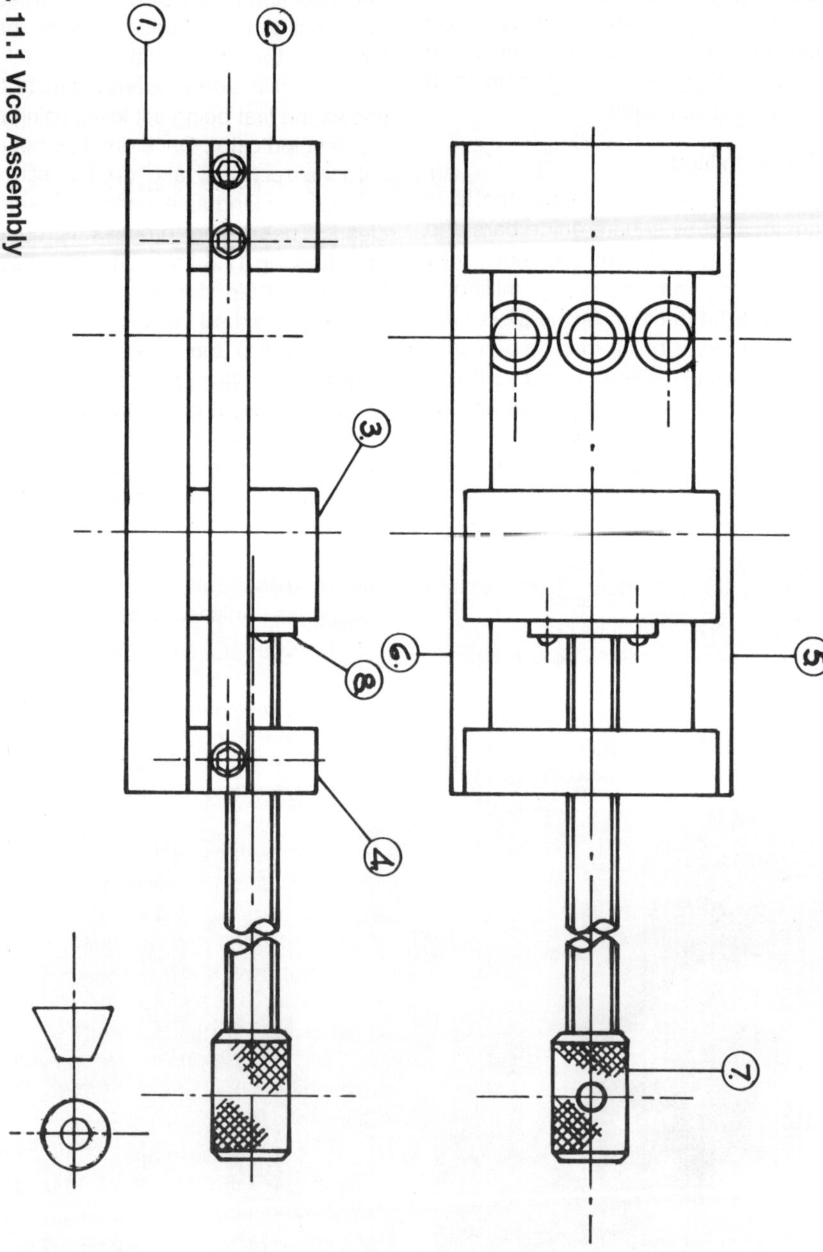

Fig. 11.1 Vice Assembly

happened in the final rolling or drawing and could have been a reason why it was an off-cut. Any small imperfection can be a nuisance when marking out or setting up for a machining operation.

A little milling

Like the larger vice I made, the jaws are located by square guide bars and the best way to cut the slots they locate and run in, is by milling. I marked the position of the slots first, using a broad black marker pen as a base colour. Then I cut with a hacksaw, just inside the lines and as deep as I dared. This got rid of some of the metal and would make life easier for the Unimat, which is my milling machine. A hacksaw, used carefully, is a great roughing tool, as long as the user doesn't get excited and cut too deep.

Milling technique

The jaws and thrust block were milled one at a time, clamped against the fence of the milling table and held down with a bridge clamp. **Fig.11.3** shows the first being set level, using a dial test indicator. Once one has been set, the rest will take up the same position, as long as everything is kept clean. The milling process is quite easy and **Fig.11.4** shows it under way. I used a 3/16in slot drill for roughing out and finished with a 6mm, no significance in the sizes, it was just how they came out of the drawer. I found a depth of cut of about 0.5mm enough and the lathe made unhappy noises at that, so I put a drag on the cross slide by half locking it, the saddle being locked between cuts. A little thin oil helped the cutting and gave a reasonable finish. When the slotting was finished, I de-burred and

Fig. 11.3. Setting a jaw ready for slotting.

put jaws and thrust block aside. By one of those happy accidents, the blocks needed no adjustment for height and sat nicely for the slotting.

Base

The base material was squared off and cut to length the same way as the other parts. The holes were marked and drilled next. **Fig.11.5** is of one of the holes which had to be counterbored for the cap-head screw which holds the front jaw in position. The same size was used for the thrust block. A 1/4in drill was just right for the head of a 4mm cap-head screw. The drill was followed by a slot drill to flatten the bottom and get the right depth. The other holes, shown in **Fig.11.6** are for clamping the vice to the lathe cross slide or other positions when in use, and some 1/8in reamed holes for locating the thrust block and front jaw; more about those later.

Lining up

The thrust block and front jaw were clamped in position and the holes for the M4 screws spotted through. After drilling and tapping the holes, the jaw and block were assembled to the base and checked with the dial indicator to see if everything was in line and square. I used an accurate V-block for checking.

The assembly was clamped on the lathe and the dowel holes drilled. Once again the height of the machining table was right and needed no packing. **Figs 11.7** and **11.8** show the alignment and drilling respectively. Reaming was a hand job, to a depth which allowed the dowels to be a tight fit in the base and a sliding fit in the jaw and thrust block, in case they had to be taken apart.

Fig.11.4. Milling the slot in a jaw.

Guide bars

The guide bars, **Fig.11.9** were the other parts drilled on the machining table. I knew the height from the top of the cross slide to the lathe centre line, so a simple sum gave the thickness of packing to put under the bars to bring them on centre. **Fig.11.10** shows the drilling.

Fig.11.11 and **11.12**, the front jaw and thrust block both specify M3 tapped holes for the screws to secure the guide bars. I was too clever and thought I could use up some 5BA screws. Unfortunately, the head of a 5BA cap-head is 0.215in giving little margin for error in the counterboring, which I did with a 7/32in slot drill. Had I used the M3 screws, a 3/16in slot drill would have done the counterboring without leaving an ugly witness mark, like those in the photo of the finished vice, **Fig.11.16**. The lengths of the guide bars were left oversize, so that they could be trimmed when everything was finished.

Adjusting screw

I was lucky with the screw and found one almost ready-made which only had to have a clean up and a bit of turning. It was one of a batch made to check the programme of an automatic capstan. They were to be thrown away, so I liberated a few.

The one I used was 5/16in BSF with a 12mm knurled head. It needed a spigot and an undercut machined, details in **Fig.11.9**. I drilled a cross hole in the head to take a tommy bar. If the screw is to be made from scratch, I'd recommend a finer thread for a better locking effect. 5/16in UNF or 5/16in brass would be suitable. **Fig.11.14** shows the undercut being machined at the spigot end.

Finishing the jaws

It is vital that all the holes for the adjusting screw line up. The best way to do this drilling is to assemble the vice. At this stage everything was tight and the moving jaw was solid; it was attended to later.

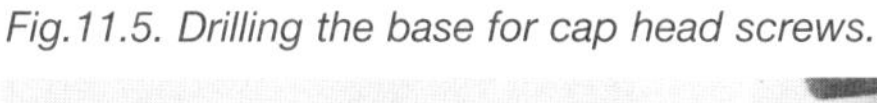
Fig.11.5. Drilling the base for cap head screws.

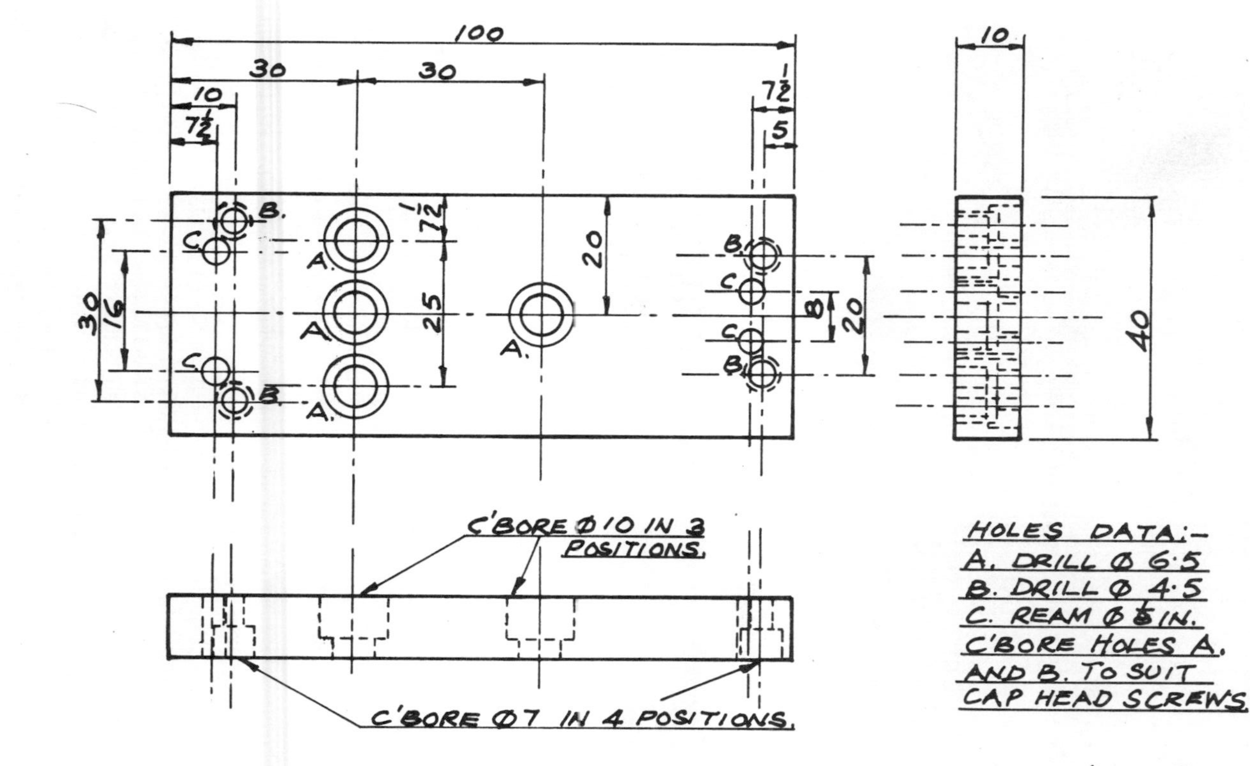

Fig. 11.6 1. Vice Base - B.M.S.

Dimensions in millimetres
except where stated

With the jaws, thrust block and guide bars in position, the assembly was clamped to the lathe cross slide, using the holes marked 'A' on **Fig.11.6** and the T-nuts belonging to the lathe. **Fig11.15** shows the assembly ready for drilling with a little packing to get the height right. Two small bridge clamps did the clamping and it had been set true in line. In **Fig.11.15** the drill shown is a pilot. I always use several drills in gradually increasing sizes, to make it easier for the lathe, especially when the hole is a deep one. I drilled through the thrust block and 5mm into the moving jaw with the pilot drill, then opened it up to 6.5mm The thrust block was drilled 17/64in, the tapping size for 5/16in BSF. It was left in the lathe after drilling, so that the tap could be started in line. With the tap held in the drill chuck and the saddle eased back, the tap can be pulled round by hand and will start square. It only needs a few threads to be cut and the rest will follow.

When the thrust block was tapped, the parts were taken apart and all the burrs and sharp edges taken off, generously on the outer surfaces. The 6mm slots in the moving jaw were skimmed with a fine file, so that the guide bars would slide in them, the ones in the thrust block and fixed jaw can be left tighter. The two M3 tapped holes in the moving jaw were left till the retainer, **Fig.11.13** was made, then they could be spotted through.

Retainer

This was a simple piece, made from 1.5mm steel, chosen because the parting tool I used for undercutting was that size. It could be a bit larger but the dimensions of 25 x 15mm look about right. When finished, it can be clamped in position and the holes spotted through. The screws could be M3 or 6BA. Round- or cheese-headed screws are best, do not be tempted to use cap-heads as the fiddle to use a key in there has to be experienced to be believed. If the retainer is tight in the undercut, ease it a bit.

Fig. 11.7. Setting the thrust block ready for drilling.

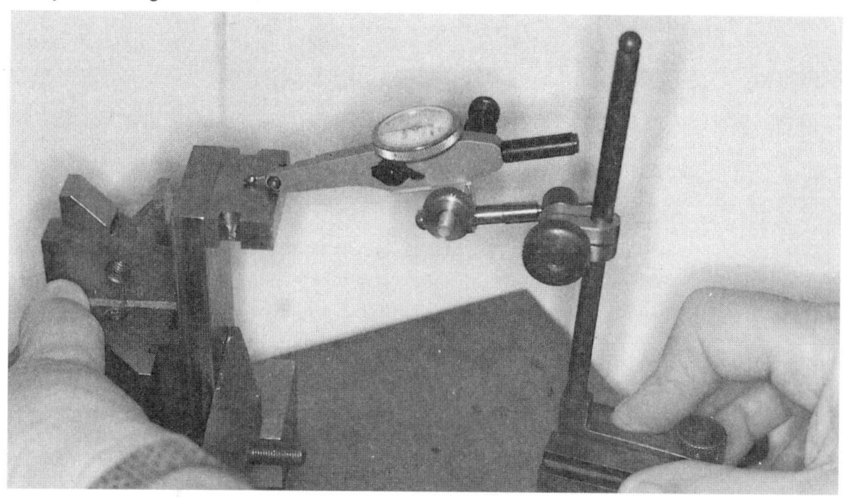

Final fitting

When everything fits, take the vice to pieces and check again for burrs and sharp edges. Next, make sure that the moving jaw moves. It will probably be too tight for the screw to move it, so file small amounts off the bottom surface till it does. A bit tight won't matter, because it will ease a little with use, just a little draw filing should do . If the jaw is too tight to move by hand but will move nicely with a tommy bar, that will be right. A smear of Vaseline under the jaw and in the slots where the guide bars fit will help.

Last things

When everything works, the guide bars can be filed off flush with the fixed jaw and thrust block.

Figs.11.16 and **11.17** show the vice in use, for a drilling job, and also for milling using a vertical head.

It was a quick attachment to make, thanks to using mostly stock sizes. Although it was designed for the Unimat, it can be used on any drilling machine. The holes in the base could be used to fit a flanged base, or perhaps a rotary one. If it is used in line on the Unimat cross slide, it needs a packer underneath to raise it, or it will foul the cross slide handle.

Tests

The maximum it will hold when fully open is 45mm and in between the guide bars, just over 30mm.

I tested for lift of the moving jaw when tightening. With a dial test indicator registering on the top of the moving jaw, there was no movement when it was tightened, so the guide bars eliminate the vexing problem of lifting. It is an easily-made and useful attachment.

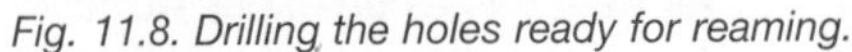

Fig. 11.8. Drilling the holes ready for reaming.

Fig. 11.10.Drilling the guide bars.

Fig. 11.14.Undercutting the screw to take the retainer.

Dimensions in millimetres

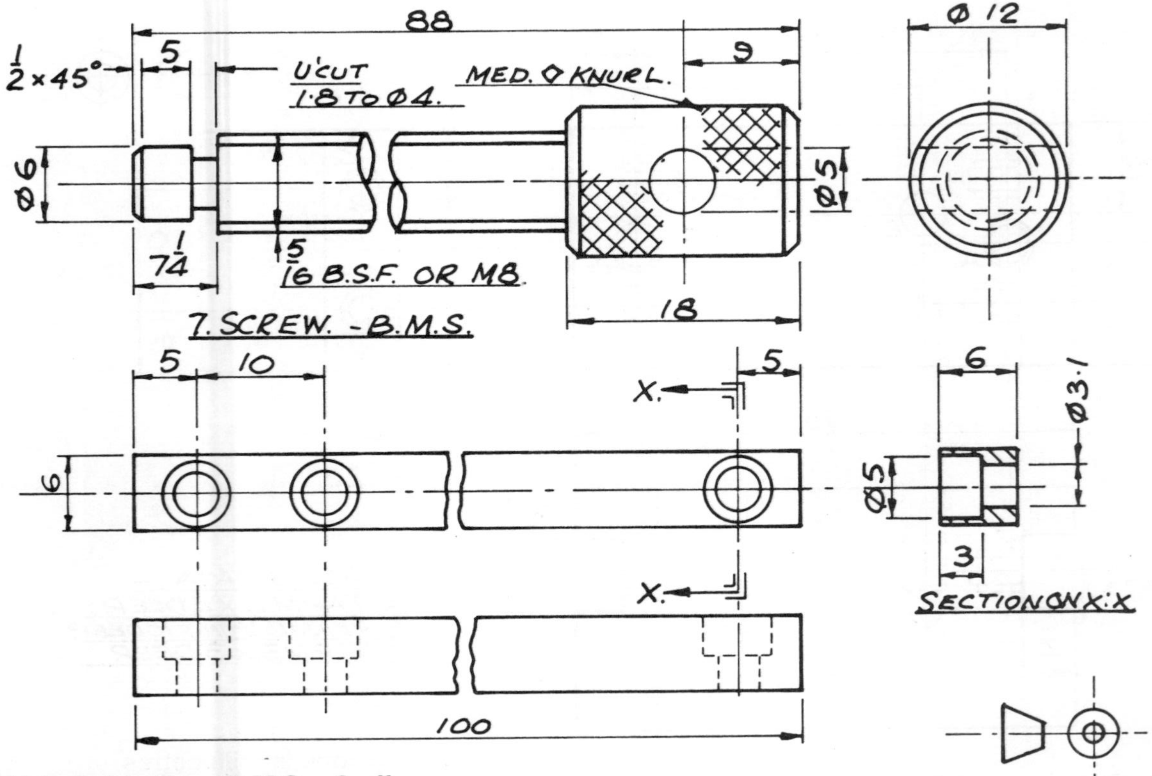

88
5
9
Ø 12
½ × 45°
U'CUT 1·8 TO Ø4.
MED. ◇ KNURL.
Ø6
Ø5
7¼
5/16 B.S.F. OR M8.
18
7. SCREW. - B.M.S.
5
10
5
6
X.
X.
6
Ø3·1
Ø5
3
SECTION ON X:X
100

Fig. 11.9 Guide Bar - B.M.S. - 2 off

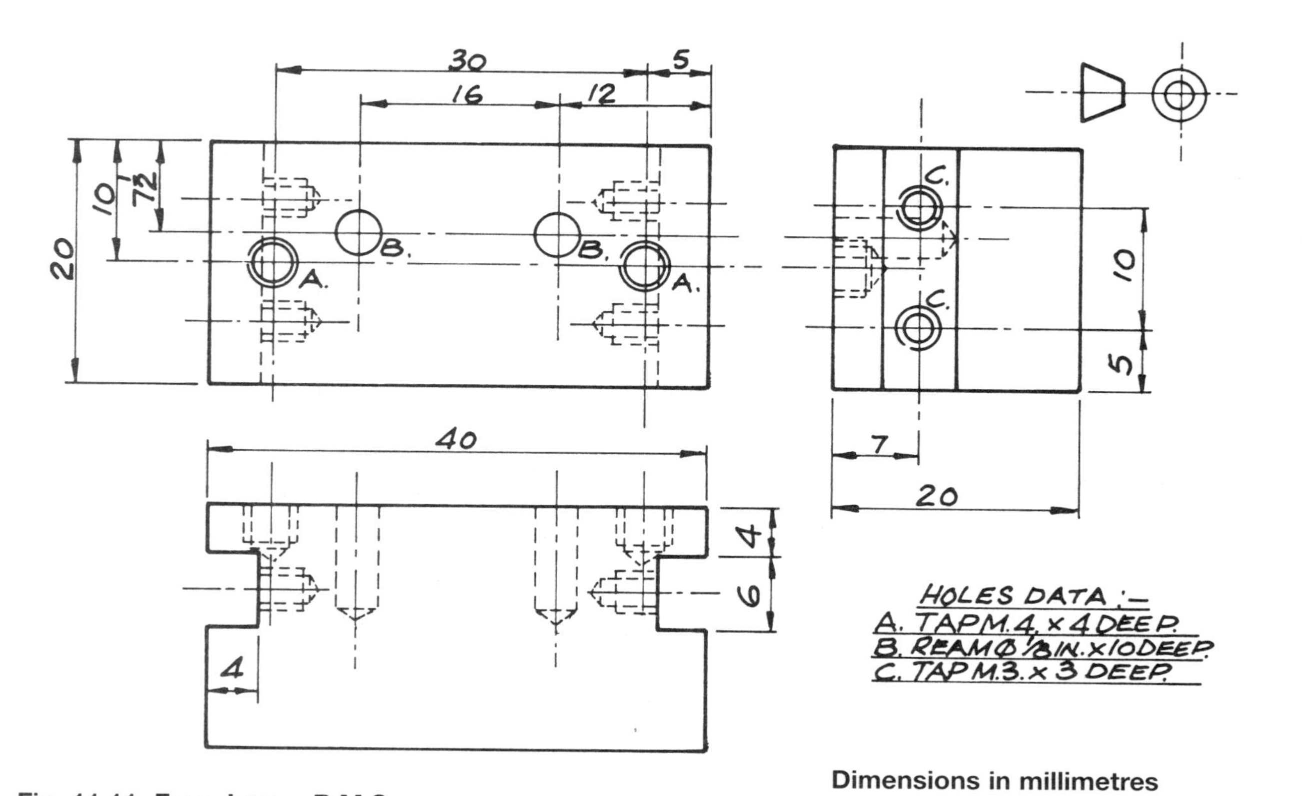

Fig. 11.11 Fron Jaws - B.M.S.

Dimensions in millimetres
except where stated

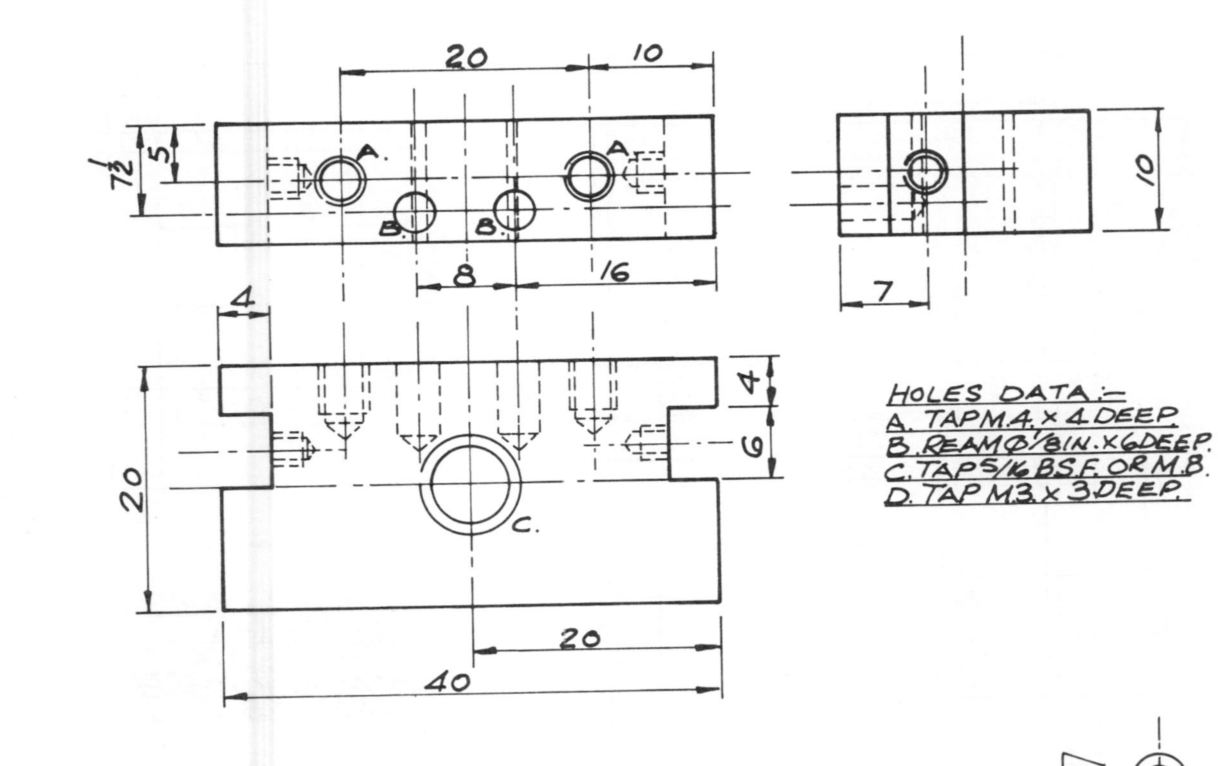

Dimensions in millimetres
except where stated otherwise

Fig. 11.12 Thrust Block - B.M.S.

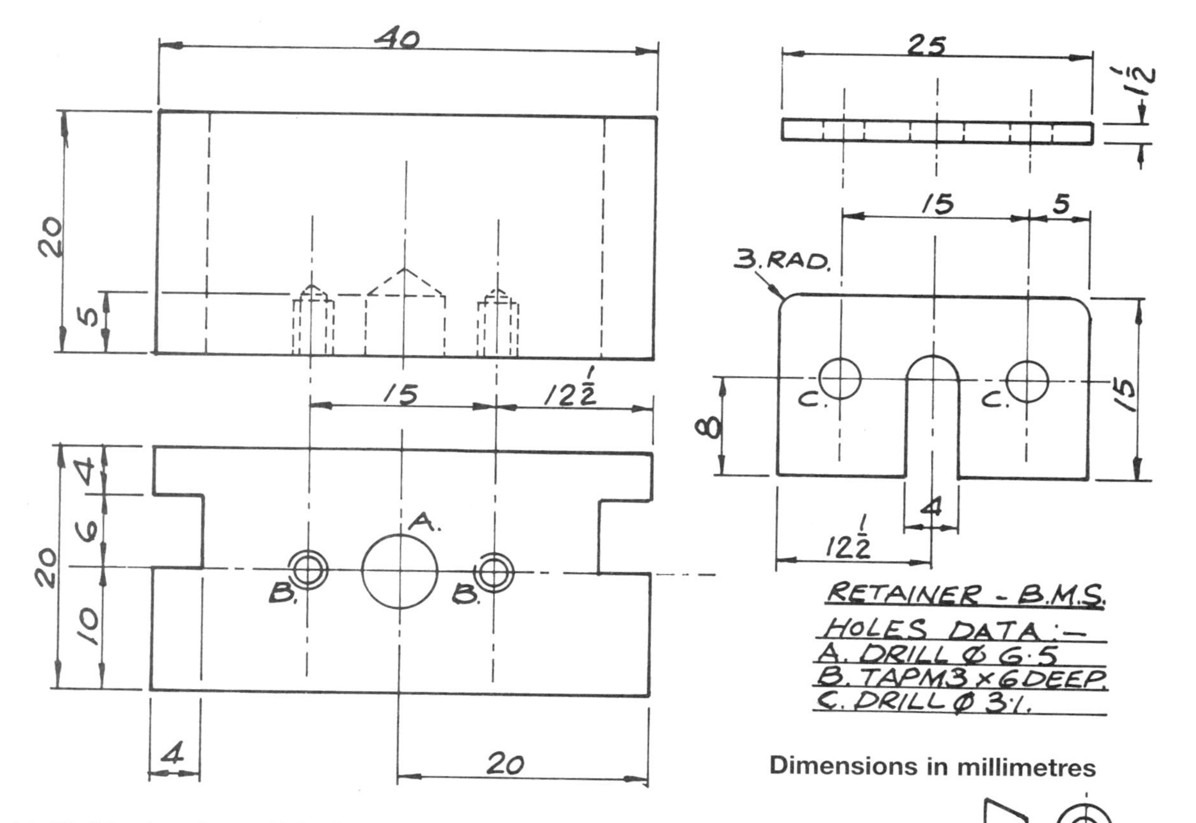

Fig. 11.13 Moving Jaw - B.M.S.

Fig. 11.15. Drilling a pilot hole through the assembly.

Fig. 11.16. Using the vice for a drilling operation.

Fig. 11.17. Milling a component.

Chapter 12

A Fine Adjustment For A Digital Caliper

For a birthday a few years ago, my wife gave me a digital calliper.

Compared with the vernier calliper I had used for a long time it had lots of obvious advantages. It will do all the measuring the vernier one did and save a lot of mental arithmetic. It also cancels out one source of error by showing the exact reading: on a conventional vernier there could be an error of a couple of hundredths of a millimetre or the equivalent in thousandths, built in as a reading error. The other great advantage is having an immediate conversion from metric to imperial at the touch of a button. A lot of my work has to be a mixture of the two. I can also leave my vernier set up as a height gauge with the home-made modifications I've made. It saves the hassle of taking it apart every time I want to change from marking to measuring and vice versa.

One small thing

So, it does everything as well as or better than, the vernier one. Everything? Well, there is one small thing which the vernier does much better. It has a fine adjustment second to none. The digital has a thumb wheel which makes a frictional adjustment, see **Fig.12.1**. The small block which holds the wheel in

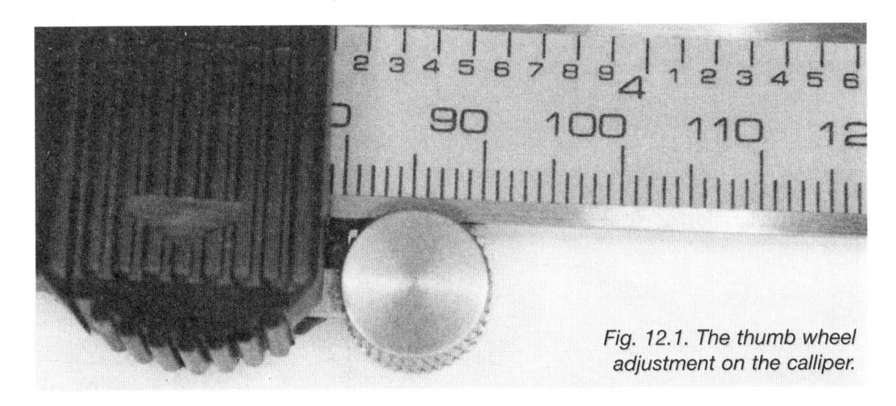

Fig. 12.1. The thumb wheel adjustment on the calliper.

position and the wheel are shown in **Fig.12.2**. A look at both photographs gives an idea of how the arrangement works. The thumb wheel has a recess which lets it make a frictional contact with the land on the calliper beam and stops it from over-lapping too much. It is not as sensitive as the conventional vernier adjustment by a long way.

I have looked at a lot of digital callipers, both in shops and in catalogues, also at the shows and they all have the thumb wheel. It seems that you can get them with solar cells, infra-red remote control and even a connection to mini processors, the only thing you are unlikely to find is one with a sensitive, easily-used, fine adjustment.

A look at the pieces

I am not a compulsive fiddler with things, or one of those who must have things to pieces as soon as they get them home. I follow the philosophy, 'if it isn't broke, don't fix it', but circumstances alter cases and I wondered if it would be possible to make a better fine adjuster.

It was very easy to get at the block which holds the thumb wheel and remove it, without doing any damage. The fixing is inside the battery compartment. When the cover is slipped off and the instrument turned upside down, all is revealed, see **Fig.12.3**. The thumb wheel is held by a small shaped block, fastened by one screw. When the screw is undone, the block and thumb wheel come off.

Fig.12.2. The retaining block and thumb wheel.

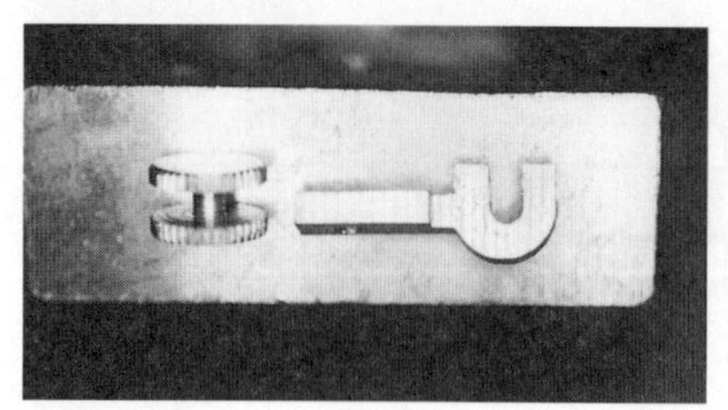

A little design work

Once it was clear that something could be done, it was time to make some sketches and put in the important dimensions. Most of the parts are quite small and the materials easy to find. The materials are what I had so others can be substituted. I used duralumin because I like the way it can be machined, filed and otherwise manipulated.

The pieces as I made them are shown in **Fig.12.4**. Check before using my dimensions as there could be differences for different makes of calliper, the most likely ones in the shape and sizes of the block which holds the thumb wheel. This block holds the studding which does the adjusting on the modification as well, so it needs to be right.

The clamp body

I usually start the job with the piece which will be the most work, or the one which is likely to be difficult. In this case it was the clamp body, **Fig.12.7**. As it would need a little accurate filing, it was a further reason for using duralumin. I had a piece of 25 x 6mm about 120mm long. I left it in the length because it is easier to clamp and do things to if it is left long. Confucius, that well known friend of engineers, had a saying for it, 'foolish man cuts to length first: wise man leaves it in a lump, till he has done all the cutting and drilled all the holes'.

Marking out was simple, the important dimensions are the width and depth of the cut-out to fit the calliper beam, 16 x 3mm. The easiest way to cut this slot is to mill it but, as it is a bit of a chore to set up the Unimat for milling, I filed it. That wasn't as difficult as it may seem, because the bulk of the waste, being duralumin, can be chiselled out. I sawed parallel slots between the 16mm lines, stopping short of the depth. The saw cuts were quite close, so the chisel didn't have much to do. I used one with a cutting edge 3/16in wide, narrow enough to be very useful in restricted spaces. It made short work of the roughing out. A 10in second-cut square file did most of the filing, followed by an 8in second cut pillar file, which was 15mm wide. I used second-cut files because they are coarse enough to shift the metal without pinning too much and the safe edge on the pillar file was useful to get into the corners.

To make sure that the 16mm dimension was accurate, I clamped a fence to the work, lined up with the marked line. A piece of square mild steel stock does the job. Do not use hardened steel and do not make it too small; it has to act as a guide, so no smaller than 6mm is best. When one edge was finished, I worked on the other one with a 4in smooth hand file, using a fence again to get the vertical edge right.

Fitting the clamp to the beam

It probably wouldn't matter if there was a bit of clearance in the fit of the clamp, but I like a nice fit, so I filed out the last bit by trying it on the beam. It just means undoing the retaining clamp at the end of the calliper which stops the depth probe flapping about. I put the clamp and screws away carefully as they aren't that big and they can easily go walkies.

Getting the depth right was a bit more taxing and needed checking with the micrometer. If the clamp body is made from 6mm material, 3mm is the dimension to aim for. Even if the saw cutting has been done carefully, there will probably be a blemish somewhere. There is on mine, as a look at **Fig.12.4** will confirm. I got a bit excited with the depth and it would not clean out. Luckily, it doesn't show when the clamp is assembled. Final fitting came later. **Fig.12.7.1** shows the clamp body.

Fig.12.3. The block and thumb wheel from underneath.

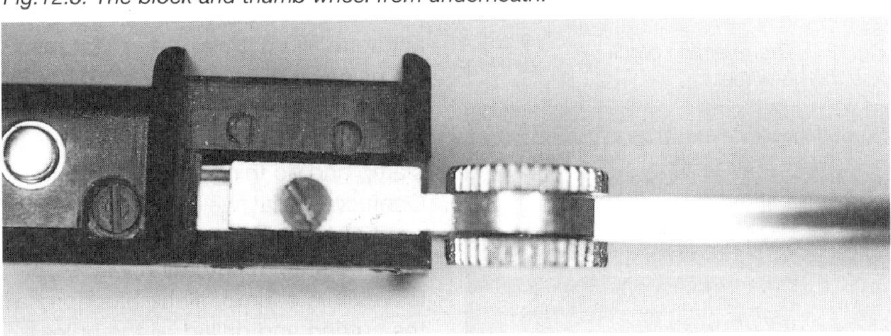

Milling the clamping pad pocket

The small cut-out or pocket in the clamp body has to be milled. It measures 8 x 1.5mm and accepts the clamping pad, **Fig.12.7.3**. It is an optional component and could be left out. I put it in because I don't like the clamping screw bearing directly on the calliper beam. The pad is there for protection.

The milling is straight forward. I used a 5/32in slot drill, which is near enough 4mm. **Fig.12.9** shows the work clamped and the milling underway, with the job left in a lump, just as Confucius suggests. The set-up is one of my normal milling ones; an angle plate clamped to the Unimat cross slide, set true and the work set vertical with a square resting on a parallel on the lathe bed. The cutting position was sighted against a scribed line and the pocket milled till the cutter just touched the filed surface. It is vital to lock the saddle for each cut.

Drilling the clamp body

Because the clamp body was relatively thin, I clamped it to a larger block for the drilling of the cross hole, clamping the assembly to the angle plate and positioning the hole centre with a small centre drill or a ground point held in the drill chuck. If you have a drilling machine, the part can be held in a small vice and drilled normally, without all the palaver. The tapped hole in the upper surface for the locking screw can be done the same way.

The cover

With the clamp body almost finished, the cover can be made. I used duralumin again, the 1.5mm thickness wasn't too important, but it shouldn't be thinner. I did the marking out for the holes in pencil, the rest was marked with a scriber. I used a nice sharp pencil so that the lines were thin. The reason for using pencil is to

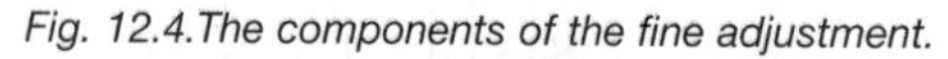

Fig. 12.4.The components of the fine adjustment.

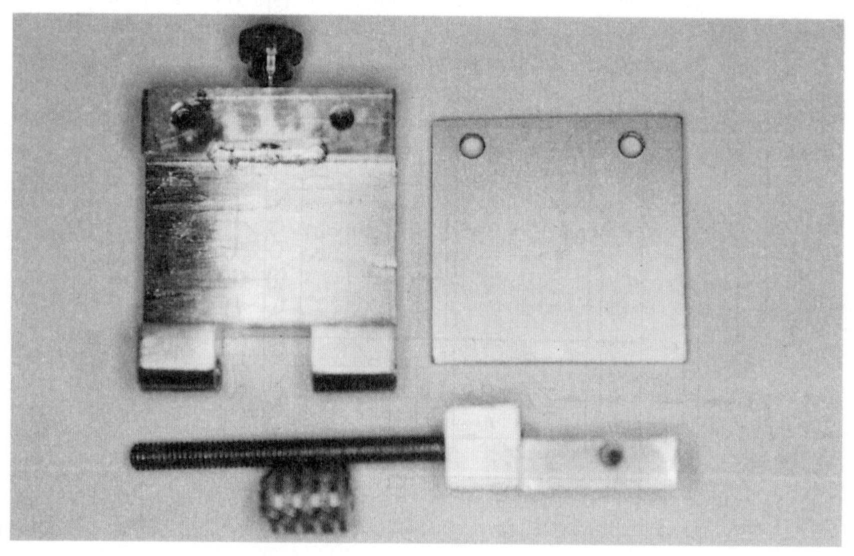

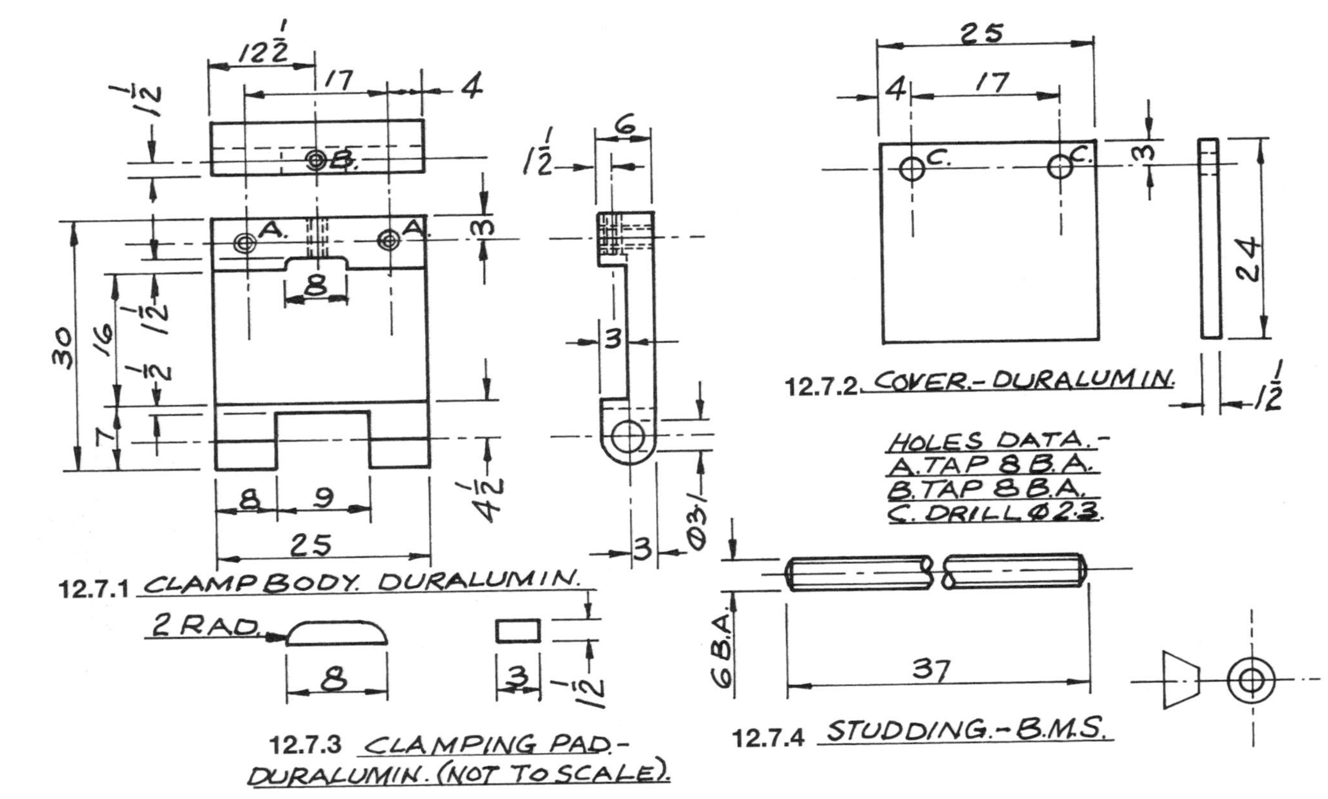
12½
17
4
25
4
17
3
24
6
1½
1½
3
8
3
16
30
7
½
8
9
25
4½
Ø3.1
3
12.7.1 CLAMP BODY. DURALUMIN.
12.7.2. COVER.- DURALUMIN.
HOLES DATA.-
A. TAP 8 B.A.
B. TAP 8 B.A.
C. DRILL Ø 2.3.
2 RAD.
8
3
½
6 B.A.
37
12.7.3 CLAMPING PAD.-
DURALUMIN. (NOT TO SCALE).
12.7.4 STUDDING.- B.M.S.
Dimensions in millimetres

Fig. 12.7

avoid having to get rid of the lines when finishing, also it is good practice when marking anything which may have to be bent, a scribed line makes a very good stress point. When the cover was shaped and drilled, it was clamped to the body and the holes spotted through. **Fig.12.10.** shows the Mark 1 cover being drilled. I intended to use four screws, but found that two were enough, so the Mark 1 was discarded. Note that the material was left oversize again for the drilling and cut to size after as it makes clamping and setting much easier.

When I had spotted the holes, they were drilled and tapped in the body. I chose 8BA. because I had a couple of chrome-plated round-head screws that looked small and neat. I was careful tapping them and used the smallest tap wrench I had; small taps don't like too much leverage. I also used a tapping drill a little larger than the book size as it made things a bit easier on the nerves.

Fitting the clamp

The 9 x 7mm cut-out in the clamp body was cut and filed, then body and cover assembled and tried on the calliper beam. In spite of all the care in the making, it needed a bit of easing. A little work with a fine file got it to slide nicely. Once it did, the clamping pad, **Fig.12.7.3**, can be made. The fit was checked again with the pad in position and the cover screwed on. It could have needed a bit more easing but I was lucky and all was well. The cover dimensions are shown in **Fig.12.7.2**.

Clamp screw and adjusting nut

The remaining components are shown in **Fig.12.8**. I haven't specified the type of knurl for the screw or nut. It isn't easy to get a good knurl with the Unimat, I have to use a full size knurling tool and just press hard by hand. I got some sort of pattern on the nut and supplemented it with some V-grooves.

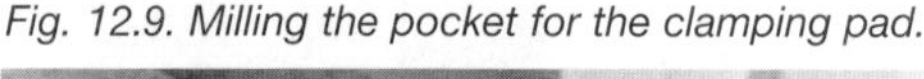

Fig. 12.9. Milling the pocket for the clamping pad.

Dimensions in millimetres

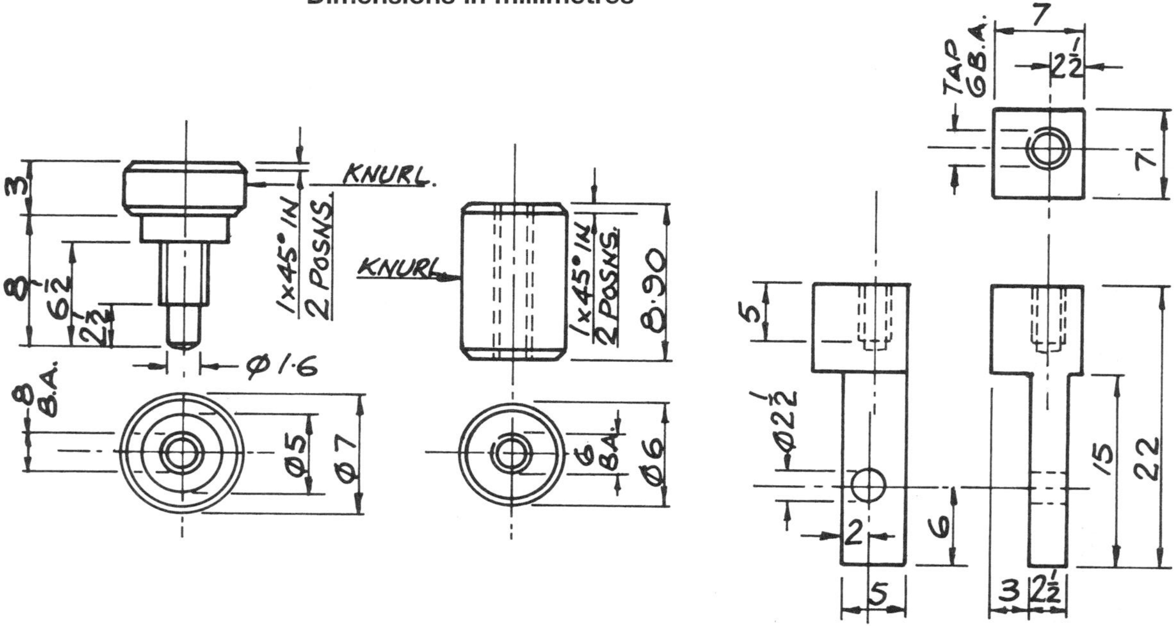

Fig. 12.8.1 Clamp Screw 12.8.2 Adjusting Nut B.M.S. 12.8.3 Stud Block - Duralumin

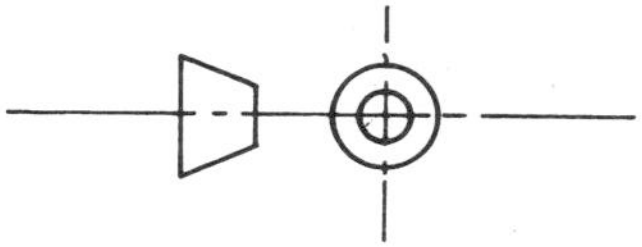

Fig. 12.8

Drilling and tapping the nut was no trouble and the chamfers were done with the V-tool which did the grooves. **Fig.12.8.2** shows the nut.

The best way to make the clamp screw, **Fig.12.8.1** is to adapt an existing one if one can be found. I had one with a straight knurled head which didn't take much altering. The drawing shows what it looked like when finished. If it has to be made, it should be possible to file fine grooves in the head to form a fine knurl, something I have often done with small parts. A straight knurl looked alright because it matched the existing locking screw.

Stud block

This is the most awkward part to make and the dimensions must be checked first because the ones I have given in **Fig.12.8.3** are those which are right for my calliper. They could be different for different makers. So to be safe, the block should be drawn and dimensioned first.

I started by making a 7mm square of duralumin 23mm long, drilling and tapping taper tap only, so that the stud would jam up tightly when screwed in. Then I drilled the 2.5mm hole and when all the drilling had been done, I filed the rest of the shape. When all the drilling and tapping was done, the final shaping was completed.

Studding

The studding I used was a long 6BA screw with the head cut off, trimmed and chamfered. I made it 37mm long, it was cadmium plated so it looked right. The 37mm length was what remained of the screw once the head was gone, so there was no significance in the dimension and within 5mm each way it wasn't important. If the studding is plain unplated steel, it could be oil blacked. **Fig.12.7.4** gives the dimensions.

Checking the stud block assembly

I screwed the studding into the stud block till it jammed. Then I took the thumb wheel and block off and replaced them with the new block and studding. I left the securing screw half tight and slid the clamp over the studding, when it slid nicely I tightened the screw and fitted the adjusting nut. If the clamp won't slide, the 3.1mm clearance hole can be opened up a little, but no more than to 3.25mm.

Last touches

I went over everything and checked for burrs. I took a few off more generously than I already had, after all, I was going to handle it. As the clamp body and cover were duralumin, they took a nice finish. The radius at the bottom of the clamp was blended in neatly. The retaining clamp and screws to fasten the depth probe were replaced and the job was finished.

Fig.12.12 shows the assembly for reference and **Fig.12.13** shows the completed fine adjustment. It doesn't look unsightly and it works a treat, making the measuring and setting a lot more sensitive, without any major modifications and with no damage to the original tool.

Since I made it I have kept looking for one with a similar adjustment, so far without finding one. Perhaps I am the only person who cannot use the thumb wheel.

Fig. 12.10. Drilling the holes in the cover, the material left over-size and the positions marked in pencil.

Fig. 12.13. The completed fine adjustment.

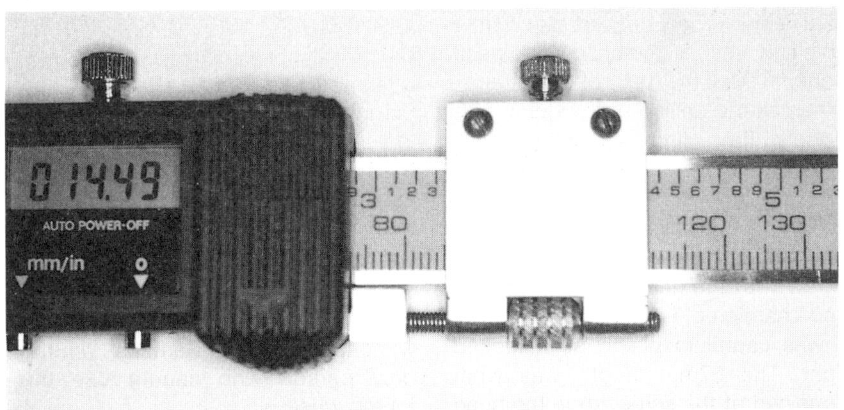

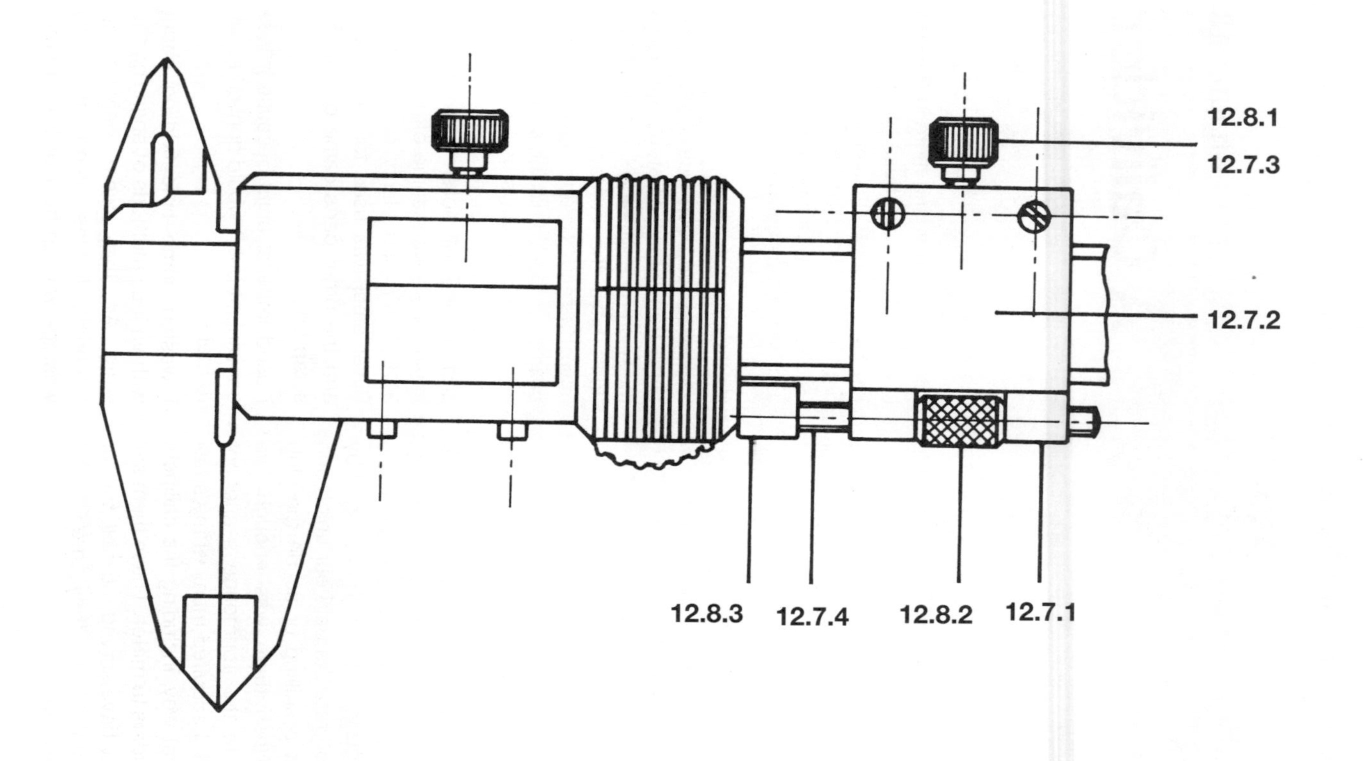

Fig. 12.12 Digital Caliper Fine Adjustment

Chapter 13

A Calivider

Some time ago, I made a calivider. You've never heard of such a thing?

Not surprising, I had to call it something, and as it can be used as an outside calliper, inside calliper or dividers, I thought the name was well chosen.

When I was a second-year apprentice, my turning apprentice master had a set of small round-legged callipers. I would have loved a set, but the best I could afford whilst earning a mere 35 shillings a week, was the 6in flat-legged type. However, to quote Confucius, 'it is no light thing to endure poverty uncomplainingly', we had no choice and if we complained, no one ever listened anyway. There was, though, a tool club organised by the union rep. We paid our union sub and put a shilling or so on the club card. When there was enough, we took it to the ironmonger's and got 10% off. I acquired many of my small tools that way, including the callipers and dividers to match. I have them still and they have served me well, but for a Unimat user they are a bit cumbersome.

I designed something more in the size I yearned for all those years ago. **Fig.13.1** shows the assembly and **Fig.13.2** the finished article fitted up as dividers. By changing the inserts, it can be used as callipers.

Materials

It would have been nice to make the parts from brass or steel, and have them chrome or nickel plated, but I don't have the contacts I used to have. Instead, I had some bits and pieces of duralumin of a grade we knew in the old days as L70. It is as strong as mild steel, easier to machine and file and will polish up to a good finish. There were some off-cuts from 3/16in strip and plenty of 1/4in rod. Silver steel was used for the inserts and the other parts came out of the scrap box.

I used imperial units because it was convenient but it would convert easily to metric.

I wasted some time fiddling about with various methods of springing the legs. As they were only scrap materials I was using, the only wastage was an hour or two of time.

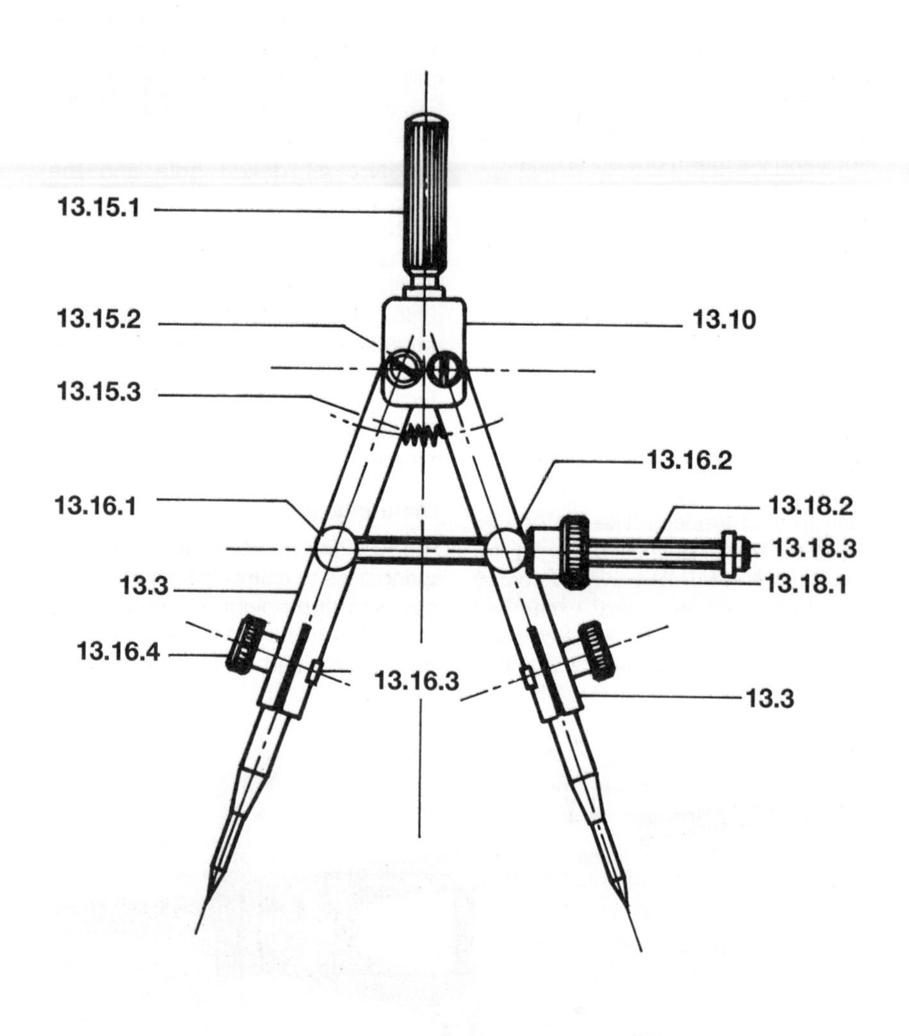

Fig. 13.1 Calivider Assembly

The method shown in the assembly drawing seemed to be the least troublesome, so that was what I used.

Legs

These were the main parts, **Fig.13.3**, made from 3/16in roughly square duralumin. It was a trimming from some strip and three sides were as stock and the fourth one soon cleaned up. **Fig.13.4** shows the setting up for drilling one of the holes. As usual, I left the material in the length for all the drilling and cut to length afterwards.

The most important feature of the legs is the 1/8in hole to take the inserts. It had its difficulties because four-jawed chucks will not close down to grip 3/16in stock and another way of holding had to be found. The best and simplest method was to use a split bush to hold the legs, like the one in **Fig.13.5**. These bushes are easy to make and can be set easily to centre for the drilling and reaming operations. When each leg had been faced, drilled and reamed, I put the bush away where I could find it again; they are always useful.

Because I have no 1/8in reamer, I used a D-bit to ream the hole to fit the inserts. If a reamer is used it should be a machine one, but if a hand one is the only one available, drill deeper than **Fig. 13.3** specifies, 5/16in or 19/32in will clear the taper of a hand reamer.

The No. 44 drilled hole and the tapping size for 6BA were both drilled by the same method as for the 1/8in spring hole in **Fig.13.4** and after the No. 43 drill for the 6BA tapping, I used a No. 34 drill to take out the first two threads of the tapped holes, so that the posts which screw into them would screw flush with the surface of the legs, about 1mm should be enough.

The tricky bits

The 0.020in slots which give the springiness to clamp the inserts in the legs were a problem. My only milling saw is too wide, but I remembered a time when I had to slot some 12BA

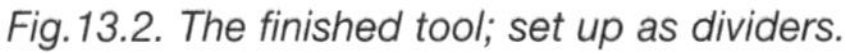

Fig.13.2. The finished tool; set up as dividers.

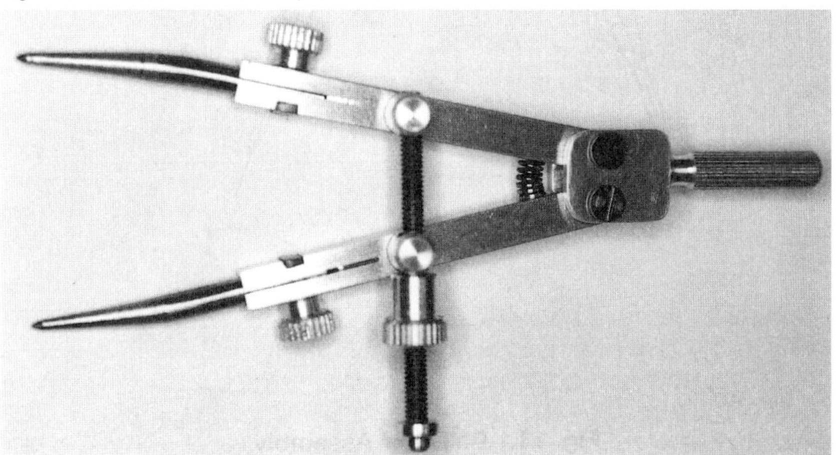

screws and the stores had no suitable saws. I'd had to improvise by making a fly cutter from a standard punch. Like most of us, I don't throw anything away if there's a chance it may be useful, so I hunted it down and it was just what I needed. It was set up as in **Fig.13.6**, with the leg against a fence, clamped to the cross slide with packing to suit. A smear of black marker pen made it easy to see what was happening. The leg was turned over to do the other side because the cutter wasn't long enough to reach in one go.

An alternative method is shown in **Fig.13.7** using a razor saw started at a very shallow angle, so that it doesn't wander. There is a good chance that any saw with a set on the teeth will wander, so the razor saw is best.

The 3/32in slot which locates the T-shaped screw needed another home-made cutter, the one in **Fig.13.8**. It has very roughly-made teeth and was made for cutting wood. The teeth are so rough that I have shown it rotating, to save my embarrassment. It did the job beautifully. Once again there is an alternative, see **Fig.13.9**, a modified Swiss file, which I used to clear out the corners of the slot. A small square file, followed by a similarly modified Swiss file would cut the slot but need more care.

After I had done the tricky bits, the rest of the work on the legs was quite easy; two No. 50 holes to clear the T-screws and the No. 44 holes for the pivot screws. Then I sawed and filed the legs to length and did the radii, finishing being left till later.

Clamp

Fig.13.10 shows the clamp, made from 3/16in square x 1/2in duralumin. The slot was milled by clamping it to the side of the Unimat toolpost, with packing to get it to the right height. **Fig.13.11** shows the setting up, using a ground point to pick up the centre line, and **Fig.13.12** shows the milling almost completed. I used a 3/16in end mill and the slot was a good fit on the

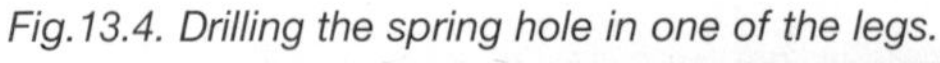

Fig.13.4. Drilling the spring hole in one of the legs.

legs. The clamp was finished by drilling and tapping the 8BA holes and the clearance ones and rounding the corners off.

Finger grip

This part posed another little problem. I have no straight knurling tool, so I had to improvise. I clamped a V-tool on its side, indexing with the Heath Robinson arrangement in **Fig.13.13**. A strip of aluminium was bent to a very long U-shape, one end clamped to the motor support plate and the other filed to a shape which located in the teeth of the small drill chuck. It made a quite acceptable knurl. I made it fairly fine but it could have been made coarser by increasing the depth of cut. The indexing took a while, long enough and quiet enough to listen to one of Puccini's longer arias.

As shown in **Fig.13.15.1** the rest of the job was ordinary turning and threading with a few chamfers, see **Fig.13.14**. The domed end could be a chamfer if it would look better, it's up to the maker.

Pivot screws

These two were plain turning and threading again, with special attention to the diameter 0.086in specified in **Fig.13.15.2** This will fit the 8BA clearance holes in the clamp nice and snugly. When preparing to cut the threads, I made the length about 1/8in longer than I needed and reduced the extra bit to 0.075in. This let the die take a scrape for the first few threads so that it started square; the extra can be faced off when finished. When I'd finished the screws and chamfered the heads, I cut the screwdriver slots with a junior hacksaw using a blade which had been used a bit, so that the blade was worn; it was near enough the 0.020in.

Spring

The only other part in **Fig.13** is the spring. I found the one I used in my small collection of springs. It doesn't have to be exactly as on the drawing, as long it does what it should. It does though, have to be smaller than 3/16in outside diameter, or it will not fit the legs.

Fig. 13.5. Using a split bush to hold a leg for drilling.

Fig. 13.6. The fly cutter used to cut the 0.020in. slots in the legs.

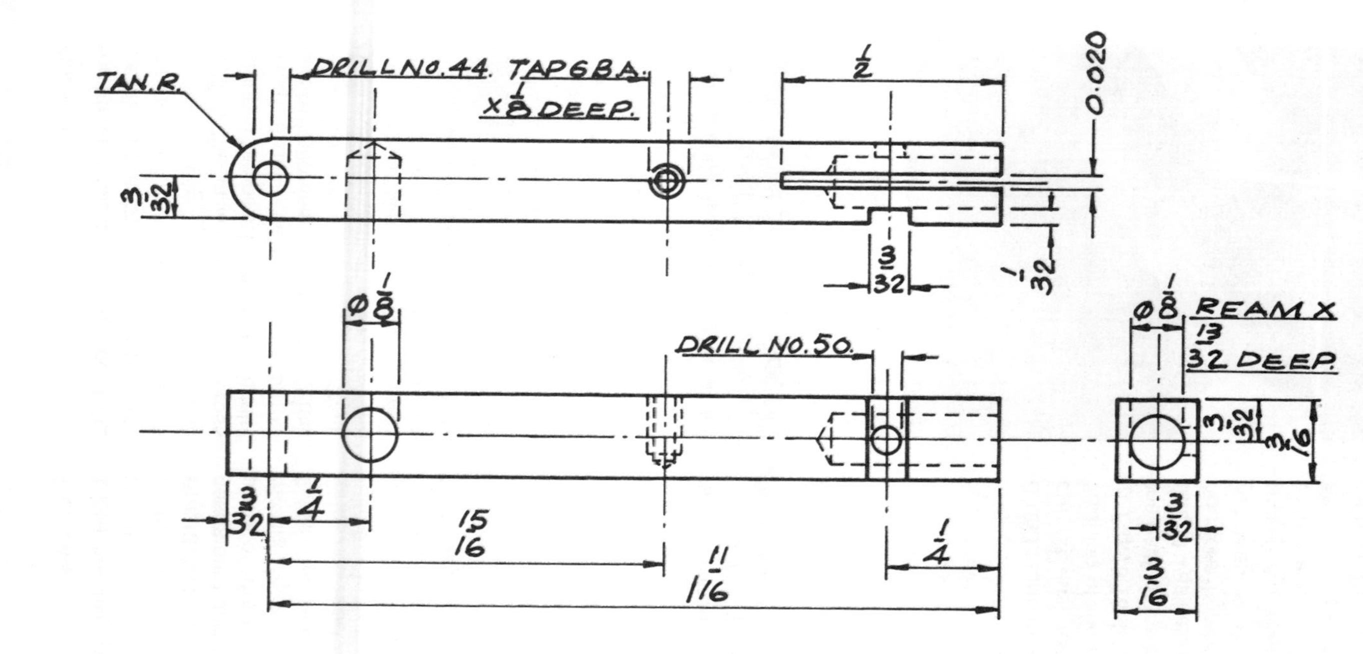

Leg - Duralumin - 1 off R.H. 1 off L.H.

Fig. 13.3

Dimensions in millimetres except where stated

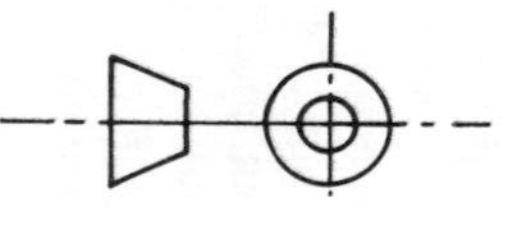

Posts

For these, I cut a piece of the 1/4in duralumin a lot longer than I needed. The reason for leaving it long can be seen in **Fig.13.17** where the piece was held in the crutch centre for cross drilling. Clamped by a small parallel clamp, it gave me plenty of room to work at it. When I'd drilled the cross holes the rest of the turning was done. One post was drilled clearance, the other tapped 6BA, dimensions are in **Fig.13.16**. On assembly, the post with the clearance hole may need the hole easing a bit, so that it will pass easily over the adjusting thread. The faces of the posts where they meet the leg surfaces may have to be lightly skimmed, so that they are flush when they are lined up. The tapped hole in part **13.16.1** should not be tapped right through; taper tap only is the best way of making sure that the studding used for adjustment will go tight for the last couple of threads, if the tap is not allowed to cut right through.

Fig. 13.7. Another way of slotting the legs.

T-screws

There are two of these, **Fig.13.16.3** and they are like miniature T-bolts. I used 1/4in diameter mild steel and shaped the sides last. The threading needs care and should be started the same as the pivot screws, by giving the die a good start. The trouble with small threads is that they are prone to stripping, especially if too much end pressure is applied, like too much backing up with the tailstock. I have found it best to start them off in the lathe, then finish off in a vice; it is much more sensitive.

Filing the sides of the T-shape and final fitting can be left till the assembly. There will be a little gentle filing to be done on the shanks of the screws, I found this so when I fitted them to the slots in the inserts. I faced the heads of the screws at high speed with very light cuts, holding them very lightly in the chuck.

Nuts

These two had to be straight knurled, so I used the same method as for the finger grip, but made the grooves deeper, so that it would give a good feel. I did enough for the two and added a bit for holding in the chuck, drilled, tapped and chamfered, then cut off, just leaving the facing and finishing of the head. Dimensions are in **Fig.13.16.4**. To face and chamfer the back of the head, a piece of 10BA thread was held in the chuck and, with no more than 5/32in sticking out, the nut was screwed on. The cutting pressure is self-tightening, so it is safe to face and chamfer, taking small cuts at high speed, the speed being reduced for the chamfer.

Dimensions in millimetres except where stated

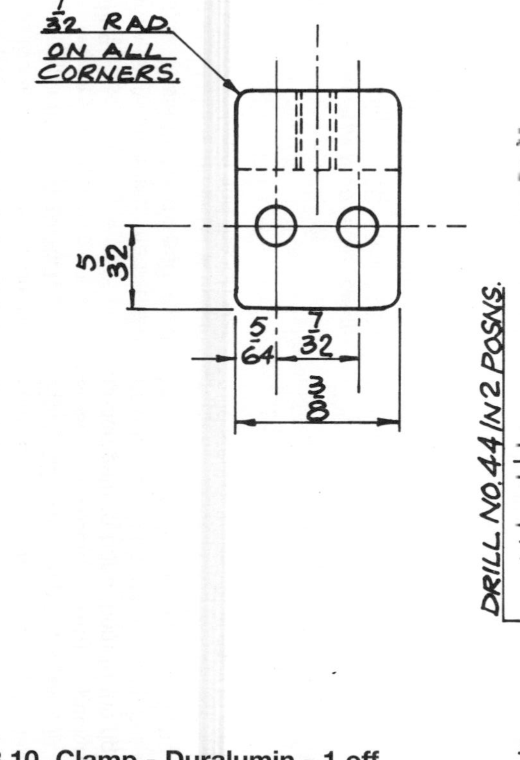

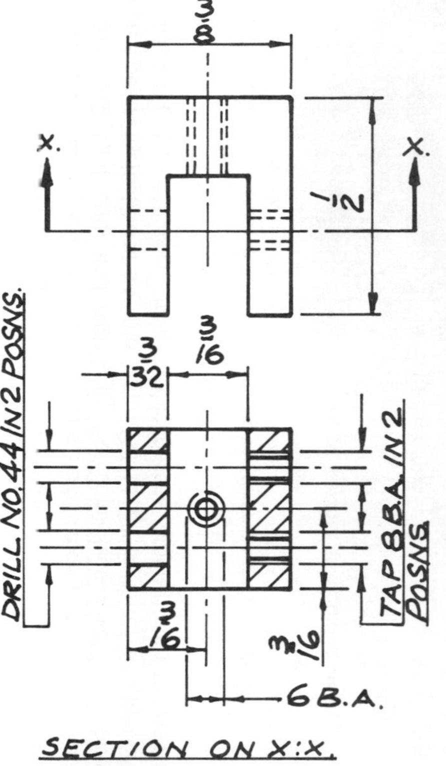

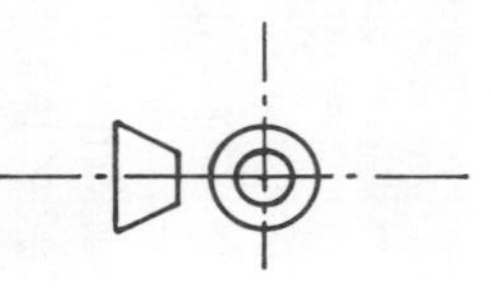

Fig. 13.10 Clamp - Duralumin - 1 off

Adjusting nut

This nut is larger than the other two, to give it a more comfortable grip. It was made in the same way as the smaller ones, dimensions in **Fig.13.18.1**.

Studding

If some 6BA studding had been available, I would have used it. It wasn't so I cut the head off a screw, faced and chamfered and the job was done.

End cap

This was an awkward little piece, made by tapping a 6BA hole 1/8in deep in a piece of 3/16in diameter duralumin, sawing off at just over 5/32in and turning the rest by holding it on a short length of thread, so that the faced surface was tight up against the chuck jaws. Like the other nuts done this way, light cuts and high speed are best. **Fig.13.18.3** shows the details.

A bit more milling

All of the silver steel inserts have to be slotted to fit over the T-shaped screws. One way is to mill them, **Fig.13.19**. They were clamped in a small V-block, with packing underneath to bring them to the right height. I checked that the slot was in the middle of the diameter by doing a trial run. It can be done in brass or mild steel or whatever is easy to cut. A 1/16in slot drill or end mill will cut the slot. I clamped a piece of soft material over the top so that the work wasn't marked.

It was a little-by-little process and could not be rushed. There was an alternative, shown in **Fig.13.20**. The slot was roughly sawn and opened out with a Swiss file. As most hand or flat Swiss files are over 1/16in thick, some modification was needed. I have several small files which have been ground to all sorts of shapes and thicknesses, among them the one in

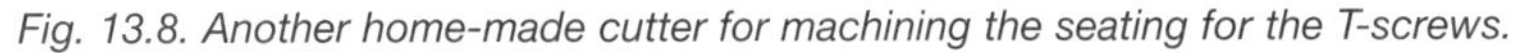

Fig. 13.8. Another home-made cutter for machining the seating for the T-screws.

the photograph. It takes a very long time to use the filing method and I don't advise it. Milling is much better and I used one of the Dormer mini mills with a very short cutting length to give it strength.

Two useful gadgets

When the inserts had been slotted, I made a couple of things to make life a bit easier when holding and forming them. One was a tweaking iron, a length of 10mm diameter mild steel with a 1/8in hole drilled 1/2in deep in one end. **Fig.13.21** shows it in use for bending one of the outside calliper inserts. It provides leverage. The other aid was a clamp made from two pieces of mild steel, 6 x 10mm, 12mm long. They were clamped together with a thin shim between them and drilled 1/8in through the centre lengthways. When separated and the shim taken out, they will clamp a 1/8in rod. They were very useful for holding the inserts without doing any damage, for instance, when putting in the 10 degree kinks in the calliper inserts.

Outside calliper inserts

These were the most awkward of the three shapes. The large radius can be bent round a 7/8in former, which is what I did. I used the piece of aluminium in **Fig.13.21**, with some thick cardboard to protect the insert from the vice jaw. It had to be done carefully, so that the slot lined up with the bend. I put the 10 degree kink in with the tweaking iron. The dimensions are shown in **Fig.13.23**. After I had bent the radius, I flattened the sides by filing, see **Fig 13.25**. A short length of aluminium with a 1/8in slot was used to clamp the inserts to a wooden base, so that they were protected. When I had flattened the sides to 1/16in, I filed the tip radius and angle.

Inside calliper inserts

I turned these to the taper first with the compound slide set to 4 degrees. I used the four-jawed chuck to get the insert running true, my three-jawed chuck isn't the last word in concentricity these days. Using the four-jawed chuck made use of the

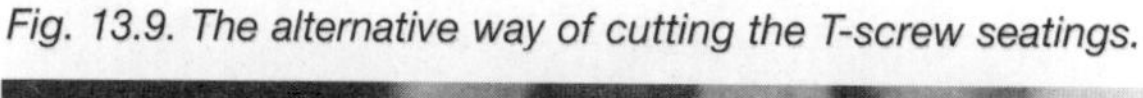

Fig. 13.9. The alternative way of cutting the T-screw seatings.

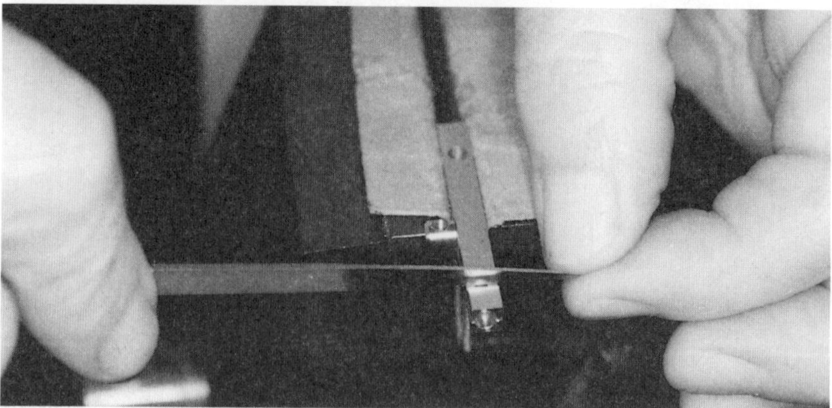

clamping block, see **Fig.13.26**, this shows one of the inserts being set true with my verdict indicator and small magnetic base, two items I wouldn't be without. I cut both inserts to length and tapered them till they measured 0.050in at 1/16in from the tip. The dimensions are shown in **Fig.13.24.1**. Finally, I rounded the tips and polished with fine emery.

I bent them to the inside calliper shape with round-nosed pliers, using the clamping block to hold in the vice and the tweaking iron did the 10 degree kink again.

Divider inserts

The method was the same as I used for the inside calliper, the only difference was that the tips came to a 45 degree point. This is my preference for dividers, but those who like their points like needles can feel free to do as they wish. I'll stay with the version in **Fig.13.24.2** because I find them stronger and needing less sharpening.

Assembling

There were one or two adjustments. Firstly, the T-screws had to fit nicely in the cut-outs in the legs. I did this by using small files to square out the sides and bottom of the cut-outs till, when an insert was in position and the nut tightened, there was no daylight showing when held against the light. It was also helped by gently filing the head of the screw, it is surprising how useful it is to take burrs off generously when fitting a tenon into a slot and the head of the T-screw is a sort of tenon.

The shanks of the T-screws had to be very slightly flattened on the sides till they fitted the slots in the inserts. I've given no dimension for this in **Fig.13.16.3** because it is only the minimum to make them fit. It needed a lot of care because it is very easy to get too excited and take off too much. It is also not easy to hold small and fragile components like those, so I used a mini vice, which is more

Fig. 13.11. Lining up for cutting the 3/16in slot in the clamp.

Fig. 13.12. The clamp, nearly finished.

Fig. 13.13. The crude indexing gadget for straight knurling.

sensitive than the bench vice and less likely to cause damage. It was an awkward piece to hold, so the way I did it is shown in **Fig.13.27**. The nut is screwed on enough to leave the section to be worked on in position. For those who haven't a mini vice, the same thing could be done using a small parallel clamp to hold the screw and nut and putting the clamp in a vice.

Final adjustments

When I had finished I tried the three pairs of inserts to make sure that they lined up. I used the tweaking iron to make small adjustments and when I was satisfied, set about the hardening and tempering. I only did the first 1/2in or so and tempered to a brown colour on the tips. I had the use of the gas stove, with permission of course, and it delivered enough heat to do the job.

Fig. 13.14. Finishing the finger grip.

Fig. 13.17. Cross-drilling the posts in the crutch centre.

Dimensions in inches

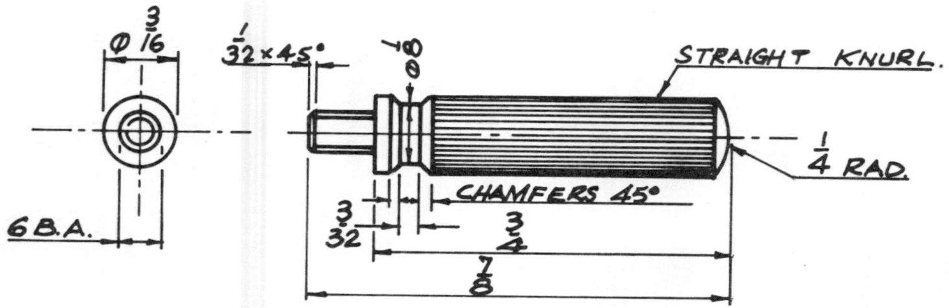

Fig. 13.15.1 Finger Grip - Duralumin - 1 off

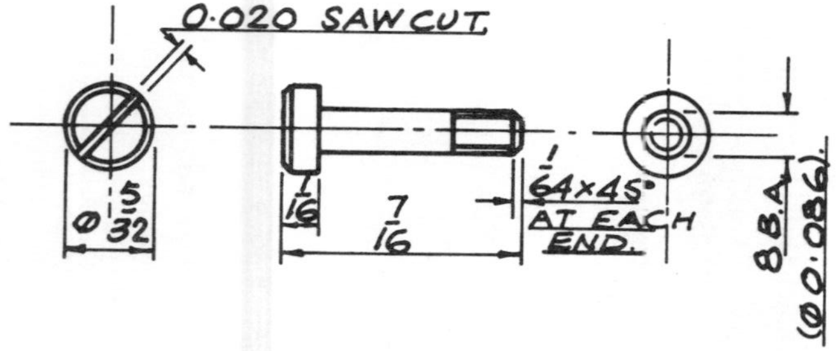

Fig. 13.15.2 Pivot Screw - B.M.S. 2 off

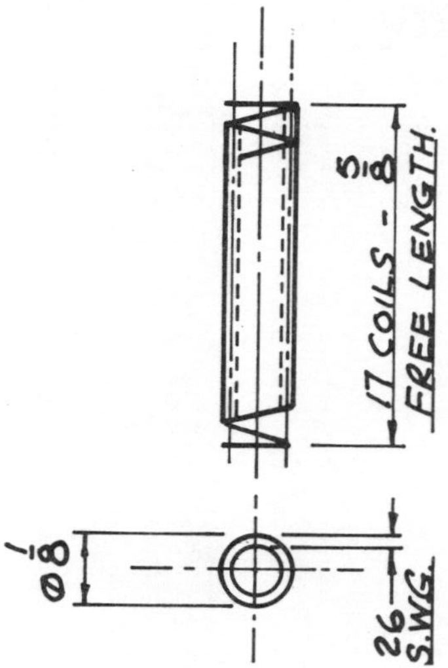

Fig. 13.15.3 Compression Spring - 1 off

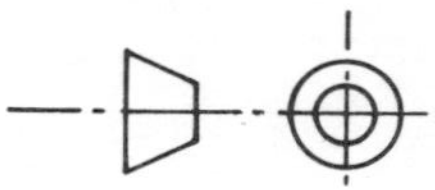

Fig. 13.15

A small butane torch would do the same and also the bluing of the studding, pivot screws and T-screws, to make them look nice. Heat to a dull red and quench in oil. Be careful not to overheat, because small parts get very hot very quickly and anything brighter than dull red will make them scale when quenched. This always looks unsightly.

Where I had to, I used Loctite to seal and lock parts in place and the threaded post and the end cap were the ones which needed it. **Fig.13.28** shows all the parts and **Fig.13.29**, **13.30** and **13.31** shows the calivider being used as, dividers, inside calliper and outside calliper. It was a useful and interesting exercise in small machining and fitting.

Fig. 13.19. Milling the slots in the inserts.

Fig. 13.20. Another way of slotting the inserts.

Dimensions in inches except where stated

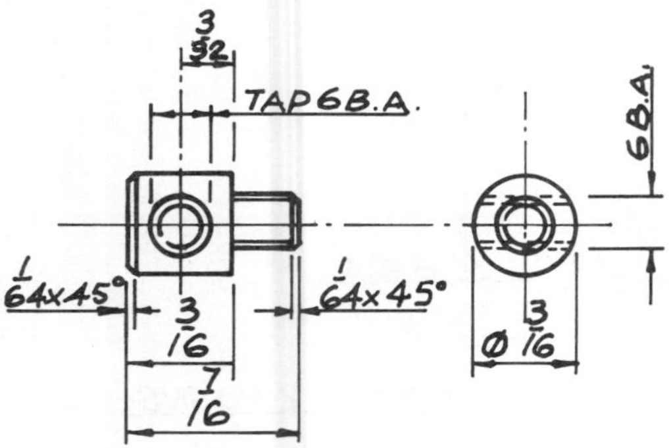

Fig. 13.16.1 Threaded Post - Duralumin - 1 off

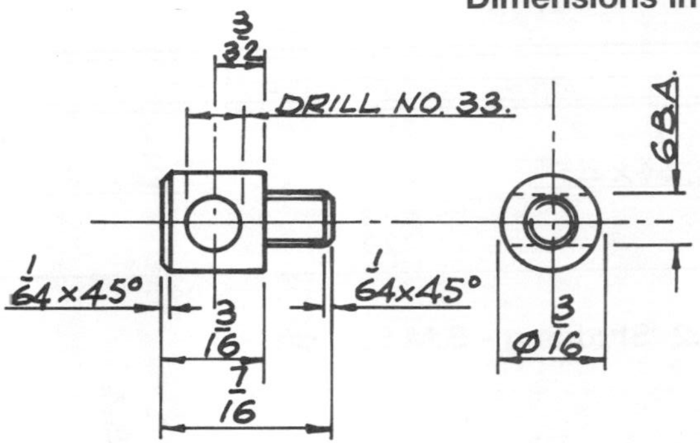

Fig. 13.16.2 Clearance Post - Duralumin - 1 off

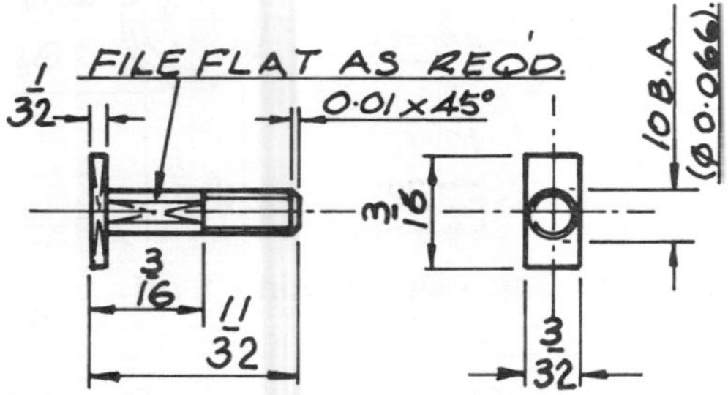

Fig. 13.16.3 Screw - B.M.S. - 2 off

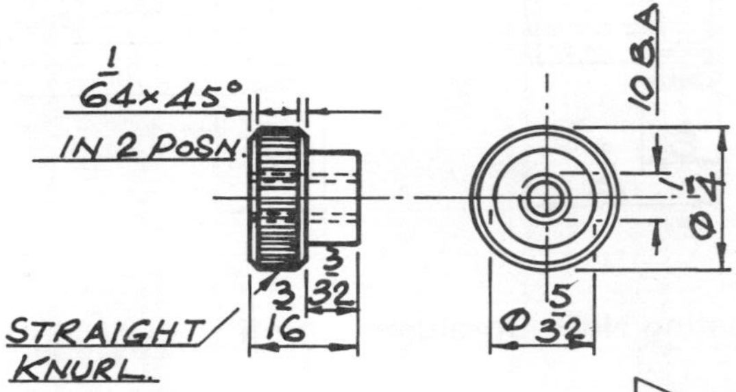

Fig. 13.16.4 Nut - Duralumin - 2 off

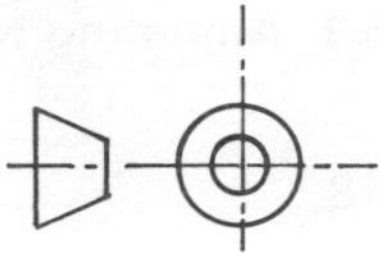

Fig. 13.16

Dimensions in inches except where stated

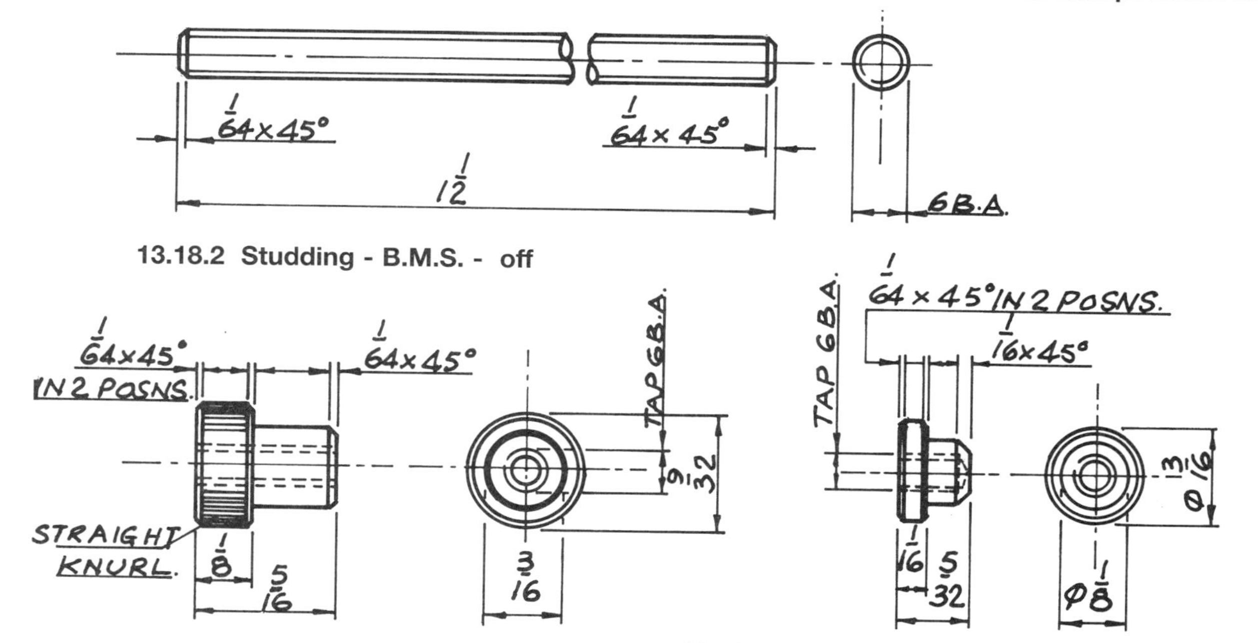

13.18.2 Studding - B.M.S. - off

13.18.1 Adjusting Nut - Duralumin - 1 off

13.18.3 End Cap - Duralumin - 1 off

Fig. 13.18

Fig. 13.21. The tweaking iron used to bend the outside calliper shape.

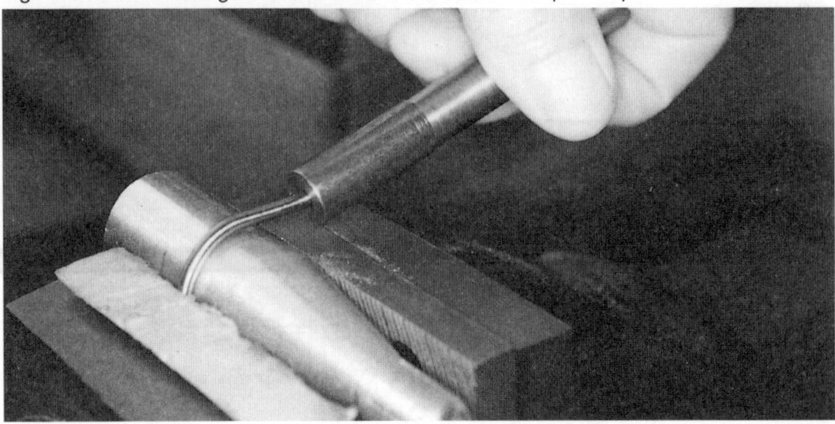

Fig. 13.25. Flattening the side of a calliper insert.

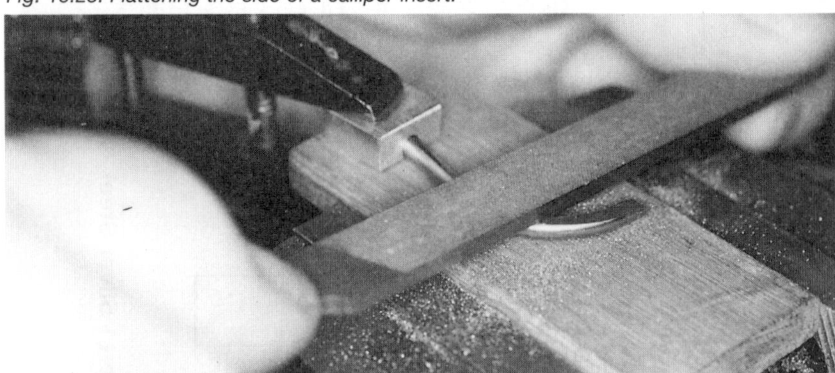

Fig. 13.26. Using a split clamp to hold an insert in the four jawed chuck for tapering.

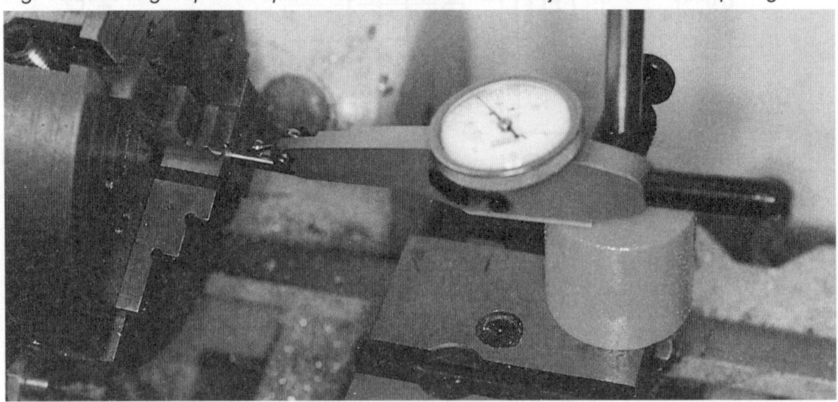

Dimensions in Inches

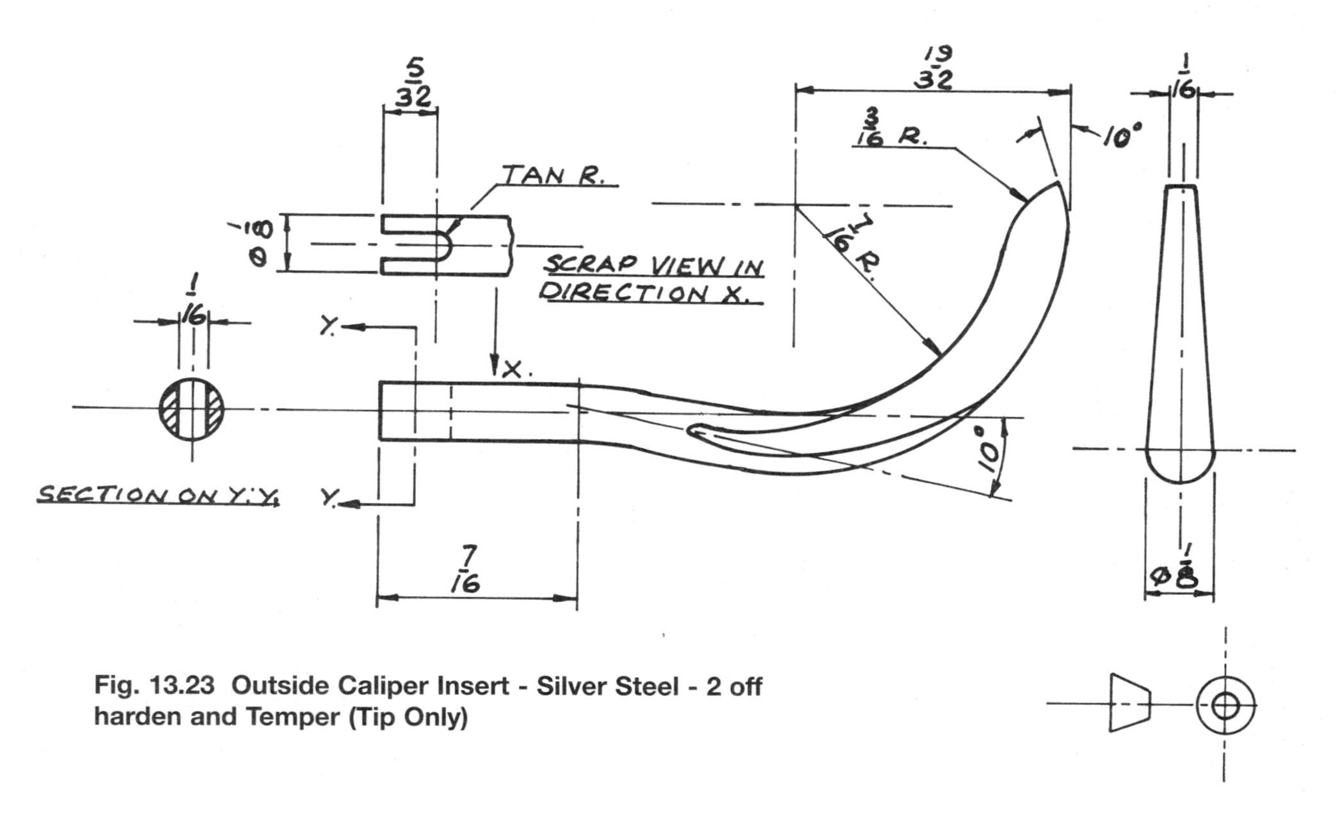

Fig. 13.23 Outside Caliper Insert - Silver Steel - 2 off harden and Temper (Tip Only)

Dimensions in inches

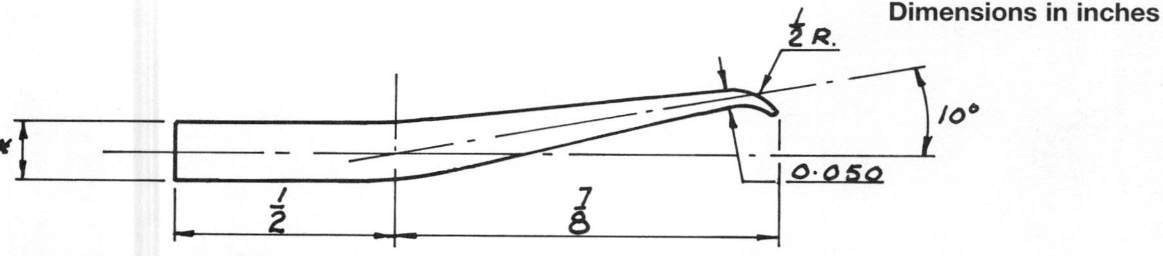

Fig. 13.24.1 Inside Caliper Insert - Silver Steel - 2 off
harden and Temper (Tip Only)

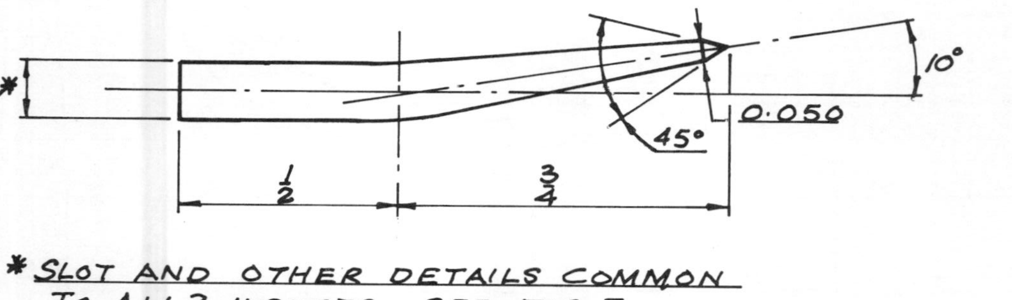

* SLOT AND OTHER DETAILS COMMON
TO ALL 3 INSERTS - SEE FIG. 7.

Fig. 13.24.2 Divider Insert - Silver Steel - 2 off
harden and Temper (Tip Only)

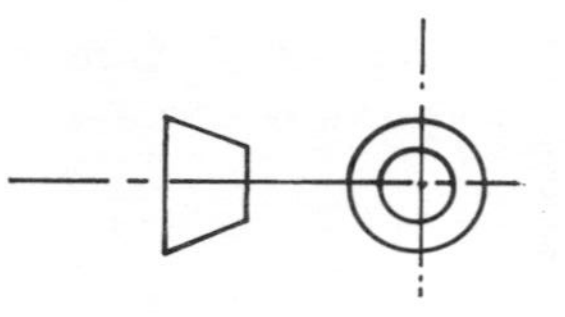

Fig. 13.24

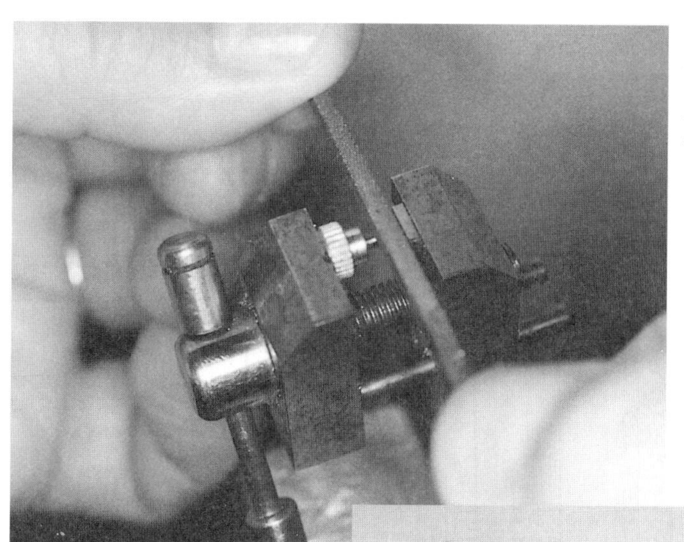

Fig. 13.27. Holding the T-screw in a mini vice to file a small flat.

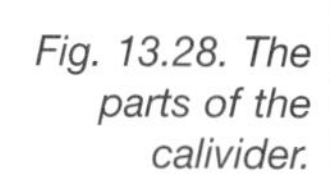

Fig. 13.28. The parts of the calivider.

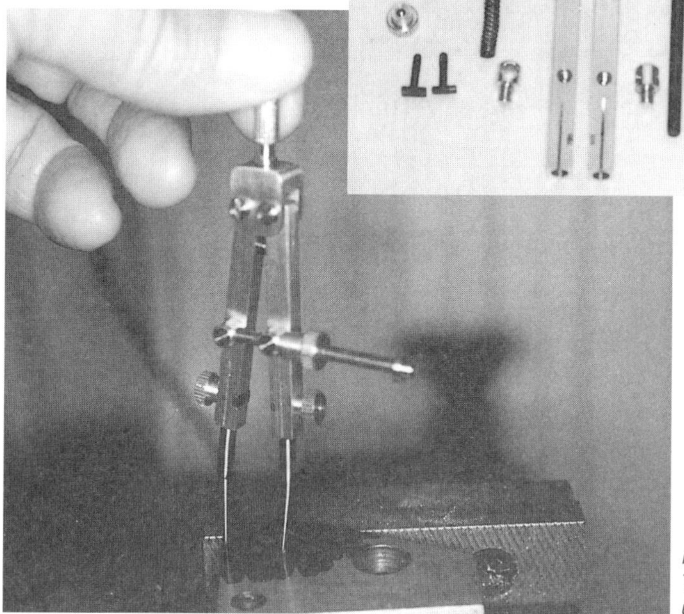

Fig. 13.29. The instrument used as dividers.

Fig. 13.30. Used as an inside calliper.

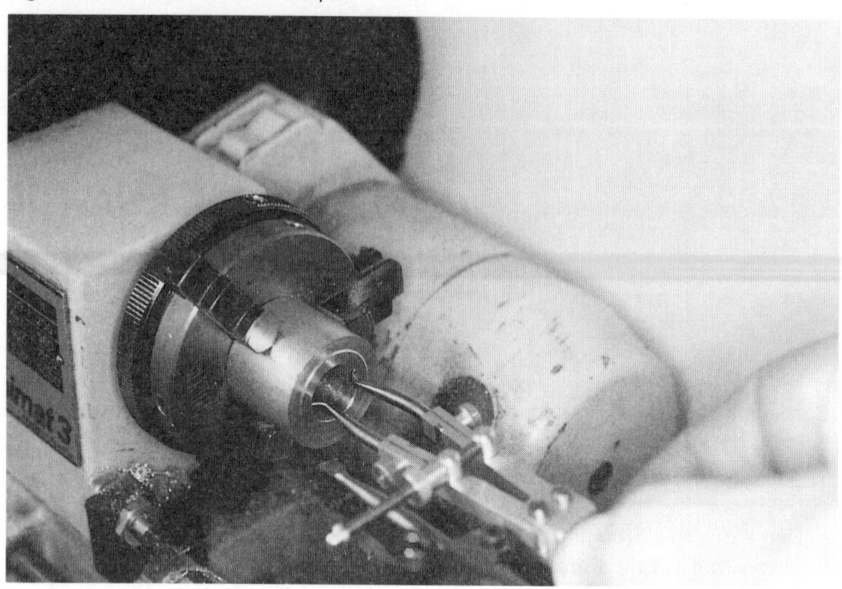

Fig. 13.31. Used as an outside calliper.

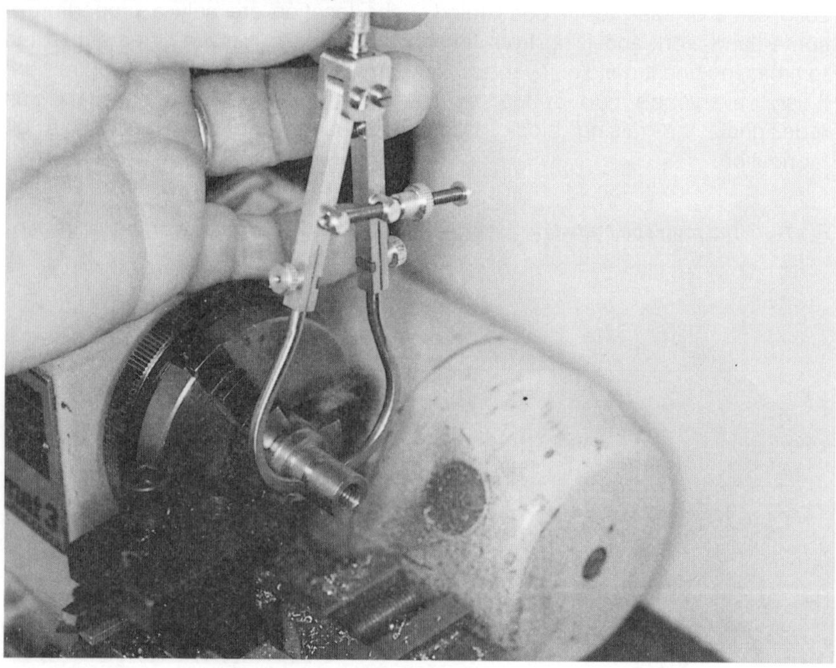

Chapter 14

A Raising Block For The Unimat 3

Sometimes a job comes along which is too big a diameter for the Unimat.

The way round this is to increase the swing over the bed, by making a raising block to lift the headstock. I've fiddled about with the idea for a long time with no more to show than the block, **Fig.14.1** which I carved out of a solid piece of cast iron. I don't mind some hand work and filing from time to time, and find it quite enjoyable, but it isn't everyone's cup of tea, so I redesigned the raising block as a fabrication.

Some design considerations

Looking at the underside of the Unimat tailstock once, when I took it off for some reason, I found that the vee and flat which fits the bed, is not a continuous shape throughout the length of the casting. The casting is ribbed, so that the shapes which do the location are only a proportion of the length, more bearers than anything. When I looked at the headstock, **Fig.14.2**, to check if it was the same, the bearers were a bit longer, but the shape was the same.

Fig.14.1. The rough first attempt.

Fig.14.2. The underside of the headstock.

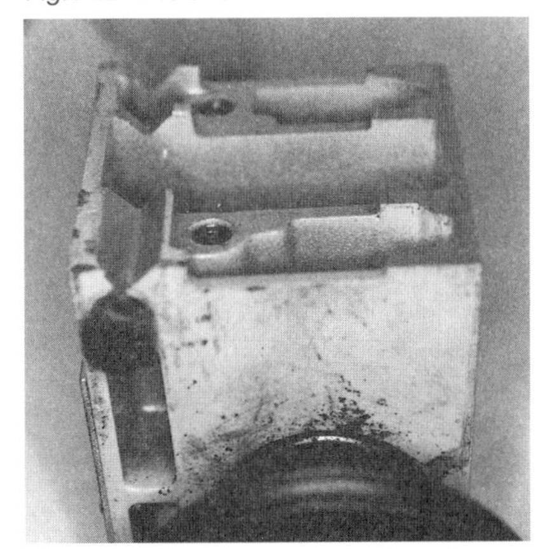

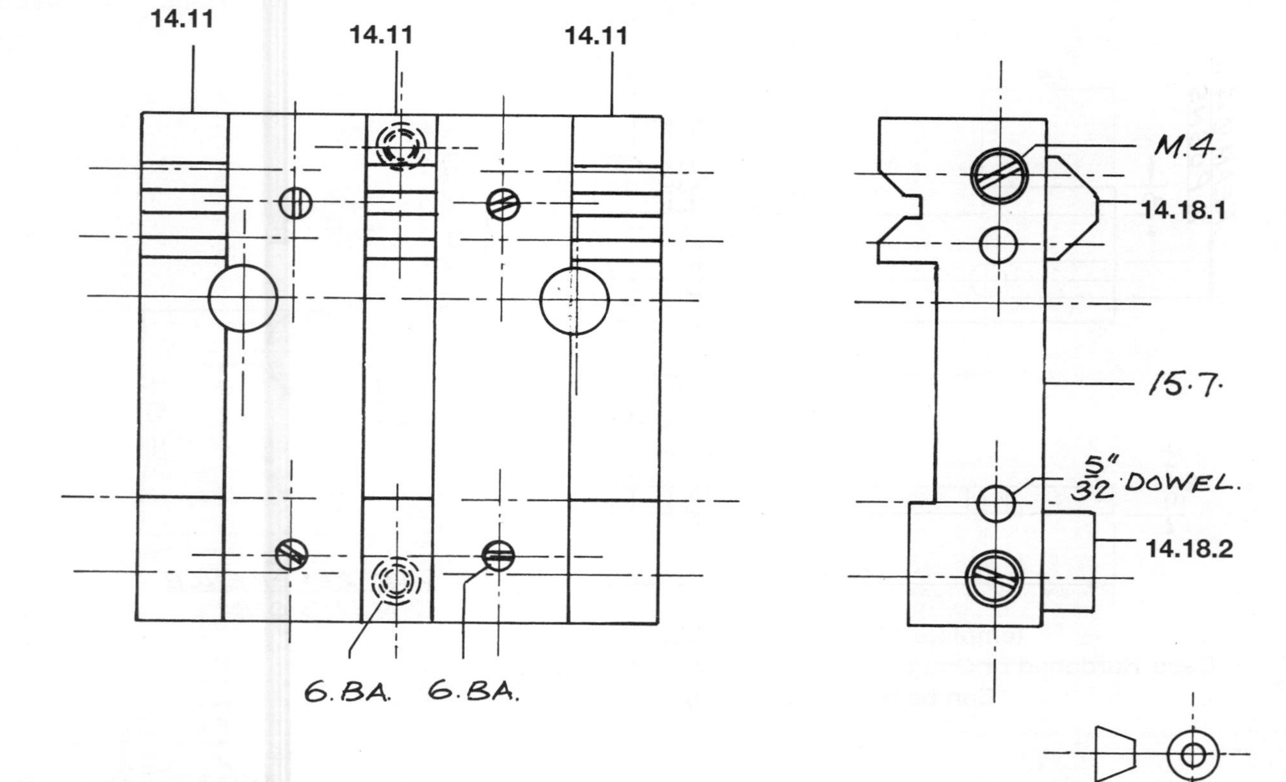

Fig. 14.3 Raising Block Assembly

Dimensions in Millimetres

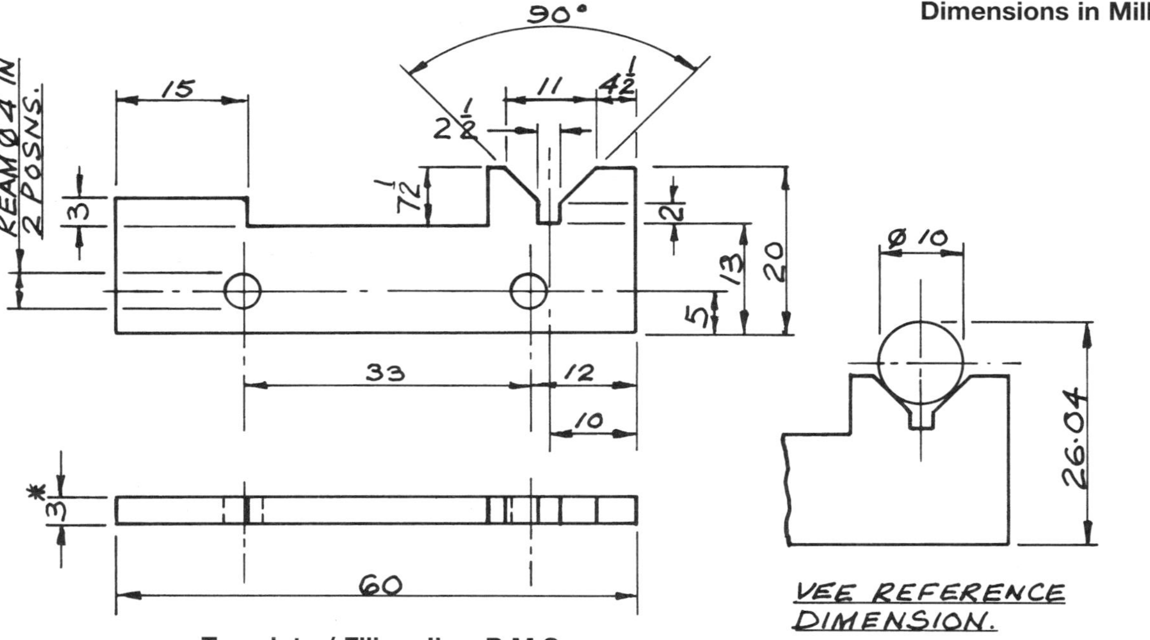

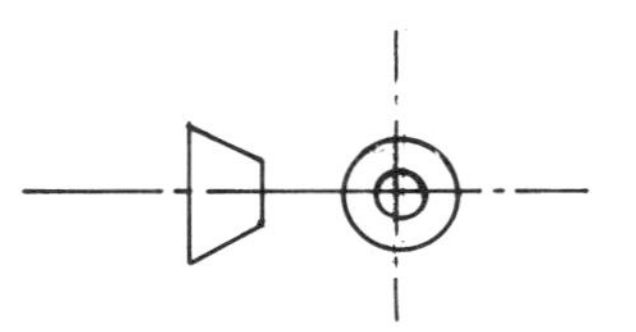

Template / Filing Jig - B.M.S.
Case-Hardened or Gauge Plate Hardened and Tempereed.
*Can be thicker (see text)

Fig. 14.4

I thought that if the lathe designers could get away with it, then so could I, especially as they used aluminium alloy and I planned to use cast iron and mild steel. My version is a block of cast iron, with three shaped inserts, two as end plates and one in the middle, see **Fig.14.3**. The inserts would fit the bed and the upper vee and flat to locate the headstock in its new position could be added as separate pieces. This would save an awful lot of machining. As Confucius once said, 'if in doubt, fabricate'.

The most important part of the job was getting the profiles of the vee and flat right and I decided to use templates. These could be used, not only for getting the shapes right, but for jigs to get the bolts and dowels in the right places.

Templates

Fig.14.4 gives the dimensions for the templates and **Fig.14.5** shows the pair just after case-hardening, the grotty finish is the look of a case- hardened part after quenching. I used mild steel and case-hardened them, but they could be made from gauge plate if it is available. They could be thicker than mine too but 3mm is the thickest I can get hot enough with my small propane torch.

Fig.14.5. The templates after case-hardening.

After filing the two pieces of 60 x 20mm steel to length, I marked out one of them, using a large black marker pen for background because it dries quickly and is excellent to mark on. I clamped the two blanks accurately and drilled and reamed 5/32in; I had some 5/32in silver steel, so I used that for dowels. I cut the dowels short, so that when they were locating the two pieces they were under flush. I used small parallel clamps to hold them together. **Fig.14.6** shows one side of the vee being finished. To keep the filing accurate, I used a piece of square stock clamped to the job in line with the marked line, to act as a fence. When the file just skids, the surface is finished. The clamped fence can be seen in **Fig.14.6**. Once the profile was as accurate as I could get it by filing, I blued the lathe bed and gently rubbed the templates on it, filing off the blue patches. This improved the accuracy and, when I was satisfied with it, I checked it for being parallel by measuring from the machined step where the tailstock clamping plate fits. My engineer's blue was, as it always is, my wife's navy blue shoe polish, with permission of course.

Case-hardening

When the templates were finished, I case-hardened them. This was a somewhat primitive process, done in the shed, where I made a hearth with the bricks which the compost bag stands on. They were ordinary building bricks and reflected the heat well enough and probably frightened some spiders very badly. My propane torch just delivered enough heat to get the templates red hot. I sprinkled them with case-hardening compound, keeping them red hot and sprinkling a bit more till they stopped bubbling and seething, then I quenched them in cold water. The hardness which results from this method is only a very thin skin, but the templates only have to do three profiles and act as a jig for a few holes and should last.

Block

When I had finished the templates, I started on the block, **Fig.14.7**. It was cut from a cast iron lump which was once the casting for a machine vice jaw. It was hard work, but with high speed steel hacksaw blades and sharp files, cast iron of that grade works well. Stock mild steel would be a much easier option, but I hadn't got any and I don't mind a bit of filing from time to time, skills have to be practised and it gives me the chance to listen to favourite tapes or CDs without graunching noises from the machinery. I can catch all the nuances of the music. I can also pick up all the bits the censor missed in the Goon Shows.

Making a block from scratch is a matter of filing the first face flat, then an edge square with it, then the opposite edge parallel and so on. **Fig.14.8** shows high areas being picked off from the surface of one of the faces and **Fig.14.9** shows a method of checking the edges for squareness. An accurate vee block was used to hold the work upright and it was rubbed against a surface plate or other flat surface which had been

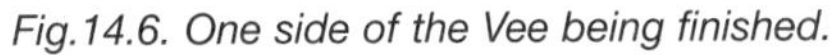

Fig.14.6. One side of the Vee being finished.

blued. With a finished face and edge held in the vee, the high spots or areas had a trace of blue which marked where to file. The blue was the shoe polish again.

When the block was to size, I put it aside and did another part. Most of the drilling was done later.

End plates

I chose 20 x 10mm stock mild steel for these and the first job was to cut and file them to 60mm long. I clamped them one at a time to one of the templates, lined up and spotted the dowel hole positions with a 5/32in drill. The reaming size drill will follow this start. I use a drill 10% less than the reamer size and it reamed a treat. I cut a couple of dowels from the 5/32in silver steel, making them 15mm long, a bit shorter than the thickness of the plate and the two templates. The templates made a sandwich with the end plate as the filling, all dowelled together. I cut the waste away with a hacksaw and filed till the file just skidded on the templates. **Fig.14.10** shows one end plate complete and one ready sandwiched for shaping. **Fig.14.11** gives all the dimensions for the end plates.

Centre plate

Because the centre plate was not so deep as the end plates, it was set up differently from the end plates. I lined up the top of the vee and the piece of 10 x 8mm clamped it and worked from there. As long as it stayed clamped once started, all was well and the shaping was the same as the others.

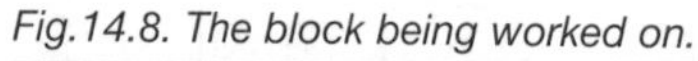

Fig.14.8. The block being worked on.

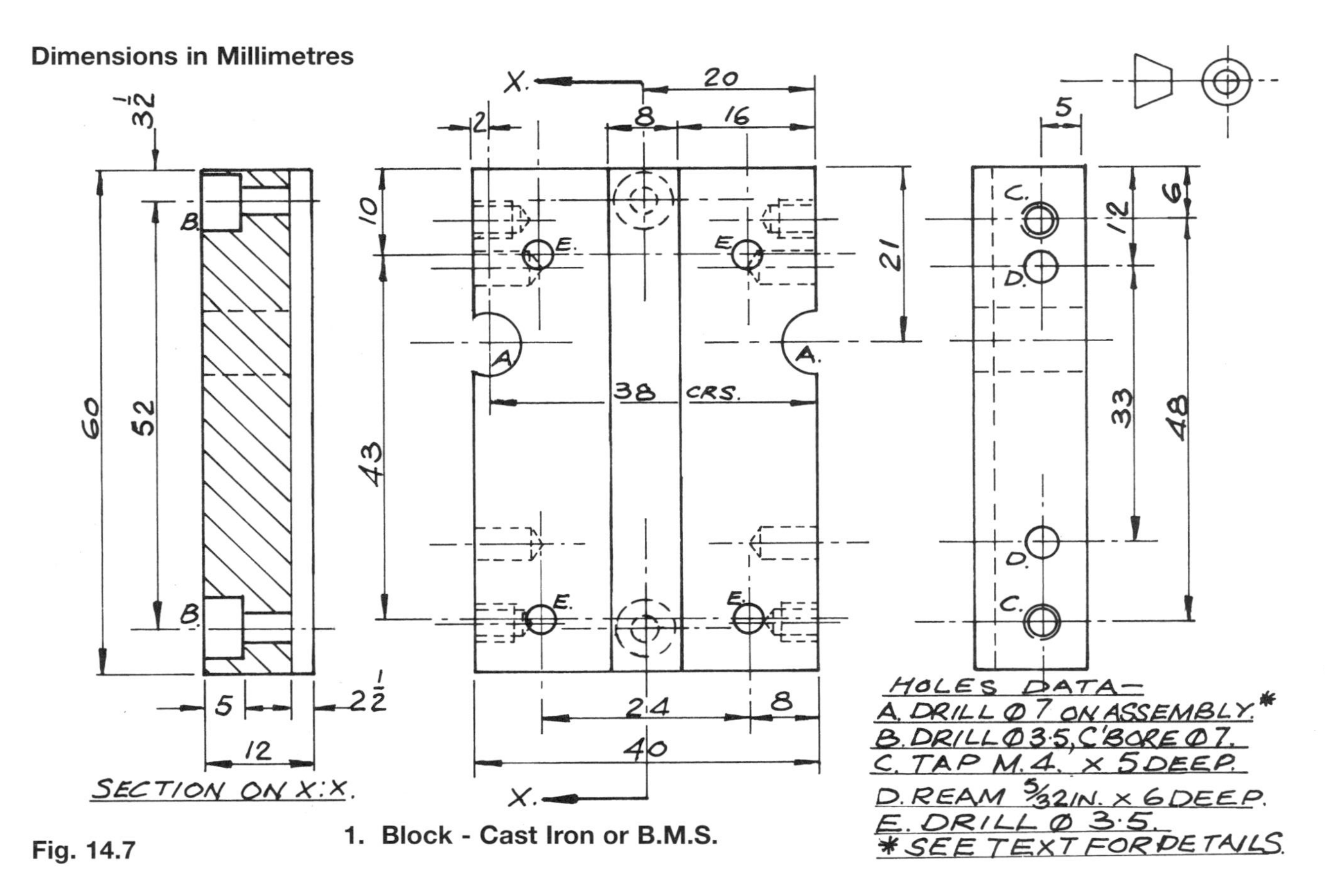

Fig. 14.7

1. Block - Cast Iron or B.M.S.

I have included a reference dimension for the vee, measured over a 10mm test bar for each of the plates. The dimension was different for the centre plate, **Fig.14.12**; it may not be the last word in precision, but I found it helpful.

When I had finished the plates to that stage, I put them to one side while the block was taken a little further. There would be more work to do on them when they were assembled, but they should be somewhere near the finished profile.

A little milling

A milled slot in the middle of the base accepts the centre plate. My method for milling this on the Unimat is to clamp a small angle plate to the cross slide and set it true. **Fig.14.13** shows the block being milled. Because the cross slide travel would not allow milling right to the end, the last little bit had to be filed. I used packing to lift the block far enough to position it with the slot near enough on centre, a little one way or the other would not matter. The cutters used were a 1/4in slot drill for roughing and a 5/16in one for finishing. The 5/16in will mill out a slot which fits the centre plate nicely with a bit of filing with a fine file.

I locked the saddle for each cut and put a bit of a drag on the cross slide by half locking it. It didn't stop the lathe making a bit of a noise, but it did well. I saw, on a television programme, that the technicians making bits and pieces for a James Bond film were using a Unimat 3. So, I reckon that if the machine is good enough for 'Q' to make 007's gadgets, it will do all I want it to do.

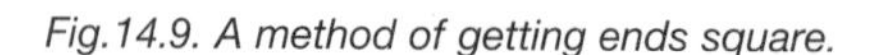

Fig.14.9. A method of getting ends square.

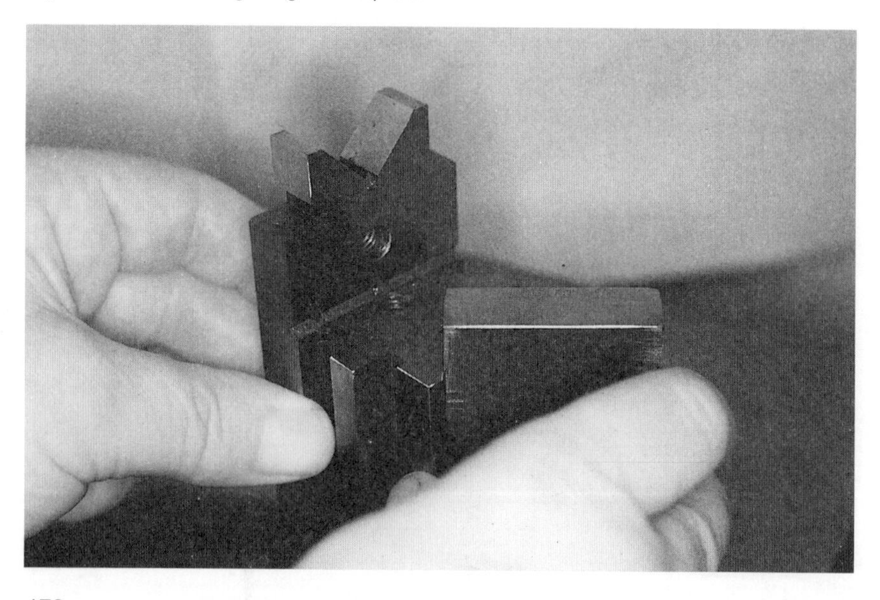

Fitting the end plates

With the slot milled and the end plates ready for positioning, it was time to do some drilling. Because the lathe has to do all the drilling as well as the turning and milling, it is sometimes a bit of a problem. This time it was difficulty with clamping and I found it wasn't easy to find clamps which would accommodate the block with the end plates as well. The solution was to stick the end plates to the block with Loctite. I cleaned everything, smeared the end plates with the Loctite, lined them up and clamped them for an hour while I did something else. It worked well and held tight while I did the drilling and reaming of the dowel holes.

The holes marked 'C' in **Fig.14.7** were drilled with the tapping size for M4. They were tapped while stuck together, through the end plates and into the block. A sharp tap with the hammer handle released the end plates and the holes shown in **Fig.14.11** were drilled 4.5mm and counterbored 7mm. Be careful to follow the instruction on the drawing and counterbore one end plate right-handed and the other one left-handed. If different screw sizes are used, the counterbore size may have to be changed. The sizes I have chosen are a guide and can be changed to suit as long as they do the job.

Fig.14.10. One end plate finished and one 'sandwiched' ready for shaping.

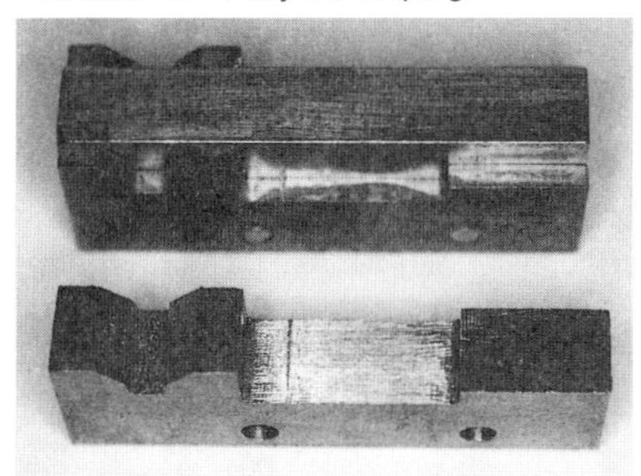

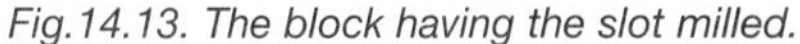

Fig.14.13. The block having the slot milled.

At this stage the clearance holes marked 'E' in **Fig.14.7** can be drilled. I was careful to keep these as accurate as possible because they fasten the upper vee and flat. I also drilled the holes 'B' and counterbored them.

I assembled the end plates and centre plate after spotting the 6BA holes and drilling and tapping them in the centre plate. **Fig.14.14** shows the assembly being checked for parallelism; it was within 0.05mm which I thought acceptable.

Finishing the vees and flats

The profiles of the plates had, up to this stage, been reasonably good but to fit really well, there was more work for me.

I blued the lathe bed again and rubbed the assembly lightly along it. The high spots were filed off and I repeated the marking and filing till I was satisfied. It took time and was tedious but I carried on till the blue was marking on all the surfaces. **Fig.14.15** shows the filing well underway. I used a three-square Swiss file because it bends slightly and has a cutting edge in three positions. As it took a bit of time, I put a couple of drops of light oil with the engineer's blue/ shoe polish to stop it drying out too quickly. It made the filings clog the file a little, so I had a file brush handy.

The final alignment of the vee was an important feature to get right, so I

Fig.14.14. Checking for parallelism.

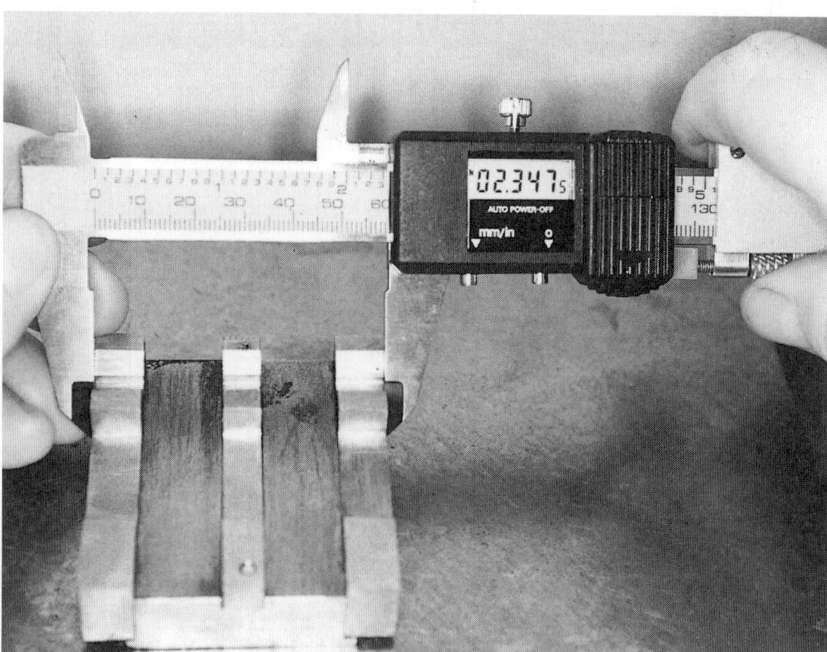

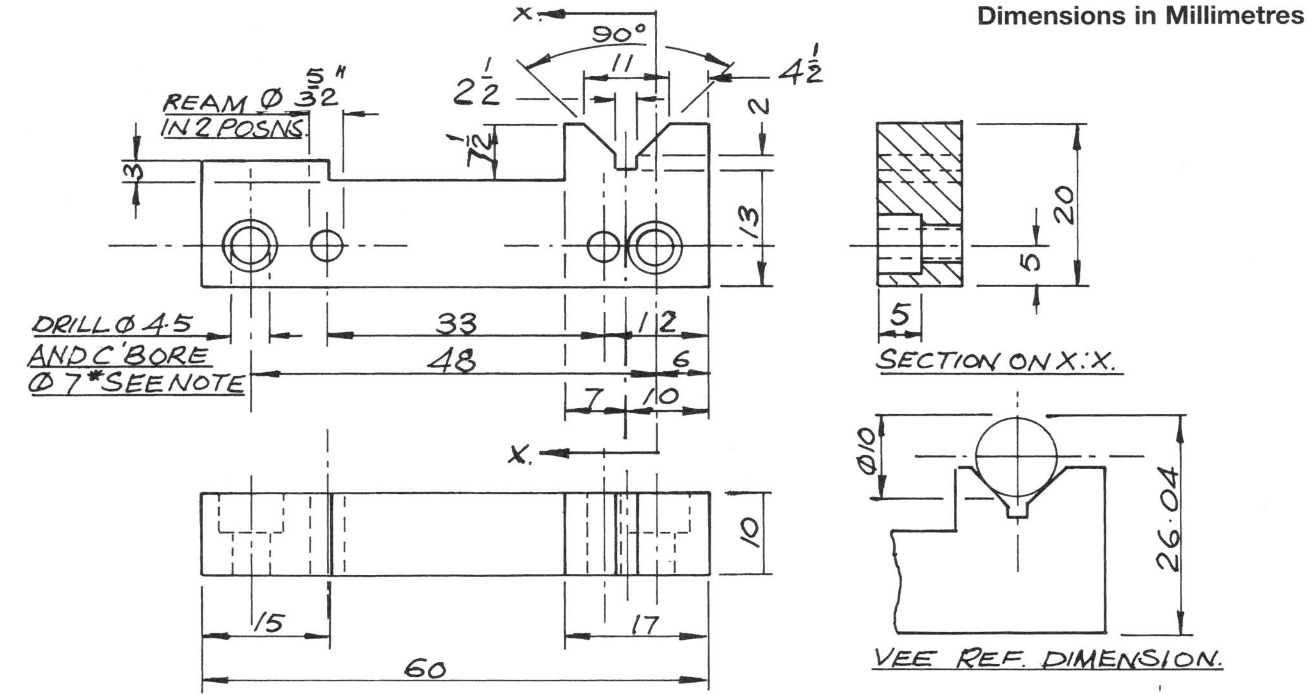

2. and 3. End Plate - B.M.S. 2. As Drawn
3.* With ø 7 C' Bores Opposite Hand

Fig. 14.11

Dimensions in Millimetres

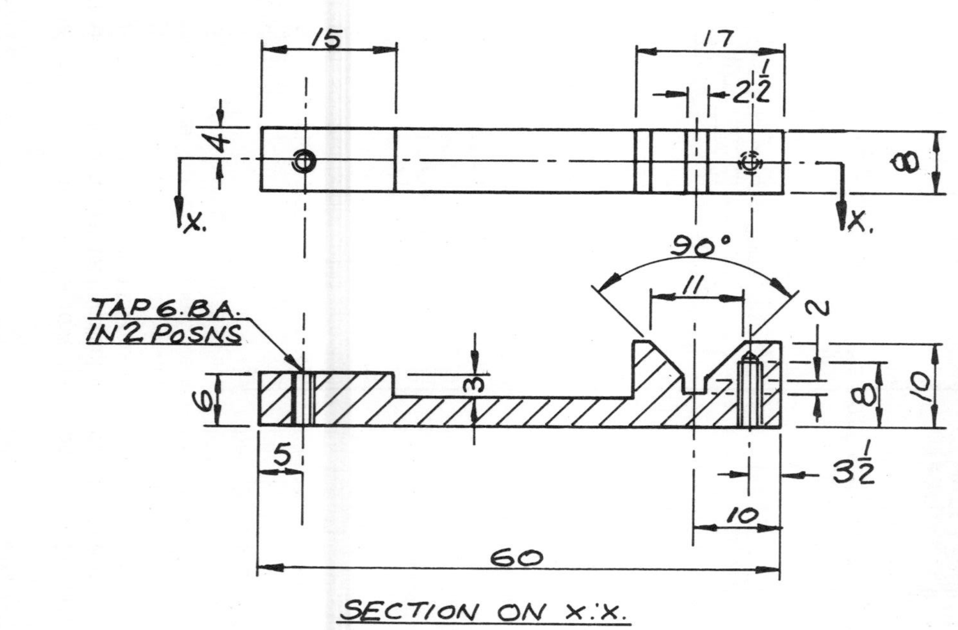

4. **Centre Plate - B.M.S. - 1 off**

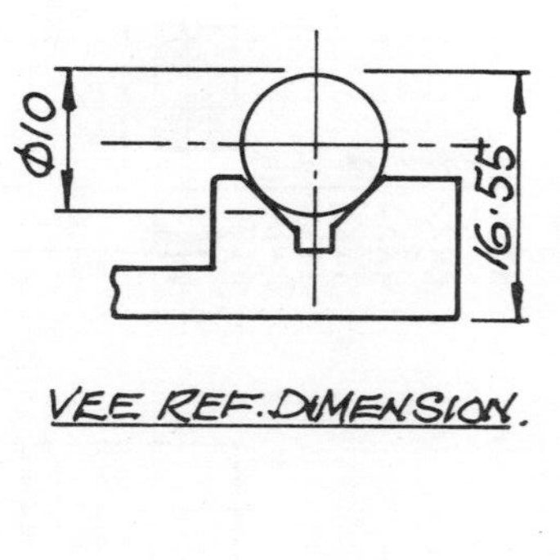

Fig. 14.12

checked with a test bar across the three vees and a dial test indicator. **Fig.14.16** shows this, with **14.17** as an alternative method with a vernier height gauge. So far so good, I still had a few more components to make.

Upper vee

This piece, **Fig.14.18.1** was cut from 12mm square bright mild steel. It made a vee about 16.5mm at the base which was plenty wide enough. It is a good idea to normalise the bar before cutting it in half, as the stresses put in by the cold rolling or drawing will make it bend when it has been cut to shape. Normalising is an easy process, the material is heated to bright red and allowed to cool at its own rate. The books insist that it must be kept out of draughts while cooling, but I've never found it makes any difference, although I have never done it in a howling gale. It was academic, for my torch will not get that size of material hot enough, so I cut it and bent it back straight afterwards. I checked it for straightness by the method shown in **Fig.14.19**, laying it in the vee of the assembly and measuring it along the length.

Fitting the upper vee

It is essential that the upper vee lines up with the lower one, which was a bit of a head-scratcher. I used the templates again and the set-up is shown in **Fig.14.20**. The templates were clamped across the upper vee and block and the assembly lined up

Fig.14.14. Checking for parallelism.

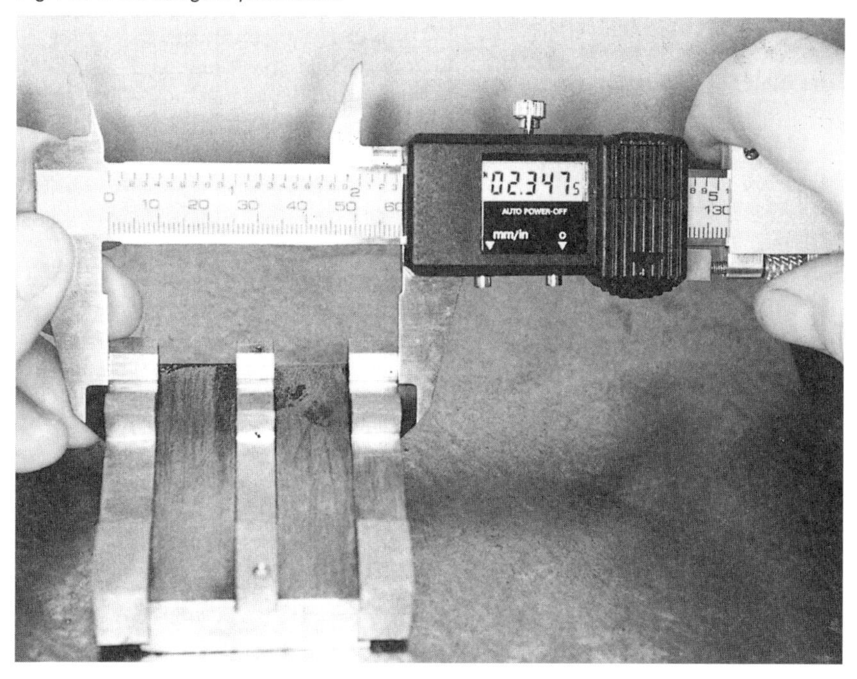

by pushing it against an accurate register, in that case the base of a very accurate vee block. A piece of 6mm square steel supported where the flat would be. When everything was clamped tight, the holes for the screws were spotted through. I used my Black and Decker for that but a spotting punch would do just as well.

Drilling the holes in the vee needed a bit of fiddling about. I clamped a vee block to the face plate on the Unimat and put the vee in that. Two hands were just about enough, three would have been better. The holes could be drilled right through, but I thought it would look unsightly, so I drilled them to give a full thread 4mm deep. As the screws are small they will locate and clamp at this depth.

Upper flat

This was an easier job than the vee. I used 12 x 6mm bright mild steel, the right height to bring the block level. The material was not thick enough to get a blind hole in, so the 6BA holes had to go right through.

Fig.14.15. Picking off high spots from the assembly.

When the vee and flat were screwed home, I did another alignment check **Fig.14.21**. The dial indicator stylus bore on the flank of the vee, while the assembly was slid to and fro.

The last operation on the complete block was to drill the two holes marked 'A'. The 7mm was an arbitrary size, chosen so that they could be slotted or opened up on final assembly to the headstock. They let the 6mm bolts holding the headstock to the bed go through. I drilled by stages as usual, opening up gradually. **Fig.14.22** shows the raising block in position, it lifts the headstock enough to swing 140mm diameter over the bed.

A small difficulty

Due to the way the Unimat motor assembly is fitted to the machine, there is no way that large diameters can be held close to the chuck or spindle, without fouling the motor. To avoid this the work would have to stick out from the headstock about 60mm. This would invite loud bangs and much damage, unless all the large work could be done on a mandrel, supported by another raising block under the tailstock.

My solution was to move the whole motor assembly back, by making an extension to the lathe spindle and standing the motor plate off on pillars. Both the spindle extension and the pillars are shown in **Fig.14.23**. They are a simple turning job as long as the important dimensions are accurate. Those were, the 10mm diameter on the extension and the 12.9mm and 14mm ones which fit the driving pulley. During the machining, there was a bang and everything went

Dimensions in Millimetres

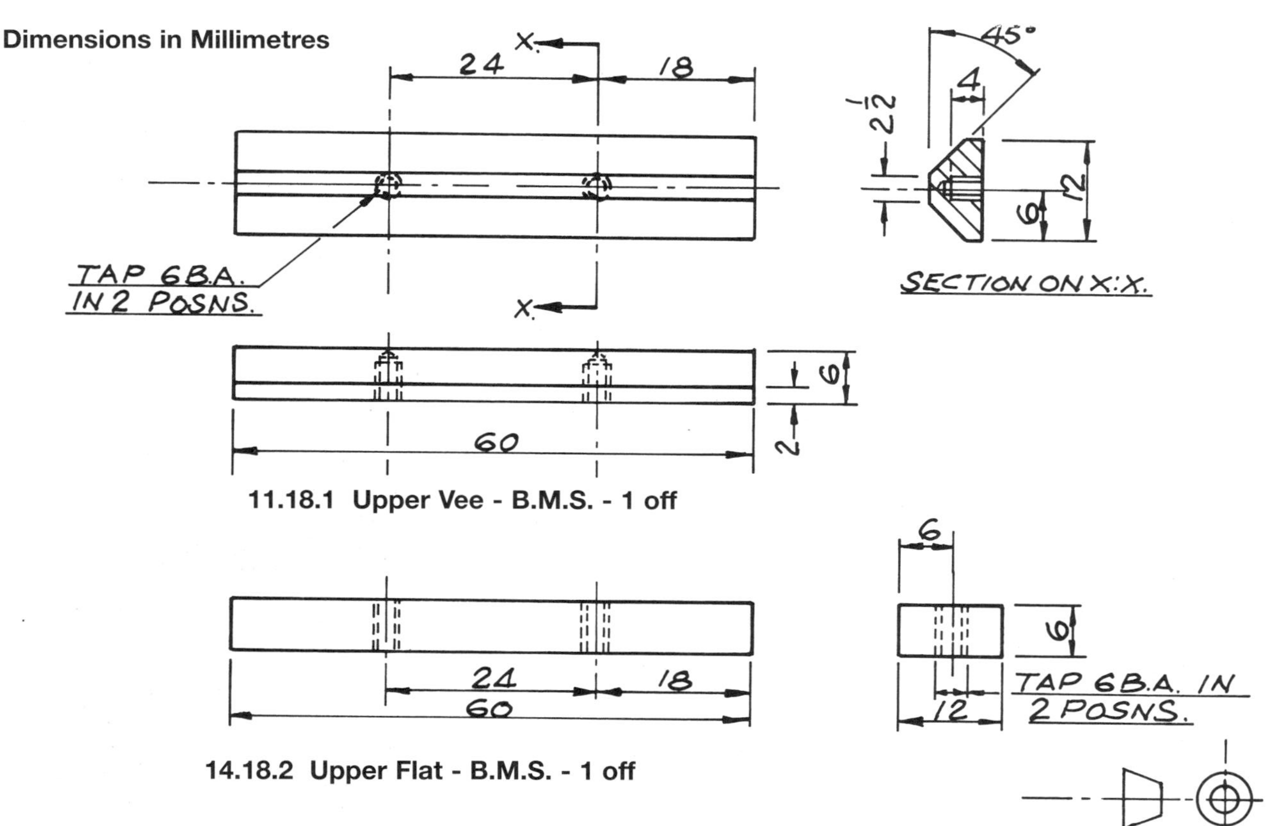

11.18.1 Upper Vee - B.M.S. - 1 off

14.18.2 Upper Flat - B.M.S. - 1 off

Fig. 14.18

slack. The small driving belt had broken and it was a weekend. Rather than stop everything, I used the same substitute as I do for the large belt, a suitable vacuum cleaner belt. They are made from thicker material than the '0' rings supplied with the lathe and they work just as well because they bear on the flanks of the pulley. They do, however, leave a black deposit on the pulleys and surrounding parts and tend to be a bit sticky. I usually correct this by using talcum powder or French chalk. I was caught that time without any, so my wife gave me some old face powder; the lathe smelled lovely for a while.

The two pillars replace the bolts which fasten the motor plate to the headstock, the bolts used to fasten the motor plate to the pillars in their turn. The assembly in the new position is shown in **Fig.14.24**.

Fig.14.16. Checking alignment of the Vees.

Fig.14.17. An alternative way of checking alignment

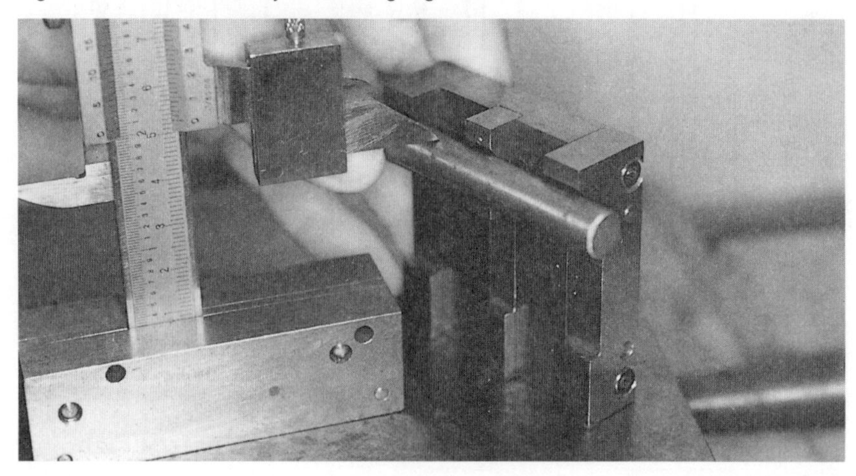

Two more items were made to complete the job. One was the locking pin shown in **Fig.14.25**. It locks the extension spindle by screwing into the tommy bar hole in the lathe spindle just to the right of the pulley. I had tapped this hole previously for another attachment. A 2BA will give a good thread and a thin nut can be used to lock if necessary, but I have found that small machining errors make it a tight enough fit. Also in **Fig.14.25** the last component to be made was an extension for the tool post, once again, stock material and a simple drilling job.

That concludes the making. To assemble the raising block, the cap-head screws are removed from the underside of the headstock and replaced with 50mm ones which will go through the new assembly. I found it was a good idea to take the motor plate off while fitting the block as things get a bit fraught with the various parts trying to go their own way.

Fig.14.26 shows the sort of work I had in mind for the accessory. I wouldn't attempt to machine work using that set-up, I'd want a support of some sort as well as the mandrel it is mounted on, preferably in the tailstock, and there is the rub. To really finish the job, I need a similar raising block for the tailstock. I have the block shown in **Fig.14.1**, all it needs is an upper vee and flat. That's how it goes, one thing leads to another, but that's model engineering!

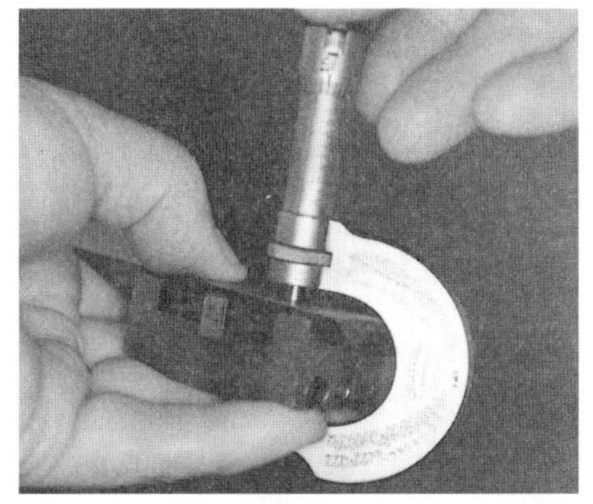

Fig.14.19. Checking that the upper Vee is in line.

Fig.14.20. Using the templates to line up the upper Vee.

Fig.14.21. Another check for alignment of the upper Vee.

Fig.14.22. The completed raising block in position.

Fig.14.24. The extension spindle and pillars.

Fig.14.26. A mock-up of a suitable operation which would need the raising block, (see text).

Dimensions in Millimetres

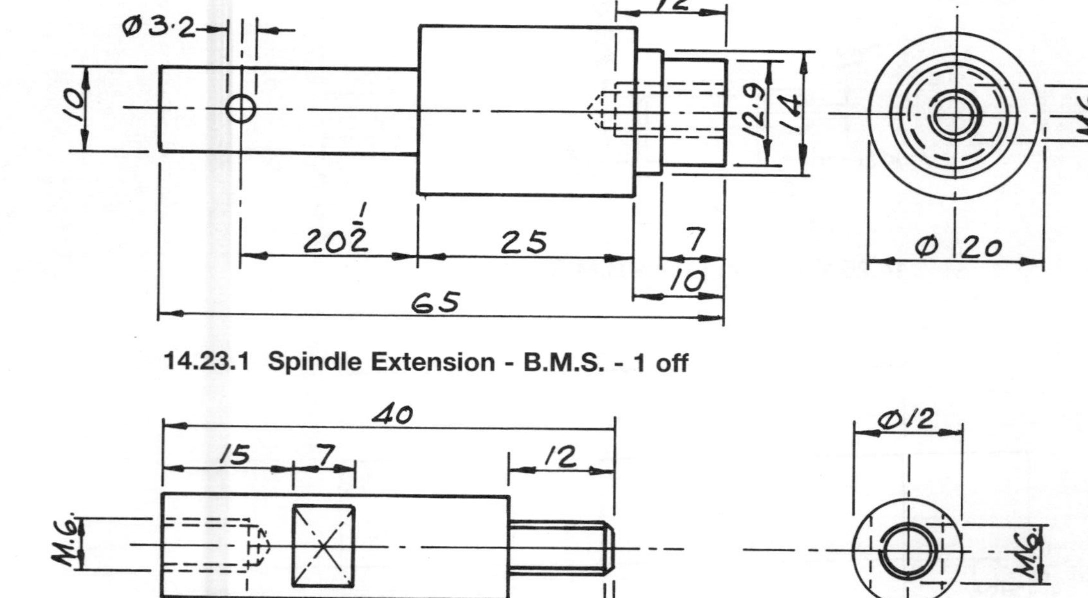

14.23.1 Spindle Extension - B.M.S. - 1 off

14.23.2 Pillar - B.M.S. - 2 off

Fig. 14.23

Dimensions in Millimetres

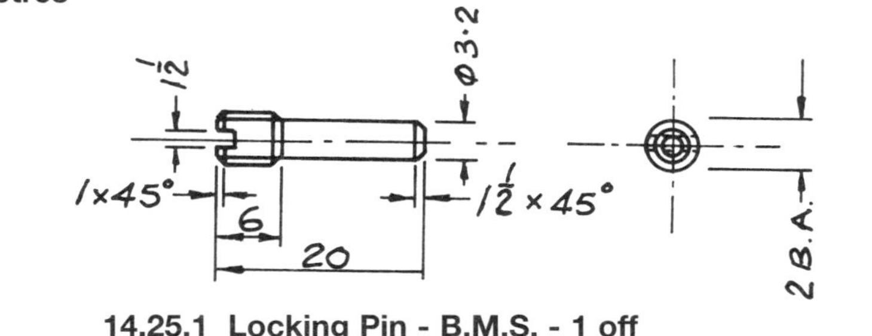

14.25.1 Locking Pin - B.M.S. - 1 off

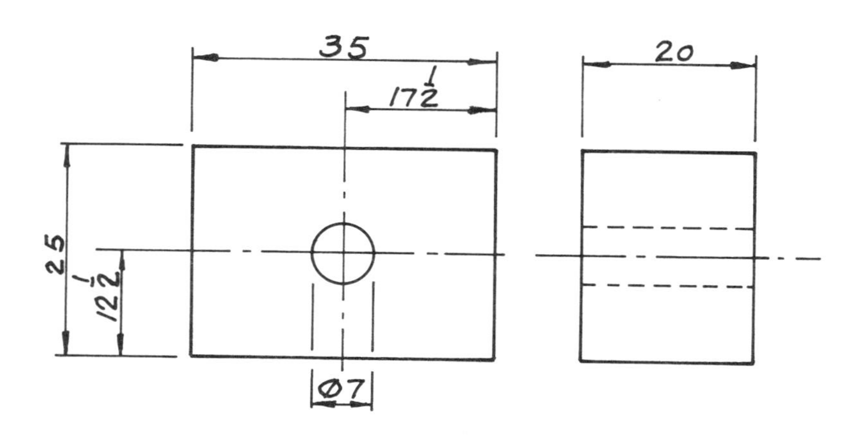

14.25.2 Tool Post Extension - B.M.S. - 1 off

Fig. 14.25